D1130983

The Price Advantage

Founded in 1807, John Wiley & Sons is the oldest independent publishing company in the United States. With offices in North America, Europe, Australia, and Asia, Wiley is globally committed to developing and marketing print and electronic products and services for our customers' professional and personal knowledge and understanding.

The Wiley Finance series contains books written specifically for finance and investment professionals as well as sophisticated individual investors and their financial advisors. Book topics range from portfolio management to e-commerce, risk management, financial engineering, valuation, and financial instrument analysis, as well as much more.

For a list of available titles, visit our Web site at www.WileyFinance.com.

The Price Advantage

Second Edition

WALTER L. BAKER
MICHAEL V. MARN
CRAIG C. ZAWADA

John Wiley & Sons, Inc.

Published by John Wiley & Sons, Inc., Hoboken, New Jersey.
Published simultaneously in Canada.

For general information on our other products and services or for technical support, please contact our Customer Care Department within the United States at (800) 762-2974, outside the United States at (317) 572-3993 or fax (317) 572-4002.

Wiley also publishes its books in a variety of electronic formats. Some content that appears in print may not be available in electronic books. For more information about Wiley products, visit our web site at www.wiley.com.

ISBN 978-0-470-48177-6

Printed in the United States of America

10 9 8 7 6 5 4 3 2

For
Ashley, Nancy, and Gail

Contents

Preface

As we approached the task of writing this second edition of *The Price Advantage*, we revisited a few basic questions—questions that our readers might have as well. Why a book on pricing? Why a book by McKinsey & Company? And finally, why a second edition now? Let us begin by addressing these basic questions.

WHY A BOOK ON PRICING?

Pricing, although one of the most critical management functions, remains one of the most misunderstood and undermanaged functions at many companies that are otherwise high performers. Pricing is far and away the most sensitive profit lever that managers can influence. Small changes in average price translate into huge changes in operating profit.

Although more companies have made gains in pricing in recent years, too few businesses have successfully tapped into the full potential that improved pricing holds. Even thoughtful general managers often feel helpless to make real progress on the pricing front. Many managers do not know where to begin to get a handle on identifying the exciting performance upside that pricing so often holds. And those who identify this upside struggle to really capture and sustain it.

This book is not designed to be an exhaustive review of the considerable body of pricing theory that has accumulated over the years. To the contrary, it has been written as a practical pricing guide for that thoughtful general manager who has been tempted by the unrealized promise of improved pricing and, perhaps, frustrated by attempts to translate pricing theory into bottom-line impact for his or her business. It is intended to provide a logical and structured approach for identifying where the most precious sources of untapped pricing opportunity reside in a business, along with practical, case-illustrated guidance on how to capture and sustain that opportunity.

WHY A BOOK BY MCKINSEY ON PRICING?

Over the past 20 years, pricing has become one of the most frequent areas in which we have helped businesses across every continent (except Antarctica!) to improve their performance. These companies represent a rich and diverse range of industries, including industrial goods, consumer packaged goods, consumer durables, banking, telecommunications, chemicals, retailing, high-tech products, basic materials, insurance, pharmaceuticals, and transportation. To support our service to clients, McKinsey has invested more than $25 million in developing practical knowledge in pricing over the past five years alone. We are credited with having developed and advanced a majority of the most useful contemporary pricing frameworks—the pocket price waterfall and the value map are just two examples.

WHY A SECOND EDITION NOW?

Since the first edition of *The Price Advantage* was published five years ago, much has changed. First, our knowledge has advanced significantly in a number of areas—areas of growing currency and relevance that were not included in the original edition. A new chapter is devoted to the topic of managing price wisely over the course of a product's lifecycle. In an ever-growing number of product categories, for example, high-tech products, consumer durables, and medical devices, product lifecycles are compressing, which makes this a topic of broad application and significance.

Included in this edition is an entirely new part titled "Advanced Topics," which were not covered in depth in the first edition. This includes Chapter 12, "Complexity Management," which addresses issues that complicate the pricing challenge, including the complexity of pricing custom-configured products, pricing when the number of individual products sold is extremely high, and pricing through a large and distributed sales force. Chapter 13, "Tailored Value," explores issues around tailoring value to specific customers and markets, including segmenting price, pricing product line tiers, dealing with "razor/razor blades" offerings, and pricing new products and integrated solutions. Chapters 12 and 13 contain sections of information that do not apply to each and every business; but when they do apply, we have found that they are often central to a company's realization of *the price advantage*. Chapter 14 "Software and Information Products," is also new and discusses how to tackle the unique challenges of pricing software and information-based products.

Second, the legal landscape has also continued to evolve since we wrote the first edition. The United States' pricing rules have evolved and enforcement has been generally more aggressive. EU pricing law and enforcement has moved closer to and, in some cases, surpassed that of the United States in severity. Likewise, pricing and antitrust law in many Asia-Pacific countries is gradually becoming more strictly defined and aggressively enforced. Chapter 9, "Legal Degrees of Freedom," has been updated to reflect the changing degrees of legal freedom that companies must operate within today. Furthermore, we have updated language throughout this second edition to avoid pricing wording and phrasing that might be more likely to raise legal red flags in the current legal environment.

Finally, we have heard from businesses around the world asking for more details on how to build a sustainable capability in pricing; that is, what does a high-performing pricing infrastructure look like today and how do you best move an organization in that direction. Our overarching framework, "The Three Levels of Price Management" from the first edition, has been extended to include a cross-cutting pricing infrastructure level; Chapter 6, "Pricing Infrastructure," is completely new and dedicated to issues of pricing infrastructure—where we have synthesized our experience in helping companies build high-performing organizations, processes, and tools. So, as we mentioned above, much has changed since we published the first edition back in 2004—so much that we deemed the writing of the second edition of *The Price Advantage* timely and warranted.

STRUCTURE OF THE BOOK

This book is organized into six main sections. Part One describes *the price advantage* and explains why it is worthwhile for businesses to pursue that rare but valuable advantage. It then lays out our overarching framework for identifying and ultimately capturing pricing opportunity. This framework, the three levels of price management plus pricing infrastructure, provides the integrating thread that weaves through the book and is applicable to most business situations.

Part Two explores each of these three levels plus pricing infrastructure in considerable detail. Part Three addresses unique pricing events that almost any company might have to face on an occasional basis. Part Four explores some of the boundaries of *the price advantage*—boundaries that may affect a company's degrees of pricing freedom and boundaries that companies can expand to find opportunities beyond the fundamentals covered in Parts One and Two. Part Five covers a variety of advanced topics, as mentioned earlier. Part Six is devoted to the practical enablers and constraints to making enduring and positive pricing change happen, including a detailed case study and some final thoughts. In addition, the Appendixes are designed to provide some useful examples of the application of core frameworks discussed in the book, an overview of key points in pricing law, a list of acronyms and abbreviations, and instructions for accessing a functional demo of *Periscope*, a web-based pricing tool that has been loaded with realistic transaction data for a hypothetical company. This book contains a number of disguised cases to illustrate pricing concepts, frameworks, and insights. These cases are rooted in McKinsey's extensive client work in pricing, and client identities are heavily disguised to assure protection of confidential client information and strategies. The location and nature of opportunities identified are consistent with the underlying cases, and the magnitude of improvements shown by these examples is real.

Unless otherwise noted, when we talk about a company's "product," we are referring to that company's comprehensive product, service, and support offering to customers. This convention allows for more economical word usage throughout the book.

Acknowledgments

As we embark on this journey for a second time, we do so with a full understanding and appreciation of the level of support it takes to write a book. As with the first edition, our colleagues, our clients, our firm, and our families continue to support us in extraordinary ways. To them we extend a hearty thank you in the hope it captures our true appreciation for what they have contributed.

We start our acknowledgments with the "godfathers" of pricing. Those that saw the power of pricing before the rest and persisted in sharing the story—Kent B. Monroe, Tom Nagle, Dan Nimer, and Arleigh Walker. And to the leaders at McKinsey & Company who supported and invested in the development of our pricing knowledge—David Court, Tom French, Marc Singer, Robert Garda, Philip Hawk, Ralf Leszinski, Andrew Parsons, Hajo Riesenbeck, and Rob Rosiello—thank you for believing in us and the impact we could have for our clients. We also want to recognize the tremendous support of Eric Roegner, an author on the first edition. Eric's ideas and contributions remain at the foundation of this edition.

There are some special people who accompanied us on this journey and we would like to take the time to recognize them. Cheri Eyink served as our undaunted project manager. Beyond driving the process of creating this second edition with resolve and enthusiasm, she acted as an irreplaceable thought partner to the authors—adding content, insight, and clarity at every turn. Sarah Smith was our trusted editor—pushing us to express in written word the knowledge we had gathered over many years of serving clients. She gracefully and persistently challenged us to share our best with our readers in a clear and concise manner. To them both, we are grateful.

A number of past and current McKinsey colleagues contributed their deep content expertise to this book, including John Abele (postmerger pricing), Scott Andre and Robert Musslewhite (market strategy), Daniel G. Doster (solutions pricing), Dieter Kiewell (pricing tools and implementation), Andy Kincheloe (lifecycle pricing), Stephen Moss (pricing infrastructure), Adolfo Villagomez (market strategy), and John Voyzey (price wars). Special thanks to Gene Zelek, partner and chair of the Antitrust and Trade Regulation Practice Group at Freeborn & Peters LLP in Chicago (legal issues). In addition, we would like to thank current and past McKinsey colleagues who made significant contributions to the knowledge we shared here: Kevin Bright, Hugh Courtney, Gareth Davis, Tom Dohrmann, David Dvorin, Jonathan Ford, Amit Jhawar, Kristine Kelly, Michal Kisilevitz, Eric Kutcher, Eric Lin, Glenn Mercer, Jamie Moffitt, Derick Prelle, David Rosenberg, David Sackin, Mike Sherman, Philippe Stubbe, and Florian Wunderlich. Thanks also to George Gordon, partner and co-chair of the Antitrust/Competition Group at Dechert LLP in Philadelphia and Lynda Martin Alegi, of Counsel in Baker & McKenzie LLP's EC Competition and Trade Unit based in London.

We would also like to take this opportunity to thank the editing and publishing experts at the *McKinsey Quarterly*, past and present, including Don Bergh, Stuart Flack, Allan Gold, Rik Kirkland, and Allen Webb, as well as those at John Wiley & Sons, including Bill Falloon and his team.

Mary Turchon spent countless hours taking care of all of the details required to publish a book. Creating exhibits, scheduling meetings, formatting text; the list could fill pages. Her excellent skills and willingness to help out in a crunch are deeply valued. We would also like to recognize the research assistance provided by Danica Reed and the graphics support of Janet Clifford and Mary Ann Brej.

We close with recognition and appreciation for the hundreds of McKinsey & Company consultants that have worked alongside us over the past 30 years, expanding our knowledge and bringing the power of pricing to thousands of companies. And to our clients, who opened the door to their businesses and allowed us to be a part of their transformations.

Pricing Fundamentals

Part One describes what *the price advantage* is and explains why this is such a worthwhile and profitable advantage to pursue. This part also introduces an overarching framework for identifying the magnitude and location of pricing opportunities—and for sustainably capturing those opportunities.

308

Pricing Fundamentals

CHAPTER 1

Introduction

What's your advantage? What capabilities distinguish your company most from its peers, allow your business to perform better than your competitors, provide the foundation for superior returns to your shareholders? Is it a cost advantage—do you purchase better and manufacture more efficiently than your competition? Is it a distribution advantage—are your products sold through the best wholesalers, retailers, and locations in your markets? Is it a technology advantage or an innovation advantage? Or is yours a brand advantage or a capital structure advantage or a service advantage?

For all of the advantages that businesses pursue, there is one powerful advantage that is accessible to virtually every business, but actually pursued by too few—and ultimately achieved by even fewer. That advantage is *the price advantage*.

Setting prices for goods and services is one of the most fundamental management disciplines. It is, in truth, unavoidable. Every product and service sold since the beginning of time has had a price assigned to it. Setting that price is among the most crucial, most profit-sensitive decisions that companies make. Ironically, very few companies price well. For a host of reasons, few ever develop anything resembling a superior, business-wide, core capability in pricing. In other words, few companies build pricing into the distinctive business advantage that it can be.

In this book, we discuss the details of creating and sustaining *the price advantage*, where pricing excellence generates superior returns to shareholders and enables a company to invest in sustaining its advantages in other areas. But first, let us look at why getting pricing right is so important, and why so few companies realize this advantage.

THE POWER OF 1 PERCENT

Why is it so vital to get pricing right? Because pricing right is the fastest and most effective way to grow profits. The right price will boost profits faster

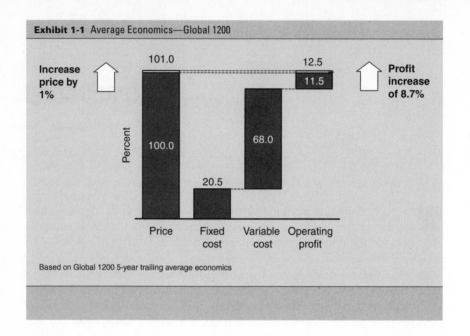

Exhibit 1-1 Average Economics—Global 1200

Based on Global 1200 5-year trailing average economics

than increasing volume; the wrong price can shrink profit just as quickly. The exhibit above illustrates this dramatically. In Exhibit 1-1, the average income statement of the Global 1200 (an aggregation of 1,200 large, publically held companies from around the world), shows just how quickly the right price can create profit. We use a five-year average to reduce sensitivity to yearly economic variations.

Starting with price indexed to 100, we see that fixed costs (items like overhead, property, and depreciation that do not vary when volume changes) amount to an indexed average of 20.5 percent of price. Variable costs (expenses like labor and materials that shift in tandem with volume) account for 68.0 percent. This leaves an average return on sales (ROS) of 11.5 percent.

Now, given these Global 1200 economics, what happens if you improve your price by 1 percent? Price will rise from 100 to 101. Assuming volume remains constant, then variable costs will remain constant as well—as will fixed costs. Operating profit, however, rises from 11.5 percent to 12.5 percent, a relative increase of 8.7 percent.

The clear message is that very small improvements in price translate into huge increases in operating profit. When you talk about creating a pricing advantage, you may have to recalibrate your thinking about how large a price increase needs to be to have a meaningful impact. Pricing

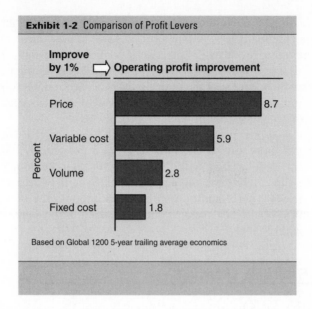

Exhibit 1-2 Comparison of Profit Levers

Based on Global 1200 5-year trailing average economics

initiatives that increase average prices by only a quarter or a half percent are important because they bring disproportionate increases in operating profit. A 1 or 2 percent price improvement is a major victory with significant profit implications. Find 3 percent—and many companies can, once they start looking—and operating profit can jump by more than 25 percent, if your cost structure is similar to the Global 1200 average.

Not only that, but pricing is far and away the most powerful profit lever that a company can influence. Continuing with average Global 1200 economics, Exhibit 1-2 illustrates the impact on operating profit when individual levers improve by 1 percent while other factors stay constant. Pricing has by far the strongest impact, raising profit by 8.7 percent.

Variable cost is the second most significant one, increasing operating profit by 5.9 percent for every 1 percent decrease in costs. However, most companies have already wrung a lot out of variable costs in recent years through purchasing and supply management initiatives, labor productivity improvements, and other measures. As a result, continued improvement in variable cost structure has become increasingly difficult.

Fixed cost decreases have an even smaller effect on operating profit. A 1 percent improvement generates only a 1.8 percent operating profit increase. While making other cost-cutting efforts, companies over the past decade were also busy trimming fixed costs; as with variable costs, further improvements have become elusive.

The low impact of volume increases on operating profit can be a real surprise to many managers. A 1 percent increase in unit sales volume only increases operating profit by 2.8 percent, if per unit prices and costs remain constant. This is less than a third of the impact of a 1 percent improvement in pricing. But which lever gets the majority of the attention and energy from marketing and sales people? The volume lever, despite its much smaller impact on profit—a fraction of what pricing delivers.

Unfortunately, the pricing lever is a double-edged sword. No lever can increase profits more quickly than raising price a percentage point or two, but at the same time nothing will drop profits through the floor faster than letting price slip down a percentage point or two. If your average price drops just a single percentage point, then, assuming your economics are similar to the Global 1200 average, your operating profits decrease by that same 8.7 percent.

THE PRICE/VOLUME TRADEOFF

This inevitably leads us to the age-old question of the price/volume/profit tradeoff: If I lower my price, can I increase volume enough to generate more operating profit? Exhibit 1-3 explores how that tradeoff works—or,

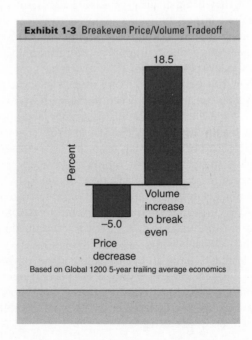

Exhibit 1-3 Breakeven Price/Volume Tradeoff

18.5

Percent

Volume increase to break even

−5.0

Price decrease

Based on Global 1200 5-year trailing average economics

more accurately, does not work. If a business takes steps that effectively reduce average prices by 5 percent, how much of a volume increase would be necessary to break even on an operating profit basis?

With economics similar to the Global 1200 average, a 5 percent price decrease would require an 18.5 percent volume increase, just to break even, much less increase operating profits. Such an increase is highly unlikely. For a 5 percent drop in price to generate a 18.5 percent volume rise would require a price elasticity of −3.7 (price elasticity is equal to the percentage change in volume that occurs with a percentage point change in price; in this case 18.5 divided by −5). In other words, every percentage point price drop would have to drive up volume by 3.7 percent. Our experience shows price elasticities commonly reach a maximum of −1.7 or −1.8. On rare occasions, usually for consumer items purchased on impulse, it might be as high as −2.5. In the real world, −3.7 price elasticity is *extremely* rare.

As this example shows, the basic arithmetic of decreasing price and increasing volume to increase profits just does not add up. You should do this calculation using the economics of your own business to confirm how the tradeoff works for you.[1]

But the point to remember is that profits are extremely sensitive to even minute changes in prices. Each percentage point of price represents a precious nugget of profit that should be held tight to the chest and never given up without a hard fight. Unfortunately, sales reps (and often even general managers), propelled by their incentive systems, routinely negotiate away five percentage points at a time through discounts, special offers, and other inducements to close deals. Companies with a superior pricing capability—with *the price advantage*—consistently let fewer of those nuggets slip away.

MARKET FORCES ADD PRESSURE

The second reason managing pricing is so important is because even if nothing changes internally, most companies, whether selling to consumers or to businesses, face unprecedented downward pressure on prices. If nothing is done, these external forces will depress prices and erode profits quickly.

---

[1]Note that the price/volume/profit tradeoff is not symmetrical, for example, for the Global 1200, a 5 percent price *increase* would allow up to a 13.5 percent volume decrease without driving a profit decline.

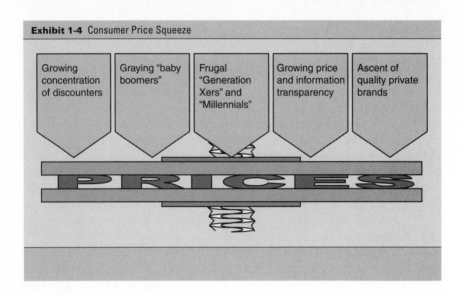

Exhibit 1-4 Consumer Price Squeeze

A combination of fundamental business and demographic changes are squeezing prices in consumer markets as illustrated in Exhibit 1-4. Discount retailers such as Walmart, Home Depot, and Costco are growing larger and accounting for ever-increasing shares of volume in their markets. These giants use their market power to extract lower prices from consumer goods suppliers. The growth of the Internet, as well as the increased use of price advertising by such discounters, makes it easier for shoppers to find and compare prices of consumer products. Meanwhile, private-label packaged goods, often sold under a retailer's brand name, have witnessed quality improvements that put added pressure on traditional brands in many product categories.

Generational shifts are leaving their mark on the consumer market as well. The baby boomers who fueled much of the rampant consumer spending over the past few decades are throttling back purchases now that they are helping children through college, supporting aging parents, preparing for their own retirement, and carrying other financial burdens. The generations behind the baby boomers are notably more price sensitive, having grown up surrounded by discount retailers of every stripe.

Business-to-business (B2B) companies are also feeling price pressure from changes in the market environment, as shown in Exhibit 1-5. Buyers are tougher and more skilled than ever in extracting every last penny of price from suppliers. Efficiency programs in recent years have unleashed newfound excess capacity into many markets. Open-book costing, in which powerful buyers insist on knowing the details of a supplier's costs for each

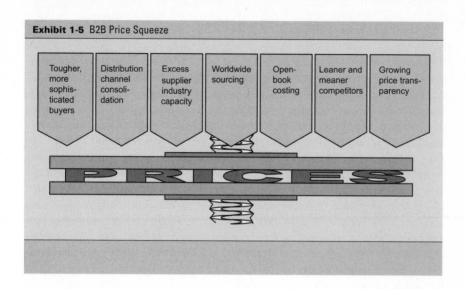

Exhibit 1-5 B2B Price Squeeze

component of a product, including individual component materials costs, direct labor, and overhead, has become more common. This greater visibility provides buyers with significantly more leverage when negotiating prices. Prices in some instances have become even more transparent, with individual customer price quotes being highly visible to not only other customers but to competitors as well—particularly if the quoted price is extremely low. We refer to this higher visibility of lower prices as "asymmetrical price transparency"—a condition that actually exerts even more downward force on prices that may already be low.

Furthermore, many industrial suppliers have already cut their own costs—have themselves become leaner and meaner—and thus generally feel more confident competing more aggressively on price to secure business. Global companies increasingly shop the world for the best prices, and then insist on those unified low prices for all their buying locations. Just as in consumer distribution, B2B distribution channels are becoming more concentrated and more powerful relative to suppliers.

The forces that are putting pressure on companies that serve consumers and businesses alike are gathering strength and are not likely to subside in the foreseeable future; indeed, they have shown no signs of subsiding since we wrote the first edition of *The Pricing Advantage* in 2004. A company that neglects pricing, that does not actively develop an enhanced pricing capability and a price advantage to combat this onslaught, will inevitably see its prices crumble away under the weight of these prevailing forces.

THE NOBILITY OF PRICING EXCELLENCE

The last reason building *the price advantage* in your business is so important goes beyond profit economics or market forces to the spirit, heart, and pride of your organization. There is genuine nobility to pricing done well. Individuals responsible for setting prices hold a sacred trust. They assure that a business gets fairly rewarded in the marketplace for products and services superior to its competitors—that there is a real payoff for being better.

The price advantage is not about gouging customers or employing tricks to gain undeserved revenues. Quite to the contrary, the real price advantage is a source of organizational pride. The highest compliment a customer can pay a supplier is to knowingly pay more for that company's goods and services. In doing so, the customer is saying, "You are higher priced, but you are worth it; you are superior to my other supplier alternatives." Businesses that, lacking *the price advantage,* fail to have their superiority rewarded with higher prices, often lose their drive—and even their ability—to continue to be superior.

WHY THE PRICE ADVANTAGE IS SO RARE

The reasons for pursuing *the price advantage* are compelling, but few companies have achieved a level of competence in pricing that could be described as *the price advantage.* Although many companies may attribute much of the double-digit profit growth that was so common in the 1990s and the mid-2000s to improved pricing practices, in fact the bulk of this growth can be traced to cost cutting and increased demand. Pricing had little to do with the profit growth during this period and remains a largely untapped opportunity.

A number of factors explain why companies undermanage the opportunities inherent in pricing and why so few businesses have ever developed *the price advantage.*

- Pricing is a complicated topic that requires the analysis of large amounts of data and customer insights, as well as the ability to influence entrenched opinions of many people—from frontline sales people to senior management.
- Under past buoyant economics brought on by strong demand and sharp cost cutting, many companies sensed little need to develop advanced pricing skills and to pursue pricing as a source of increased profits.
- Companies often did not believe that pricing was manageable. They saw prices as set by the market, by customers, or by unreasonable competitors.

- Data to support pricing decisions was either not available or not current enough to help with real-time pricing decisions.
- Price differentiation and other pricing actions were misperceived as always illegal, and therefore degrees of pricing freedom were internally limited.
- Pricing mistakes and errors were hard for most companies to detect. If your sales representative in Scotland negotiated a price that was 5 percent lower than it could have been, it was unlikely to raise a red flag at headquarters.
- Frontline pricers often had virtually no incentive to stretch for an additional percent in price.
- Senior managers often had little, if any, involvement in pricing.
- Many companies did a more than adequate job of identifying opportunities to improve pricing but failed to make changes in infrastructure, mindsets, and behaviors necessary to deliver and sustain pricing improvement.

As we show in later chapters, the obstacles outlined here are real but can be overcome with some effort. Indeed, the barriers to building pricing capabilities are not trivial, and creating *the price advantage* is hard work. But the payoff is so large that knocking down these barriers is well worth the effort.

* * *

The price advantage is a powerful advantage worth pursuing and is achievable by each and every business, but fully realized by very few. It deserves pursuit because pricing is such an extremely sensitive profit lever, with small swings in price levels generating huge swings in bottom-line profitability.

As we have shown, a 1 percent increase in price can increase your profit by 8 percent or more; a 1 percent slip in price can erode profits by that same 8 percent or more. And rare are the circumstances where decreasing price can generate nearly enough additional sales volume to offset the effects of a price cut and produce incremental profitability.

Furthermore, *the price advantage* deserves pursuit because of prevailing market forces—both in consumer and business markets—that are putting unprecedented downward pressure on industry-wide price levels and showing no signs of subsiding. Failure to take real initiative in pricing today virtually assures that percentage points of price will slip through your hands annually—and that huge chunks of operating profit will drop off your bottom line. Finally, achieving *the price advantage* can be a source of organizational pride as employees are reassured that their hard work to create superior products and services does not go unrewarded.

CHAPTER 2

Components of Pricing Excellence

The reasons, economic and otherwise, for pursuing *the price advantage* are compelling. But the sheer breadth of pricing issues in most companies makes it challenging to even know where to start. Managers must constantly deal with pricing issues that are seldom simple and isolated; rather, they are intricate and linked to multiple business aspects. Even pricing issues that may seem entirely tactical often have strategic implications and affect other prices, other customers, even competitors.

The cases below illustrate the breadth and diversity of pricing issues discussed above—and the widely different sources of opportunities they provide:

- A specialty wire company failed to recognize the industry-wide shortages created by the closing of a competitor's large European factory and consequently missed an opportunity to raise prices by at least 10 percent.
- A consumer electronics firm underpriced an innovative compact disc player because it did not realize that customers really valued the new model's special features and design.
- An automobile parts supplier inadvertently sold items to some of its smallest accounts at net realized prices lower than those charged to its largest accounts. Why? The supplier's off-invoice price structure, with items like cash discounts and program rebates, was out of control.
- A leading medical products company identified sizeable opportunities to improve prices based on aligning prices with both unique benefits to customers and local competitive situations, but only realized a small portion of the opportunity. Why? The company failed to put in place the basic tools, support and incentives required to change the behaviors of frontline sales people.

These cases clearly demonstrate issues in pricing, but the underlying problems somehow feel fundamentally different—and they are. One of the real challenges of making progress in pricing is defining the territory. When you say "price," it means different things to different people.

Depending on their points of view (their training and their jobs, among other factors), thoughtful businesspeople will understand the topic in a variety of different ways.

For economists, the word *price* fosters images of intersecting supply and demand curves and price indices that rise and fall. Economists focus on overall market price levels, using microeconomics to project broad price trends. Economists would be most intrigued with the pricing opportunity missed by the specialty wire manufacturer that failed to capitalize on the wire shortage caused by a competitor's plant closure.

Marketers view the field quite differently. For them, the primary force in play is customer perception, or, more to the point, how customers weigh their product's benefits against a competitor's offerings. If a product or service is perceived as superior to a competitor's, the marketer's pricing concern is about determining the overall price premium that the product deserves in the marketplace. If the product is inferior, the marketer tries to figure out either the price discount required relative to the superior competitor or how to improve the product offering to allow it to command a higher price. The marketer, of course, would be attracted to the pricing issues faced by the consumer electronics company that underestimated the market's reaction to its CD player.

Although savvy sales representatives may appreciate microeconomics and market positioning, their concern is usually much more about getting the price right for individual customer transactions, deal by deal—for example, negotiating the right invoice price, discounts, allowance, terms, and conditions. Most salespeople could readily relate to the dilemma of the auto parts supplier whose differences in transaction prices did not seem justified.

Finally, the organizational behaviorists would focus most on the challenges of the medical products company. They would say that the company clearly knew *what* to do (i.e., tailor prices to their unique value and local market conditions) but did not know *how* to do it—how to get people across the organization to execute pricing in a new and different way.

So who has the correct perspective on pricing? Economists, with their focus on market prices driven by supply-and-demand balances? Marketers, who focus on getting the right price relative to competing products? Sales reps, who concentrate on coming up with the correct transaction price for each specific customer? Or organizational behaviorists, with their change management orientation?

AN INTEGRATED APPROACH

Although each constituent group seems to address distinct and diverse pricing issues, these views are not at odds with each other. Rather, each perspective forms part of the broad and integrated pricing dynamic. They reinforce each other and define the components across which companies that truly excel at pricing address pricing issues, opportunities, and threats. Understanding these components—*the three levels of price management plus infrastructure* (Exhibit 2-1)—is a first step in getting a handle on the challenge of pricing.

We discuss each level in more detail in later chapters, but first let us take the executive tour of the structure.

MARKET STRATEGY

The first level of price management—Market Strategy—considers overall market price levels. The main question centers on how myriad factors—for example, supply, demand, costs, regulation, technological changes, and competitor actions—shift industry-wide prices. Companies that excel at this level better understand market trends and their underlying drivers than does

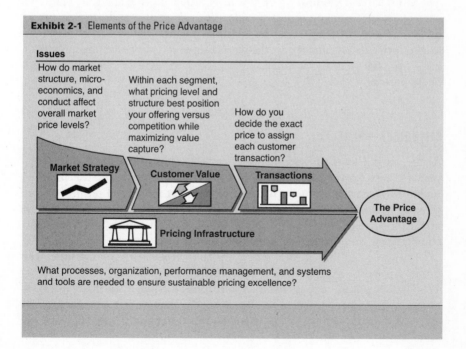

Exhibit 2-1 Elements of the Price Advantage

Issues

How do market structure, microeconomics, and conduct affect overall market price levels?

Within each segment, what pricing level and structure best position your offering versus competition while maximizing value capture?

How do you decide the exact price to assign each customer transaction?

Market Strategy

Customer Value

Transactions

The Price Advantage

Pricing Infrastructure

What processes, organization, performance management, and systems and tools are needed to ensure sustainable pricing excellence?

the competition. They invest in gaining rich insights into the near- and longer-term direction that market prices are heading. Their dedication to creating and constantly refining a fact-based understanding of available industry supply and the variables that can change it, as well as of industry demand and the market factors that can move it, positions them well. As a result, they have a deeper understanding of how market price mechanisms work and can predict market price volatility and turns in market cycles better.

Excellence at the Market Strategy level requires not only in-depth knowledge of your own company and how your actions will affect market prices, but also of the competition. Capacities, cost structures, capital investments, research and development (R&D) expenditures, and growth aspirations of other companies (including suppliers and customers) must be a part of the overall picture. In addition, companies need to weigh the potential for new market entrants.

By bringing all this knowledge together, companies can anticipate market price trends and be proactive rather than just a pawn of the market's invisible hand. Companies can adjust their tactics to take advantage of this superior understanding, for instance by avoiding long-term, fixed-priced deals just ahead of an expected upturn in market prices.

More careful monitoring at this level would have helped the specialty wire company spot the industry-wide shortage earlier and raise its prices quickly to new market levels. Its lack of vigilance at the Market Strategy level of price management cost the wire company three percentage points of price over the year and a missed opportunity to increase operating profits by 36 percent.

CUSTOMER VALUE

At the second level of price management—Customer Value—the primary issue is price positioning relative to competitors. So the question here is, within each market segment that you serve, what price level positions your offering optimally in customers' eyes on a price/benefit basis? Price actions at this level tend to be quite visible to the market—both customers and competitors. You are setting, for instance, list prices, base prices, or target prices in an often public way, telling the marketplace what you think your product is worth relative to competitive offerings.

The key phrase here is *customer perceptions*. Unless you figure out how potential customers perceive the benefits of your products compared with those of the competition, you cannot go much beyond a guessing game in setting list prices or base prices. You will not know what list price premium to seek or list price discount to take relative to which competitor. Many research tools exist to help determine and measure customer perceptions, which we discuss in later chapters.

Companies that shine at this level obsess about customers' perceptions of both their products and their price. They continually research and update their understanding of how customers perceive competitors as well as themselves, and how that all varies by customer segment. Armed with this knowledge, these companies seek justifiable price premiums, move to optimal price/benefit positions for each customer segment, and avoid destructive price competition.

The consumer electronics company failed at the Customer Value level when it launched its new CD player. Had it understood customers' perceptions of the new player's benefits, it could have set a list price 4 percent higher without sacrificing unit sales volume.

TRANSACTIONS

The third level of price management—Transactions—focuses on the exact price to assign to each and every customer transaction—in other words, what discounts, allowances, payment terms, volume bonuses, and other inducements to apply to a starting-point list price, base price, or target price. This is the most detailed, time-consuming, systems-intensive level of pricing for most companies. It generates the price the customer sees and ultimately the net revenue that the company realizes. At most companies, it entails hundreds, even thousands, of individual pricing decisions daily, usually made at multiple organizational levels.

The best companies at the Transactions level break through the complexity to gain a superior understanding of the full economics of every transaction and customer. They fully account for every discount and cost-to-serve item that swings the attractiveness of transactions. They know which customers and transactions are best for them and aggressively seek their business. They know which current customers and transactions are underperforming, know why, and take steps to improve or drop them.

If the auto parts supplier had greater discipline at the Transactions level, the over-discounting to small accounts would have been readily apparent and corrected. If it had monitored more rigorously and tightened its control on a transaction-by-transaction basis, with a full accounting of all discounts after the invoice, its average realized price could have increased by 5 percent with negligible loss of unit sales.

PRICING INFRASTRUCTURE

Pricing Infrastructure underpins the three fundamental components of pricing management (Market Strategy, Customer Value, and Transactions) we just discussed. While the first three identify *where* to look for pricing opportunities, pricing infrastructure addresses the issue of *how* to capture opportunities and profits sustainably. Pricing Infrastructure is crucial because it supports all the other components and makes them possible. Without it, much of the pricing opportunity will remain on the table. This infrastructure component addresses critical questions like what should the processes for pricing decision making look like, how should the pricing organization within a company be structured, how should pricing excellence be recognized and rewarded, and what tools—IT tools and others—are required to support pricing excellence.

The best companies avoid the trap of believing that once pricing opportunities are identified individuals across the company will just naturally change their pricing behaviors to capture those newfound opportunities. Rather, these companies are completely aware of the scale of the change management challenge of moving a business toward pricing excellence and make deliberate investments in pricing talent and skill-building, process definition, incentives, and support tools. They do the infrastructure building required to translate pricing opportunities into bottom-line impact. And as asserted in Chapter 1, "Introduction," the payoff for even small improvements in pricing is so high that it literally dwarfs the infrastructure investments in most situations

If the medical products company had created some simple support tools and training to help sales reps quantify customer benefits and had refined the sales incentive program to more richly reward higher price levels, it could have boosted average prices by at least 3 percent.

AN INTERDEPENDENT HIERARCHY

There is a natural hierarchy to the three levels of price management. The Market Strategy level is the most general, with its orientation around pricing issues that have an impact across the entire industry. The Customer Value level entails a tighter scope that focuses on value specific to customer segments, particularly on setting list or base prices by segment. The Transactions level is the most detailed, with its microscopic focus on individual transactions and customer pricing.

The three levels of price management provide a valuable way to break the broad, sometimes daunting range of pricing issues into more manageable subcategories. Determining which level a pricing issue belongs to—Market Strategy, Customer Value, or Transactions—can focus discussions and provide a useful context for finding a solution. An issue with market strategy implications would be considered in a much different light than one with only transaction issues.

Although these three levels may look independent, companies must realize that they are not; rather, all three are highly interrelated. The Market Strategy level provides a constant backdrop against which customer value price decisions are made; the Customer Value level defines the starting point for pricing at the Transactions level, by setting the list prices from which on- and off-invoice items are subtracted. Simultaneously, Pricing Infrastructure supports opportunities at all of these levels.

Companies that create *the price advantage* typically are more skilled than their competitors both at operating *within* each level and at orchestrating pricing moves *across* the different levels. These companies ensure that actions at one level reinforce objectives at the others. For example, when they expect prices to rise (Market Strategy), they avoid introducing low-priced products (Customer Value) that could put downward pressure on the market. In the same scenario, they are careful to prevent heavy discounts (Transactions) when launching a new product that targets premium market segments (Customer Value).

APPLYING TO YOUR COMPANY—PINPOINTING THE OPPORTUNITY

Where are your pricing opportunities and what are your most important infrastructure requirements to realize those opportunities? Each business will have different pricing priorities based on its unique situation. The following questions can help managers pinpoint the untapped pricing opportunity that is waiting to be discovered and delivered to the bottom line.

MARKET STRATEGY

- Do you have a fact-based projection of overall pricing trends in the market for the near, medium, and long term? How accurate have these projections been historically? Have there been major disconnects between expected and actual market price levels?
- Is that view shared across your organization so that your market-pricing behavior is consistent with those projections?
- Do you have a mechanism in place to assess specific market events, such as technological shifts, capacity additions and reductions, new

competitors, changes in component and raw material costs, and demand shifts, and their likely impact on industry prices?

- Has there been market-wide earnings pain? Are there competitors in your markets whose pricing behavior is perceived as irrational?

CUSTOMER VALUE

- Do you research customer attitudes in detail or rely on hunches and anecdotes from the sales force? Has the research led to an understanding of customer segments and of what attributes each segment values most, how each segment compares to others, and how each grades available products against the attributes it desires most? Has your company changed prices recently based on this understanding?
- Do you have up-to-date end-customer price sensitivity research that shows how sales volume changes with price? Do you use that research to assist resellers in positioning your products optimally to their customers?
- Do you collect and synthesize competitive price data routinely, both in situations where you won and lost business?
- Have you pinpointed the premium or discount that is justified in relation to competitors' prices? Do you understand how this varies by customer segment, and is this reflected in price levels and structure?
- Have there been dramatic, unexplained shifts in market share or unexpected price and/or benefit moves by key competitors?

TRANSACTIONS

- Do you monitor price performance for each transaction, including all discounts, allowances, rebates, and other incentives, whether they are reflected on the invoice or not? Does that view include all promotional as well as pricing elements? Are these price performance metrics at an aggregate level or can they also be viewed by transaction, customer, or segment?
- Do you understand how widely net realized prices vary? Do you know which customers or segments regularly pay the highest and lowest net prices? Are programs in place to attract more of the best and to fix or drop the worst?
- Do you understand how customers compare your prices to those of your competitors? Do they use invoice price or list price—and do they fully value all off-invoice discounts, rebates, and allowances that you provide?

- Do you specifically and thoughtfully differentiate price targets by customer type, size, segment, transaction size, and so forth?

PRICING INFRASTRUCTURE

- Is your company's pricing performance clear and transparent to senior managers? Do they see straightforward price monitoring that clearly shows the magnitude and sources of pricing improvement or decline?
- For pricing decisions at each level (Market Strategy, Customer Value, Transactions), do you routinely follow well-defined decisions processes? Do you have pricing reporting and information systems that support that decision making?
- Have you clearly defined and limited discounting authority and are the rules rigorously enforced?
- Do your sales and marketing forces have incentives, monetary or otherwise, to stretch for higher transaction prices?
- Is there a dedicated pricing organization that takes the initiative to continuously improve the level of pricing capability across your company? Are frontline sales and marketing people regularly trained and mentored in pricing skills?

The chapters in the next section are organized around this integrated approach: the three levels of price management plus pricing infrastructure. We explore each level in greater depth, introduce key analytic tools, and provide a number of real business cases to bring the approaches to life. These cases all represent real efforts by companies to capture *the price advantage*, although most are disguised to protect confidentiality.

We start with the most specific level—Transactions—because it has broad applicability across businesses and industries and often results in the quickest positive impact on price performance. However, it is important to note that the Market Strategy and Customer Value levels hold as much or more pricing potential for many businesses.

* * *

The range of issues that falls under the umbrella of pricing can be so broad and daunting that many companies with a sincere desire to create *the price advantage* have difficulty sorting out which ones to address and, even if they make a choice, gaining any real traction. The *three levels of price management plus pricing infrastructure* can help them logically categorize and prioritize the issues they face, eventually leading to workable, successful solutions and *the price advantage*.

The three levels—Market Strategy, Customer Value, and Transactions—progress from broad, market-wide pricing issues to specific customer and transaction issues. Businesses that have achieved *the price advantage*, when considering a pricing issue, first determine under which of the three levels that issue falls. They then employ the appropriate analytic frameworks and approaches for that level in addressing each specific pricing issue—and ultimately build/use the appropriate infrastructure to execute against those issues and opportunities.

Two

Exploring the Levels

P art Two explores and amplifies each of the components of the overarching framework introduced in Part One; that is, the three levels of price management plus pricing infrastructure. It demonstrates the core analytics that apply at each level and brings untapped pricing opportunities to light.

CHAPTER 3

Transactions

The Transactions level is the most granular level of price management. Its critical issue is how to manage the exact price charged for each transaction—that is, from a starting point list price or target price, and how to manage and apply discounts, allowances, rebates, conditions, terms, bonuses, and other incentives. Efforts at the Market Strategy and Customer Value levels focus on the broader issues of overall industry prices and relative price position within an industry. Those at the Transactions level are almost microscopic—customer-by-customer, deal-by-deal, transaction-by-transaction.

Transaction management's objective is to capture the right and best realized price for each transaction or order. Transaction pricing is a game of inches where each day, hundreds or even thousands of customer-specific (and invoice line-specific) pricing decisions determine success or failure, where companies win or lose percentage points of profit margin one transaction at a time.

But a host of obstacles can prevent companies from managing transaction pricing successfully. High transaction volume and complexity, top management neglect, management reporting shortfalls, and lack of aligned incentives can all contribute to missed transaction pricing opportunities. The sheer volume and complexity of transactions often create a smoke screen that makes it difficult to impossible for the rare senior manager who shows an interest in the Transactions level to penetrate it. Management information systems all too often do not report on transaction price performance or report only average prices that shed no real light on missed pricing opportunities for individual transactions. Rarer still is the incentive system that genuinely rewards sales and marketing individuals for achieving deal-by-deal pricing excellence. In fact, many incentive approaches, which emphasize total sales volume, discourage salespeople from taking the risk required to prevent percentage points of price from slipping away at the Transactions level.

THE POCKET PRICE WATERFALL

Too many companies focus on an incorrect or incomplete measure of price at the Transactions level. Most companies concentrate on either the list or invoice price and fail to manage the full range of components that contribute to the final transaction price.

Exhibit 3-1 shows the price components for a manufacturer that sells large rolls of linoleum to national, regional, and local flooring retailers, which in turn resell them to residential and commercial customers. The starting point is the dealer list price for this product, $6.00 per square yard. An order-size discount (based on the total dollar volume in that order) and a "competitive discount" (a discretionary discount negotiated before the order is taken) are subtracted from the list price to arrive at the invoice price of $5.78 per yard. This is the price printed on the billing invoice sent to the retailer for that order. For companies that monitor price performance, this invoice price is the most commonly used measure.

OFF-INVOICE DISCOUNTS

In almost all B2B and most consumer businesses, the pricing story does not stop at invoice price. A number of pricing components that occur after

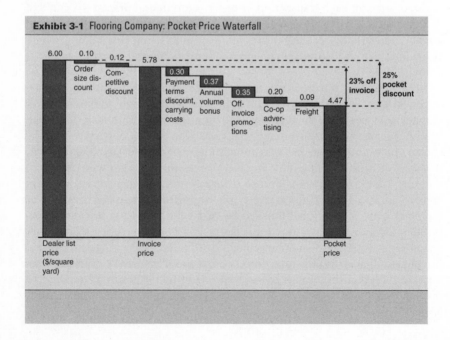

Exhibit 3-1 Flooring Company: Pocket Price Waterfall

invoice price can substantially affect revenues resulting from a customer transaction (see box). When you subtract these transaction-specific, off-invoice items from the invoice price, what is left is called the *pocket price*—the revenues that are actually left in a company's pocket from a transaction to cover costs and contribute to profit. Pocket price—not invoice price or list price—is the right measure of the pricing attractiveness of a transaction.

TYPICAL OFF-INVOICE ITEMS

The list of off-invoice items that reduce the pocket price realized by a supplier can be long. Some of the common elements include:

- Annual volume bonus: an end-of-year bonus paid to customers if preset purchase volume targets are met.
- Cash discount: a deduction from the invoice price if payment is made quickly—for instance, within 15 days.
- Consignment costs: the cost of funds when a supplier provides consigned inventory to a retailer or wholesaler.
- Cooperative advertising: an allowance usually paid as a percentage of sales to support local advertising of a manufacturer's brand by a retailer or wholesaler.
- End-user rebate: a rebate paid to a retailer for selling a product to a specific customer, often a large or national customer, at a discount.
- Freight: the supplier's costs of transporting goods to a customer.
- Market-development funds: a discount to promote sales to a specific market segment.
- Off-invoice promotions: a marketing incentive that would, for example, give retailers an additional rebate for each unit sold during a specific promotional time period.
- Online order discount: a discount offered to customers ordering over the Internet.
- Performance penalties: a discount that the seller agrees to give buyers if the seller misses performance targets, such as quality levels or delivery times.

(Continued)

TYPICAL OFF-INVOICE ITEMS (*Continued*)

- Receivables carrying cost: the cost of funds from the moment an invoice is sent until payment is received.
- Slotting allowance: an allowance paid to retailers to secure a set amount of shelf space and product positioning.
- Stocking allowance: a discount paid to wholesalers or retailers to make large purchases into inventory, often just before a seasonal increase in demand.

Exhibit 3-1 shows the series of off-invoice discounts and allowances that dropped the invoice price down to the pocket price for the flooring manufacturer. The company gave dealers a payment terms discount of 2 percent of invoice price if they paid an invoice within 30 days; it also incurred carrying costs on receivables as it awaited payment. The manufacturer offered an annual volume bonus, paid at the end of the year, of up to 8 percent of a dealer's total invoice purchases. Retailers also received promotional funding to support in-store promotions, as well as cooperative advertising allowances of up to 4 percent of invoice price if they featured the flooring manufacturer's products in local newspaper and broadcast advertising. The company also paid freight and delivery costs on all orders exceeding a preset dollar value.

Taken individually, none of these off-invoice discounts significantly affected transaction economics. Together, however, they reduced revenues an additional 23 percent from invoice price down to pocket price. The product, which was listed at $6.00 per yard, ends up generating an *average* pocket price of only $4.47 per yard, less than 75 percent of the starting list price. This 25 percent reduction from the dealer list price to the pocket price is called the *pocket discount*.

Pocket price can be a difficult number for even competent, well-intended managers to get a handle on. Accounting systems often fail to collect many of the off-invoice discounts on a customer or transaction basis. For example, payment terms discounts get buried in interest expense accounts, cooperative advertising is often included in companywide promotional and advertising line items, and customer-specific freight gets lumped in with all other business transportation expense. Because these items are collected and accounted for companywide, it is almost impossible for managers to think about, let alone manage, them on a customer-by-customer or transaction-by-transaction basis.

THE POCKET PRICE WATERFALL VIEW

Exhibit 3-1, which shows revenues cascading down from list price to invoice price to pocket price, is called the *pocket price waterfall*. Each element of the pocket price waterfall, both on and off the invoice, represents a revenue leak. The flooring company's 23 percent drop from invoice price down to pocket price may seem large, but is not uncommon. In past McKinsey client situations, the average decline from invoice price down to pocket price was 24 percent for a breakfast cereal company, 38 percent for a data communication service company, 47 percent for a furniture manufacturer, and 72 percent for an electrical controls supplier. Of course, the structure and components of the pocket price waterfall vary across companies and industries. (Appendix 1 shows sample pocket price waterfalls from a variety of businesses.)

Pricing becomes much more interesting when you adopt the pocket price waterfall view. All of a sudden, it is more than just setting list prices and standard discounts. Pricing degrees of freedom expand to managing each and every component of the pocket price waterfall. Recall our earlier discussion of the impact of a 1 percent improvement in price. Companies that use the pocket price waterfall now have many more places to look for that precious 1 percent—it does not matter whether it comes from an on- or off-invoice item. The dramatic effect on bottom-line profitability will be the same. Companies that do not actively manage the entire pocket price waterfall, with its multiple and often highly variable revenue leaks, miss all kinds of opportunities to enhance price performance.

THE POCKET PRICE BAND

The magnitude of each element of the pocket price waterfall is not the same for all customers. Starting point list prices can vary across different customer types and segments. Order size and total annual purchase volume affect discount and rebate levels. How and when customers pay their invoices affects both cash discounts and receivables carrying cost. The result is that at any given point in time, no product generates the same pocket price for all customers.

Instead of having a single pocket price, items sell over a range—often a surprisingly wide range—of pocket prices. The distribution of sales volume of a product over the range of pocket prices that a company realizes is called the *pocket price band* for that product. Exhibit 3-2 shows the flooring company's pocket price band for the single product represented in the previous pocket price waterfall. The horizontal axis is pocket price in dollars per

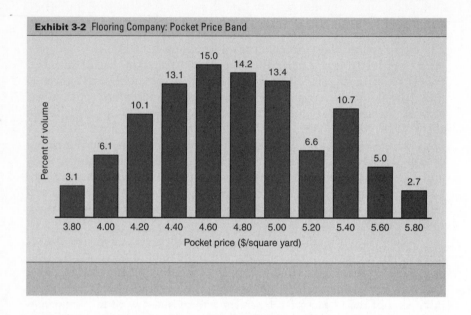

Exhibit 3-2 Flooring Company: Pocket Price Band

square yard, with higher pocket prices to the right. The height of the bars represents the percentage of volume that is sold within each pocket price range. The graph shows that some transactions for this product (2.7 percent) are generating a pocket price as high as $5.80, while others are as low as $3.80 (3.1 percent). Note that the difference between the lowest priced transactions and the highest is 53 percent. The largest chunk of volume (15 percent) is sold in the $4.41 to $4.60 range, which is near the average of $4.47.

Although the width of this pocket price band may appear quite large, much wider price bands are commonplace. We have seen pocket price bands with a range of 65 percent for an electrical controls manufacturer, 80 percent for a medical equipment supplier, 170 percent for a specialty metals company, and 500 percent for a fastener supplier.

UNDERSTANDING THE POCKET PRICE BANDS WIDTH

So wide pocket price bands exist in most businesses and industries. They are a fact of business life. Most managers do not know that they exist or, if they do know, they just let them happen. However, companies that excel at pricing understand their pocket price band and make actively managing it one of their core marketing and sales disciplines. If a manager can identify a wide pocket price band and comprehend the underlying causes of the band's width, then the company can manage and benefit from that band.

Recall the huge operating profit payoff from a 1 percent increase in average price. When, as in the case of the linoleum flooring manufacturer, pocket price varies over a 53 percent range, it is not hard to imagine how changing the distribution along the price band slightly through more deliberate management might yield percentage points of price improvement and the rich operating profit awards that accompany such improvement.

The width and shape of a pocket price band often tell a fruitful story. When managers see their pocket price band for the first time, they are invariably surprised by two dimensions: its width and the identity of customers at the extremes. The width of the pocket price band reveals the combined effect of all on- and off-invoice discounts on transaction economics to them for the first time. The pocket price band also shows the true price from customers. Customers perceived by managers as very profitable (based on high invoice price) can end up at the low end of the band, driven there by excessive off-invoice discounting that is not always transparent to managers. Some customers perceived as unprofitable end up on the high end of the pocket price band because of relatively light discounting and revenue leaks off-invoice.

The shape of the pocket price band provides the astute manager with a graphic profile of the business, depicting, among other things, what percentage of volume is being sold at deep discounts, what groups of customers are inherently willing to pay higher prices to you, and how appropriately field-discounting authority is being exercised.

WIDE BANDS SUGGEST OPPORTUNITY

Managers, dismayed by the width of their price bands, often perceive wide price bands as absolute negatives. Nothing could be further from the truth. By contrast, wide price bands almost always indicate significant pricing opportunity. They indicate potentially manageable heterogeneity in markets; differences companies can capitalize on with customers: how they value a product, how they order, how sophisticated they are, how costly they are to serve; openings in competitive situations: segments or regions where there are many versus few competitors, situations where a single competitor's strength varies widely; and finally, variability within the supplier itself: markets where it is stronger or weaker, segments where a supplier's products and services are a better fit with customers' needs, and/or sales representatives whose price negotiating skills vary widely.

So wide pocket price bands should not be seen as negative, nor should they be perceived as needing to be aggressively narrowed. Rather, they are a positive sign of rich variability and texture in the markets served—variability and texture that can ultimately be managed to your advantage. And when price bands are wide, small changes in their shape—for instance, a few more transactions at the high end or a modest improvement in pricing for a few transactions at the low end—can readily move the average price up by multiple percentage points. When price bands are narrow, such changes tend to be more difficult and have less impact on average pocket price.

So what do you do if you discover that you have a wide price band? As the case below shows, the key is to gain a detailed understanding of why your pocket price bands are so wide. That understanding will unlock the pricing and profit opportunity inherent in wide price bands.

THE SOUNDCO RADIO COMPANY CASE

The Soundco Radio Company makes aftermarket automobile radios and CD players. A car owner would purchase a Soundco radio either to replace an existing malfunctioning radio or to upgrade to higher performance. The following case shows how Soundco used the pocket price waterfall and pocket price band to identify profit leaks and regain control of its pricing system. It illustrates one way to apply the basic price band and waterfall concepts and how, if you do not manage your pricing policies around the waterfall, experienced customers can use your pocket price waterfall to their own advantage.

As background, Soundco sells its radios directly to regional and national electronics retailers, several automotive stereo catalog retailers, and electronics wholesalers who then resell Soundco radios to smaller auto stereo retailers and installers. Exhibit 3-3 shows Soundco's economics and profit structure. With return on sales (ROS) of 6.8 percent, Soundco's profitability is extremely sensitive to even small improvements in price. A 1 percent price increase with no volume loss would increase operating profit by nearly 15 percent—almost three times the impact of a 1 percent increase in volume (assuming no decline in average price).

The automotive replacement radio industry was in a state of overcapacity due to the installation of increasingly high-quality original-equipment radios in many automotive brands. Gradual commoditization made it more and more difficult for Soundco to distinguish its products from competitors. So Soundco senior management was skeptical that there was much, if any, potential for price improvement. However, they had entirely overlooked lucrative pricing opportunities at the Transactions level.

SOUNDCO'S POCKET PRICE WATERFALL

Exhibit 3-4 shows the average pocket price waterfall for one of Soundco's most common radio models, the CDR-2000. From a dealer base price of

Exhibit 3-3 Soundco Radio Company: Economics

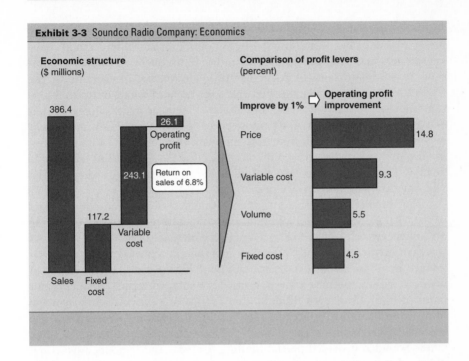

Economic structure
($ millions)

386.4

26.1
Operating profit

243.1

Return on sales of 6.8%

117.2

Variable cost

Sales   Fixed cost

Comparison of profit levers
(percent)

Improve by 1% ⇨ **Operating profit improvement**

Price	14.8
Variable cost	9.3
Volume	5.5
Fixed cost	4.5

Exhibit 3-4 Soundco Radio Company: CDR-2000 Pocket Price Waterfall

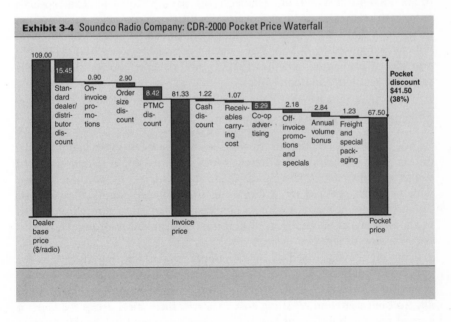

109.00

15.45
Standard dealer/distributor discount

0.90
On-invoice promotions

2.90
Order size discount

8.42
PTMC discount

81.33

1.22
Cash discount

1.07
Receivables carrying cost

5.29
Co-op advertising

2.18
Off-invoice promotions and specials

2.84
Annual volume bonus

1.23
Freight and special packaging

67.50

Pocket discount $41.50 (38%)

Dealer base price ($/radio)

Invoice price

Pocket price

$109, Soundco deducted up to four specific discounts to arrive at invoice price: (1) a standard dealer/distributor discount that varied by account channel category and averaged $15.45 per radio; (2) frequent on-invoice promotions to stimulate sales of particular products which, in the case of the CDR-2000, averaged 90 cents per unit sold; (3) a discount of up to 4 percent off base price, based on the total dollar value of an order. On average, it was $2.90 per radio; and (4) a price-to-meet-competition (PTMC) discount, negotiated customer-by-customer, to meet competitor prices. With these on-invoice discounts, the average invoice price for the CDR-2000 model was $81.33. The minimal attention Soundco paid to transaction pricing focused almost entirely on this invoice price.

That invoice price focus meant that Soundco overlooked a major part of the total pricing picture: all the discounting and revenue leaks occurring off-invoice, which resulted in an average pocket price of $67.50 (17 percent less than invoice price and 38 percent less than dealer base price). The off-invoice items included: (1) a cash discount of 2 percent for payment of invoices within specified time periods; (2) extended terms (payments not required until 75 or even 90 days after receipt of an invoice) to a handful of distributors and high-volume retail accounts. The cost of carrying these extended receivables averaged $1.07; (3) cooperative advertising ($5.29), where Soundco provided partial funding for local and regional advertising of Soundco products; (4) miscellaneous off-invoice promotions and specials (e.g., cash rebates to end-customers, awards for retailer sales personnel) at an average of $2.18; (5) annual volume bonus ($2.84), based on the total volume purchased from Soundco over the course of a year; and (6) freight and special packaging expenses ($1.23) paid by Soundco for shipping the radios to retailers and distributors.

SOUNDCO'S POCKET PRICE BAND

As one would expect, not all transactions for the CDR-2000 had the same pocket price. Accounts of different types qualified for different standard dealer and distributor discounts. Quantities ordered by accounts varied widely, which resulted in variations in order-size discounts. And PTMC discounts were negotiated with specific deals. Even more variability existed in the off-invoice items. Not all accounts paid invoices promptly, resulting in major differences in cash discounts and receivables carrying costs; and not all accounts used all of the cooperative advertising allowance for which they qualified. Wholesalers and retailers took advantage of off-invoice promotions and specials at different levels, with some not participating at all. Account size (and resulting cost-to-serve efficiencies) drove the level of annual volume bonus, and freight and packaging paid by Soundco varied

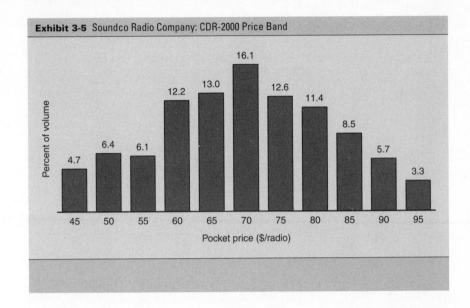

Exhibit 3-5 Soundco Radio Company: CDR-2000 Price Band

widely based on retailer location, order pattern, and special packaging needs such as information printed in multiple languages.

These differences in on- and off-invoice discount elements resulted in the wide pocket price band shown in Exhibit 3-5. The average pocket price was $67.50, but units sold for a pocket price as low as $45 and as high as $95, resulting in a 111 percent difference between the lowest and highest pocket prices. A pocket price band like this should trigger immediate questions: What are the underlying drivers of the price band's shape and width? Does this pocket price variability make good management sense and align with Soundco's market strategy? Why are pocket prices so variable, and can that variability be positively managed?

Managers at Soundco were at first surprised at the width of the price band for their CDR-2000 model but, on reflection, concluded that it was all due to and justified by differences in account sizes. Soundco had a clearly stated market strategy of rewarding account volume with lower prices, rationalizing that cost-to-serve would decrease with higher account volume. To test the assumption that variability in pocket price was explained by account size, the company plotted discounts against account size and created the analysis shown in Exhibit 3-6.

Each point on this chart represents a single Soundco retail or wholesale account. The horizontal axis shows annual dollar volume of sales through each account. The vertical axis shows pocket discount for CDR-2000 radios sold to each account. If account size were the primary driver of pocket

Exhibit 3-6 Soundco Radio Company: Pocket Discount versus Account Size

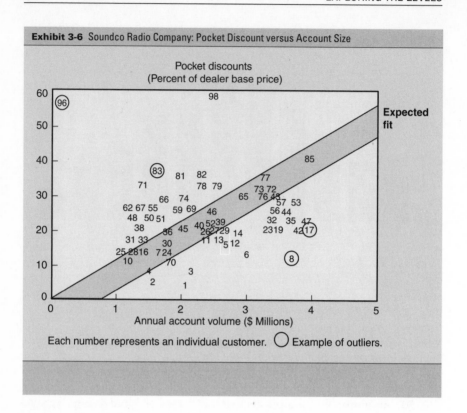

Each number represents an individual customer. ◯ Example of outliers.

price bandwidth, then you would expect the account to be in the shaded diagonal area labeled "expected fit"—that is, the larger the account, the larger the pocket discount. But the accounts are scattered—a virtual shotgun blast—showing no correlation between account size and pocket discount level. Close examination showed that some relatively small accounts, like accounts 96 and 83, were buying at very low pocket price levels. At the same time, several large accounts, like accounts 8 and 17, were buying at relatively high pocket price levels.

Perplexed by this apparent randomness, Soundco managers launched an immediate investigation to understand what explained the scatter. Soundco thought that extenuating circumstances might explain some of the smaller accounts' positioning above the "expected fit" line in Exhibit 3-6, for example, a retailer's location in a depressed market or in a region where competitive intensity was extremely high, or where Soundco's competitive position was particularly weak. In fact, this was not the case for most of the accounts. It turned out that most of the over-discounted smaller accounts had no legitimate reason to be paying such low pocket prices. Most of these accounts were just experienced, clever customers who had been dealing with Soundco for 20 years or more and knew just whom to call at Soundco headquarters to get that extra exception discount, that percentage point of extra co-op advertising, that extra 30 or 60 days to pay, the large-order size discount on small orders. They had close relationships with regional Soundco sales managers who regularly gave them preferred treatment on off-invoice promotions and specials. These favorite old accounts were granted extra discounts based on familiarity and relationships rather than on economic justification and performance. These experienced customers understood the Soundco pocket price waterfall better than Soundco and were working it against the company.

When searching for the sources of a wide pocket price band, companies should always consider variance and slippage-type price deviations, two of the major drivers of bandwidth. Soundco's customers' skillful negotiation of low prices is a classic example of what is known as a variance-type price deviation. Variance-type deviations refer to situations where two customers who should pay about the same price actually pay different prices because unjustifiably different prices were originally negotiated with each. Variance issues are best addressed by bringing full transparency to low price transactions, instituting processes to catch these deals before they make it to the customer, and rewarding salespeople for over-performing relative to their peers.

Another type of deviation to watch for is slippage. In slippage, a customer agrees to a pricing discount, condition, or term but the customer does not comply with the term and/or the supplier does not enforce it. Frequent slippage examples include customers not adhering precisely to payment terms (e.g., a customer can take a 2 percent cash discount if they pay their invoice within 30 days; they pay in 40 days and still take the 2 percent discount), customers not reaching a volume bonus hurdle but still being granted the bonus. Slippage issues are best addressed by gaining better transparency into when they occur and enforcing the agreed-to pricing terms and rules with greater consistency and discipline.

CAPTURING THE OPPORTUNITY AT SOUNDCO

After examining its pocket price band, Soundco senior management finally realized that its transaction pricing process was out of control, that decision making up and down the waterfall lacked discipline, and that no one was focusing on the sum total of those decisions as reflected in pocket price. The end result was transaction pricing that did not square with Soundco's intended strategy of rewarding account size with lower prices—a reality that was costing Soundco millions of dollars.

To correct its transaction pricing shortfalls, Soundco immediately mounted a three-part program. First, it took aggressive corrective actions to bring the over-discounted "old favorite" accounts back into line. Marketing and sales managers identified problem accounts and explained the situation and its overall impact on Soundco profitability to the sales force. Then Soundco gave the sales force nine months to fix or drop those outliers. Fixing meant decreasing the excessive discounting across the waterfall so that outlier accounts' pocket prices were more in line with other accounts of similar size. They designed a specific negotiation plan for each outlier account, focusing on the waterfall elements that were driving pocket price down most. Sales people who could not negotiate their outlier pocket prices up to an appropriate level (or drive account volume up to a level that aligned with existing discounting) were instructed to find other accounts in their territory to replace them. This well-executed pricing variance reduction initiative helped the sales force correct 90 percent of the outlier accounts over the next nine months. The sales force's newfound realization that every element of the waterfall represented a viable negotiating lever contributed much to this success. And in most cases, salespeople easily found more profitable replacement accounts for the 10 percent that could not be fixed.

Second, Soundco launched a program to stimulate sales volume in larger accounts that had higher-than-average pocket prices compared with accounts of similar size. Management singled out these attractive accounts for special treatment. Sales and marketing personnel researched them carefully and even interviewed some customers to better understand the nonprice benefits to which these accounts were most sensitive. Soundco ultimately increased volume in these accounts, not by lowering price, but by delivering the specific benefits that were most important to each: higher levels of service to some, shortened order lead times for others, more frequent sales calls for still others.

Third and finally, Soundco instituted a crash program to get the transaction pricing process under control. This program included, among other components, clear decision rules and guidelines for each discretionary item in the waterfall. It established pocket price as the universal measure of price performance in all transaction pricing performance and IT systems. It also capped discretionary on-invoice discounts at 5 percent and granted them only after a structured evaluation of volume, margin, and market impact. Individual pocket price targets were established for each product line within each account to help prevent the recurrence of the shotgun-blast chart comparing pocket price and account size. Soundco's IT department set up new information systems to help guide and monitor transaction-pricing decisions. it began tracking and allocating to each transaction all the significant off-invoice waterfall elements that were previously reported on a company-wide basis. Reporting was also created to red-flag customer situations where significant price slippage was occurring—so that sales person could see that slippage in a timely fashion and take quick action to correct it. Further, pocket price realization against those account-specific targets became a major component of incentive compensation for salespeople, sales managers, and even product managers.

From these three transaction-pricing initiatives, Soundco reaped rich and sustained rewards. In the first year of implementation, average pocket price levels increased a full 3 percent, and, while unit sales volume remained flat, operating profits swelled 44 percent. Soundco realized additional pocket price gains in each of the two subsequent years as skill in transaction price management grew across the organization. As is often the case, Soundco also received some unexpected strategic benefits from its newfound transaction pricing capability. Account-specific pocket price reporting revealed a small but growing distribution channel for radios where Soundco's pocket prices were consistently higher than average. Increasing volume and penetration in this emerging channel became a key strategic initiative for Soundco that generated further incremental earnings. The fresh and more granular business perspective that senior Soundco managers gained for their involvement in transaction pricing became the catalyst for an ongoing stream of similar strategic insights and opportunities.

POCKET MARGIN WATERFALL AND BAND

In the flooring company and Soundco Radio cases, companies were selling standard products and essentially standard services to all accounts. In such situations, pocket price is usually a representative, prescriptive measure of price performance. Generally the higher the pocket price, the higher the attractiveness of the transaction for a particular standard product.

But what about product and service offerings that are not standard—products that are tailored to specific customer applications or standard products where the accompanying service (and the cost of that service) varies widely across customers? It could be argued that in these situations, pocket price may not tell the entire story of pricing and transaction attractiveness. In such situations, the pocket price concept may require an extension to what is called *pocket margin* to be useful. The following case shows how this refinement to the pocket price waterfall works.

ALEN GLASS COMPANY CASE

The Alen Glass Company makes tempered glass used in the cabs of heavy-duty trucks (both over-the-road and off-road applications), in earthmovers, and in other construction and agricultural equipment. Although all of its products are tempered glass, no two customers share exactly the same product. For example, the windshield designed for one manufacturer's truck will not fit another manufacturer's vehicle. Each product must be designed for each specific truck or equipment manufacturer. And products vary not only in size and shape but also in annual volume and customer service requirements. For instance, some higher volume truck manufacturers require windshields and side-glass to be shipped in special containers that are compatible with material handling equipment within the truck manufacturers' assembly plants. Pocket price would clearly not provide a complete and useful measure of transaction attractiveness for Alen.

ALEN GLASS DIAGNOSTIC

Extending the pocket price waterfall to the *pocket margin waterfall* makes it relevant to this business situation. This extension still has pocket price at its foundation. Pocket margin is defined as the pocket price for a transaction minus direct product costs and any account-specific costs-to-serve. Exhibit 3-7

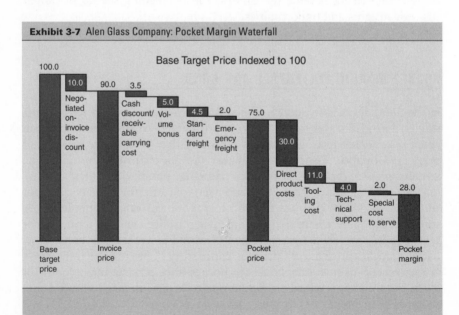

Exhibit 3-7 Alen Glass Company: Pocket Margin Waterfall

shows Alen's average pocket margin waterfall. The starting point is the base target price for each glass application. That target price is established when the truck manufacturer specifies each individual glass application. It is calculated with expected standard material and processing costs and expected annual unit volume and further fine-tuned based on the application's market segment.

For ease of comparability, we indexed this base target price to 100 and showed all other waterfall elements as a percentage of that index. So, from that base target price, a negotiated on-invoice discount that averages 10 percent of base is subtracted to yield an average invoice price of 90. Off the invoice, cash discounts and receivables carrying costs average 3.5; a volume bonus averages 5; and standard freight is 4.5 on average. Alen is also required from time to time to pay emergency freight to manufacturers, which averages 2 percent of base price. The resultant pocket price is 75 percent of base.

From pocket price, we now subtract various costs involved in customizing the product and serving the customer. These provide us with the pocket margin of 28 percent of base target price. Direct product costs of 30 are subtracted first. Alen often has to incur tooling costs for custom glass applications, which are on average 11 percent of base. Technical support varies widely by account and application, but averages 4 percent. Miscellaneous special costs-to-serve, such as special packaging or special applications support, average another 2 percent. With pocket price as its revenue foundation and direct and special costs used on the expense side, pocket margin can be an effective indicator of transaction attractiveness in nonstandard product situations. (Appendix 1 also presents a selection of pocket margin waterfalls.)

Alen, unfortunately, had traditionally focused its pricing energy on constructing the base target price for a customer product and then negotiating its on-invoice discount. It paid little attention to off-invoice price items or to costs beyond direct product costs, which were aggregated in general accounts. The result was an incomplete picture of the transaction price and transaction margin. In trying to obtain a more complete picture, it made sense to create a pocket margin band, particularly given the strong likelihood that the elements of pocket margin varied widely across customers and transactions.

Exhibit 3-8 shows Alen's pocket margin band. The horizontal axis is pocket margin as a percent of base target price. The height of the bars corresponds to the percentage of sales dollars at each pocket margin level. Alen had transactions with pocket margin as high as 55 percent and as low as a loss equal to 15 percent of target base price—altogether, a 70 percentage-point pocket margin range. Furthermore, when we applied Alen's fixed costs to its sales volume, a pocket margin of 12 percent was required for operating

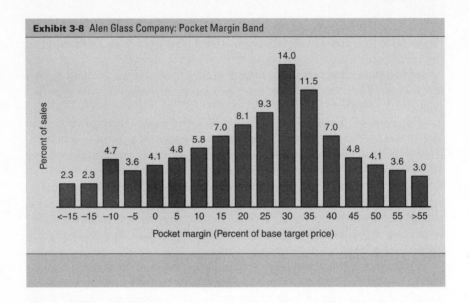

Exhibit 3-8 Alen Glass Company: Pocket Margin Band

profit breakeven. The band shows that a major portion of Alen's book of business, more than a quarter of its sales, was below breakeven.

CAPTURING THE OPPORTUNITY AT ALEN

Alen followed the same routine as Soundco as it tried to uncover opportunities within its pocket margin band. Alen sales and marketing managers put transactions at the extremes of the pocket margin band under the microscope to begin to understand the sources of the exceedingly wide variations in pocket margin. Given that they tried to apply a consistent, thoughtful discipline when setting base target price and negotiating the on-invoice discount, Alen managers were astonished at just how wide their pocket margin band was. Remarkably clear but previously unperceived patterns of business attractiveness surfaced as Alen took the hard look at its pocket margin band. Certain customer and product combinations always clustered at the high end of the pocket margin band—for example, medium volume, flat, or single-bend door glass sold to certain customers. Different customer and product combinations clustered at the low end, for example, high-volume, multibend windshields sold to other manufacturers.

It quickly became clear which types of glass applications were inherently more profitable for Alen and which were not. Unprofitable applications consistently underperformed on three elements of the pocket margin waterfall: excessive receivables carrying cost, high freight cost driven by erratic ordering behavior, and excessive per unit tooling costs driven by design complexity and overly optimistic customer estimates of annual purchase volume.

Unambiguous sales and marketing initiatives flowed directly from these granular insights into pocket margin differences. First, Alen identified and aggressively pursued every glass application that was in Alen's "sweet spot"—in other words, those that were inherently more pocket margin rich for Alen. This focus gradually increased its win rate for these jobs over time. Second, Alen applied extra care and diligence when bidding on glass applications of the type that populated the low end of their pocket margin band. They negotiated such deals much more aggressively and put in place explicit customer penalties for poor receivables performance, erratic order quantities, and unit sales significantly below the annual volume targets specified in the purchase contract. This aggressive stance caused them to lose some business that would have generated pocket margin losses anyway, and to win only when conditions were in place to move such business to pocket margin profitability. These specific customer and market initiatives aimed at the extremes of the pocket margin bands resulted in a 4 percent increase in Alen's average pocket margin and a 60 percent increase in operating profit within one year.

* * *

The Transactions level is the most detailed and precise of the three levels of price management. Here the primary issue is how to arrive at the best price for each and every customer transaction. The pocket price waterfall, a core tool, helps companies manage the full range of pricing elements, both on and off the invoice, that affect pocket price—the amount that you actually put in your pocket. The pocket price band demonstrates the often surprisingly wide degree of variability that occurs in pocket price, even when exactly the same product is offered to different customers. Understanding the sources of pocket price bandwidth—whether slippage or variance deviations—can help you manage and take advantage of it. For products that are not standard across customers, the pocket price waterfall can be refined and extended to create the pocket margin waterfall, which recognizes important product and service differences across transactions. In such situations, the pocket margin band then becomes the appropriate analytic tool for looking at pocket margin variations across customers and transactions.

Most companies just let these wide pocket price and pocket margin bands happen. As we have shown, businesses that excel at the Transactions level actively and intentionally manage the shape of their pocket price and pocket margin bands. They know the shape and composition of their bands; they know where individual customers and transactions reside on their bands and why; and they take deliberate steps to improve the pocket price and pocket margin of customers who are unjustifiably low on their bands, and to gain volume and share from customers at the high end. They modify or discontinue waterfall elements that are not effectively influencing positive behavior by their customers. They set clear targets (often account by account) for pocket price or pocket margin realization, and they monitor performance against those targets. Furthermore, they build incentives that reward sales and marketing personnel for improvements in pocket price and pocket margin by customer.

Excelling at the Transactions level is an absolute prerequisite for any business that aspires to create and sustain *the price advantage*. Excellence at the other levels of price management is fruitless unless it is ultimately delivered in the form of correct and well-managed transaction prices.

CHAPTER 4

Customer Value

T he next level of price management, the Customer Value level, is all about getting your price position right relative to competitors in every customer segment you serve. It is about finding prices that position your products correctly against competitors' products on a price/benefit basis. At this level, the focus is on price levels that are usually quite visible to customers and competitors alike, and that publicly communicate what you believe your product is worth relative to those of competitors. Here, you set the list prices, base prices, or manufacturer's suggested retail prices (MSRPs) that often serve as the starting point for negotiations at the Transactions level. Setting the "sticker price" for an automobile is the classic Customer Value level pricing decision. Even if few customers actually pay full sticker price, that sticker price is still an important and visible statement about how the manufacturer is positioning that vehicle relative to competitors; in other words, a higher sticker price indicates that the manufacturer considers that vehicle superior to its competitors in the same category.

Pricing excellence at the Customer Value level assures a just return from the investment and work devoted to developing and delivering superior products and services. It requires careful management of the crucial trade-off between benefits and price and skillful positioning of products vis-à-vis competitors' offerings. In general, price should be closely aligned with per-ceived benefits—price too low and you risk leaving substantial money on the table (and cheating yourself of the fruits of your labor); too high and you risk alienating customers and losing market share. A framework called the "value map" brings the way that the price/benefit tradeoff works to life and helps inform superior price/benefit positioning of product offerings. In this chapter, we explore in depth: (1) creating and interpreting value maps; (2) understanding how companies can change their positions on a value map; (3) understanding how customers distribute across the map; and (4) identifying variability in customer price and benefit perception.

MAPPING VALUE

Value may be one of the most overused and misapplied terms in marketing and pricing today. *Value pricing* is too often misused as a synonym for low price or bundled pricing.

The true essence of "value" reflects the tradeoff between the benefits a customer receives from a product and the price paid for it—or, more accurately, the *perceived* benefits received and the *perceived* price paid. In other words, value equals perceived benefits minus perceived price. Companies can increase the likelihood that customers will buy a product by increasing perceived benefits, decreasing perceived price, or doing both.

The fact that benefits are *perceived, and often subjective,* makes them particularly difficult for businesses to measure or manage well. Even when there are clear metrics for benefits, there can be a gap between perception and reality. Positive (or negative) past experiences with a brand or a supplier can affect perception of benefits long after the reality of those benefits has changed. So despite the fact that the quality and durability of many American cars are today on par with Japanese brands, the perception of inferior American quality has lingered on for years.

The perception element of price can be just as tricky to understand and manage. On the surface, price is a clear number where there is little basis for perception variability. But in a simple example, grocery shoppers often assume that a larger carton of orange juice is cheaper per ounce than a smaller package. This may not be the case if the retailer is offering promotional discounts on smaller sizes, making them the less expensive choice on a per unit basis.

In B2B markets, transactions are usually more complicated (with more intricate pocket price waterfalls); and even though professional buyers are often involved, there can still be important perceptual aspects to price. How price is structured, communicated, and eventually collected can easily shift a customer's perception of price level. (We look at these topics in detail in Chapter 11, "Pricing Architecture.")

CREATING A VALUE MAP

Exhibit 4-1 shows an example of a value map, a framework that demonstrates how the price/benefit tradeoff functions in real markets. Each circle in this map represents the product offering of a different company. In this basic example, perceived prices are tracked on the vertical axis and perceived benefits—which, say for a computer system, could be a combination of speed, memory, reliability, and many other factors—on the horizontal

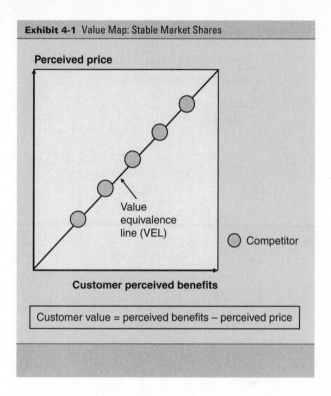

Exhibit 4-1 Value Map: Stable Market Shares

Perceived price

Value equivalence line (VEL)

◯ Competitor

Customer perceived benefits

Customer value = perceived benefits − perceived price

axis. Manufacturers with higher-priced, higher-benefit systems are in the upper right, and those with lower-priced, lower-benefit systems are in the lower left.

If a market is stable (i.e., market share is not shifting among competitors), and if perceived prices and benefits have been measured accurately, then the competitors will align along a diagonal called the *value equivalence line* (VEL), as shown in Exhibit 4-1. At any desired price or benefit level, there is a clear and logical choice of which computer to buy. In such markets, customers clearly get what they pay for. If customers want more benefits, they have to pay more; if they want lower prices, they have to be ready to forfeit some benefits. This clarity of choice virtually defines a stable market. It is important to note, however, that while market shares are stable, they are not necessarily equal. There could easily be more customers who want a high-priced, high-benefit computer than those who want a low-priced, low-benefit one.

If shares are changing across competitors in a market, then a properly constructed value map will look more like Exhibit 4-2, with some companies

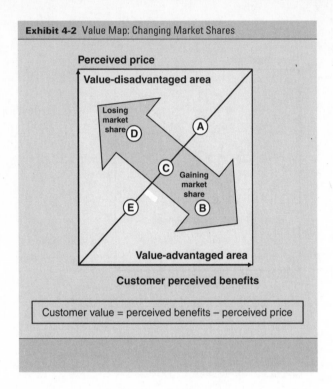

Exhibit 4-2 Value Map: Changing Market Shares

Perceived price

Value-disadvantaged area

Losing market share (D)   (A)

(C)

Gaining market share

(E)   (B)

Value-advantaged area

Customer perceived benefits

Customer value = perceived benefits − perceived price

positioned off the VEL. Company B is below the VEL in a *value-advantaged position (e.g., either more benefits or lower price)* and is gaining share. Looking at the value map, we see that if a customer wants a low-priced system, the choice is clear between companies E and B, since Company B offers a better computer at the same price. At the same time, a customer who wants a high-benefit computer also has a clear choice between companies A and B, since both offer similar benefits, but B is priced much lower.

In contrast, Company D is above the VEL in a *value-disadvantaged position (e.g., either higher price or fewer benefits).* In this position, Company E offers equal benefits for a lower price, and Company A offers more benefits for the same price. Not surprisingly, if this value map is accurate, Company D should be losing market share.

BENEFIT PERCEPTIONS

How customers perceive the benefits they will receive is one of the primary drivers of their decisions when making a purchase. It is also one of the areas where the value map can be invaluable in helping companies create a true picture of where they stand in their customers' eyes. The majority of this section will show how a company used a value map it developed with customer-based research to turn its strategy around and simultaneously increased price and gained market share.

Two primary customer research methods are used to develop value maps. The first is direct questioning of key audiences, such as structured interviews and focus groups. These open-ended, dialogue-based methods are the best way to identify the full list of buying attributes and to examine deeply why specific answers were given. The second method is tradeoff-based research, such as conjoint and discrete-choice analysis. These techniques, which require that the company already knows the relevant buying attributes, probe the customer's decision-making process by assessing how the full suite of these attributes are considered jointly. (A case study illustrating conjoint analysis is provided in Chapter 16, "The Monnarch Battery Case.")

It should be noted that a value map is relevant for the specific segment of customers who weigh benefit attributes in a similar fashion. If a subset of customers has fundamentally different requirements and places different relative importance on specific attributes, then a separate value map needs to be created for that segment; it may also require a distinct market strategy. (See Price Segmentation section in Chapter 13, "Tailored Value.")

We will now turn our attention to the practical application of the value map. The experience of a company we call Normcomp shows how internal misperception can skew value analysis and how creating an accurate value map can suggest profit-building actions. Normcomp supplied advanced computer networking systems and prided itself on its engineering skills and its ability to deliver high-technological performance at a reasonable cost. Unfortunately, Normcomp had begun losing market share.

Based on Normcomp's *internal* understanding of how customers perceived benefits and price in its market, the company built the value map shown in Exhibit 4-3. Perceived price was believed to be straightforward because industry prices were scrutinized carefully by outside analysts, published routinely, and highly transparent. The mix of volume discounts, rebates, and payment terms offered by computer makers was on average fairly standard. Normcomp was also comfortable with its internal understanding of the benefit attributes that drove customers' systems choices. It believed customers chose networking systems based primarily on processor speed and system reliability.

Using its internal views on benefits and price, Normcomp plotted itself and its key rivals—Preemco, Keecomp, and Baseco—on the value map. The

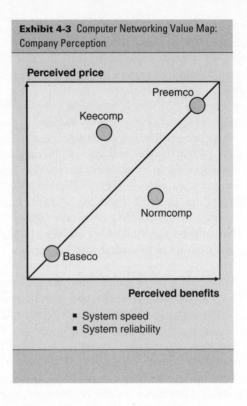

Exhibit 4-3 Computer Networking Value Map: Company Perception

Perceived price

Preemco

Keecomp

Normcomp

Baseco

Perceived benefits

- System speed
- System reliability

company saw itself in a value-advantaged position, meaning that it should have been picking up rather than losing market share. Preemco was the obvious premium competitor, ranking highest in price as well as in system speed and reliability. But compared to Keecomp, Normcomp's computers were not only cheaper but also faster and more reliable. Company managers were stumped to find an explanation for their server's disappointing market performance. Why were they losing share instead of gaining it as their value map seemed to predict they should?

Normcomp faced a common problem. The company's managers understood its products well, but not its customers. Although managers thought technical superiority was important, they had never taken the time to research the attributes that customers actually considered when choosing network servers. To determine exactly what perceived benefits drove customer choice, Normcomp's marketing department stepped back from its assumptions and commissioned a market study. Sixty buyers in Normcomp's targeted customer segment were interviewed about their criteria for selecting a network server supplier.

THREE TYPES OF BENEFITS

The benefits that suppliers provide to their customers fall into three categories: functional, process, and relationship.

Functional benefits relate to the physical nature or performance of the product. These benefits can be, for example, processor speed for a computer, flow rate for a pump, purity of a chemical, the acceleration of a sports car, or the taste of a candy bar. Because benefits in this category are usually the easiest to measure and compare against competitors, it is often the first—and too often the only—category considered.

Process benefits are those that make transactions between buyers and sellers easier, quicker, more efficient, or even more pleasant. Examples of these benefits include ease of access to product information; automated restocking or reordering systems; online or electronic data interchange (EDI) payment options; or a drive-through pharmacy pickup window. In some markets, process benefits can provide more of the benefit differential between suppliers than functional benefits.

Relationship benefits are those that accrue to a customer who enters into a mutually beneficial relationship with a seller. These benefits include softer relationship benefits like a customer's emotional connection to a brand or personalized service, as well as more tangible relationship benefits like differentiated loyalty rewards or exchanges of information that provides benefits to both customer and supplier. In many markets these relationship benefits are becoming increasingly powerful drivers of actual buying behavior.

The first steps were to understand clearly which benefits were important to customers and to compare Normcomp's relative performance in those areas against the competition. Using conjoint analysis, Normcomp identified the key perceived benefit attributes and their relative importance. The results, shown on the left-hand side of Exhibit 4-4, revealed that system speed was indeed important. However, the next attributes, in order of importance, were professional services (the technical skills of the sales and professional staff), system interoperability (the ability to communicate with other systems), and system reliability.

Further insights arose when Normcomp compared its performance against the competition based on these attributes. Although system speed was important, as the right-hand side of Exhibit 4-4 shows, all of the main

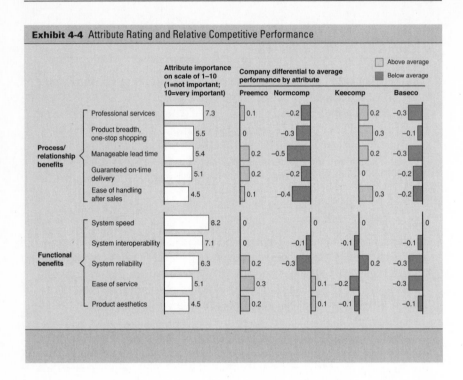

Exhibit 4-4 Attribute Rating and Relative Competitive Performance

players were comparable. Normcomp's slight system speed advantage over Keecomp was not a critical factor.

Normcomp's internal point of view on how customers perceived price levels across the competitors was shown to be directionally correct. However, Keecomp performed much better than Normcomp in other benefits such as the perceived quality of professional services and system reliability, which were key differentiators for customers.

Exhibit 4-5 shows the revised, more accurate value map based on *customer* perception of benefit attributes and the performance of suppliers against the key drivers of customer decisions. Because Keecomp scored well on the attributes most important to customers, it sits in a value-advantaged position despite its higher price, which explains why it was gaining market share. Normcomp has shifted into a value-disadvantaged position since it performed relatively poorly on the attributes most closely linked to buying decisions. The reasons for Normcomp's poor market performance were now clear.

Armed with these fresh insights, Normcomp began a crash program to tackle its problems. Many of its customers faced compatibility problems

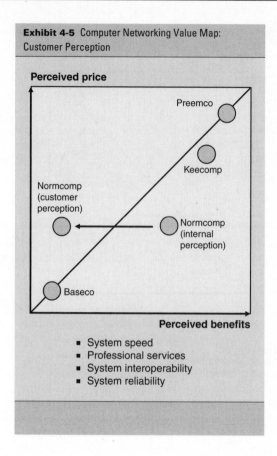

Exhibit 4-5 Computer Networking Value Map: Customer Perception

Perceived price

Preemco

Keecomp

Normcomp (customer perception)

Normcomp (internal perception)

Baseco

Perceived benefits

- System speed
- Professional services
- System interoperability
- System reliability

linked to their enterprise resource-planning (ERP) systems, as well as configuration. These problems were corrected with a minor rewrite of the software and the introduction of a standardized configuration tool. Reliability problems from an earlier generation continued to taint the market's perception of Normcomp's new system, so the company mounted an aggressive marketing campaign to demonstrate the reliability of the latest model. Finally, the sales force and professional staff were given new training and improved configuration tools that simplified the sales process and better matched customer integration requirements.

Within six months, Normcomp shifted its position on the value map dramatically, as shown in Exhibit 4-6. Customer perception of the benefits of Normcomp's new systems improved so much that it was able to increase its price by 8 percent and regain 5 percent of market share. The price and

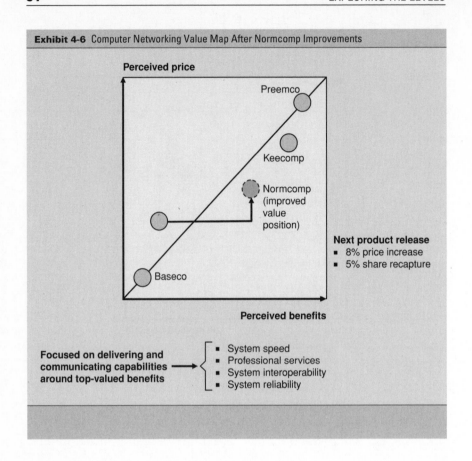

Exhibit 4-6 Computer Networking Value Map After Normcomp Improvements

Perceived price

Preemco

Keecomp

Normcomp
(improved
value
position)

Next product release
- 8% price increase
- 5% share recapture

Baseco

Perceived benefits

Focused on delivering and communicating capabilities around top-valued benefits →
- System speed
- Professional services
- System interoperability
- System reliability

volume increase more than doubled the company's operating profits in this product line.

What does the Normcomp case show us about managing value? First, the key to success often starts with gaining a clear understanding of the real attributes driving customer choice and their relative importance. Trusting internal perceptions of which attributes drive customer choice, rather than information from customers themselves, can be a fatal mistake. In many situations, softer, nontechnical attributes like perceived reliability, support quality, and the ease of doing business can match or outrank measurable technical features in the minds of customers, especially when multiple suppliers can meet most customers' minimum technical requirements.

Normcomp sold its products directly to its end customers. However, there are often intermediaries (or channel partners) between supplier and end-customer. These intermediaries run the gamut from retailers and distributors, who may include a company's products on their shelves or in their catalogues, to value-added resellers (VARs), who perform a wide range of services linked to the product. Whatever the relationship, the partner is an integral component in the delivery of benefits and value to the customer and must be carefully managed. Such partners add complexity to any attempts to understand a company's value position.

Companies dealing with channel partners face an unavoidable quandary: partners' economics are based on getting the best price from suppliers, suggesting it would be smart to play down a product's actual benefits when dealing with suppliers. But a partner must actively promote the product to customers—in other words, emphasize these same benefits. This conflict makes it more difficult for the supplier to get an accurate gauge of end-user demand and the benefits being delivered to and through its channel partners. Although the water here is murkier, a company must try to understand the benefits delivered to and through its channel partners just as well as those delivered to end-use customers.

PRICE PERCEPTIONS

Price levels, just like benefit levels, are *perceived*; and companies influence the perception of price in any number of ways, including how they communicate and structure it. (A more complete discussion of this topic is included in Chapter 11, "Pricing Architecture.")

Understanding customers' price perceptions can be as challenging as pinpointing benefits perceptions. In B2B and consumer environments alike, price can be a sensitive subject to research directly with customers. As discussed in Chapter 3, "Transactions," a seller may not realize what its real pocket price is. Customers faced with multiple levels of discounting and diverse price structures across competitors may also find price comparisons inherently difficult. For example, a buyer may think one supplier is higher priced than another based on invoice price, while in reality that supplier might be the less expensive option when off-invoice discounts are fully considered. In other examples, a brand's low-price reputation may cause consumers to perceive its price as lower than it actually is or, conversely, a brand's reputation for high quality may trigger higher price perceptions even as it tries to enter a more cost-conscious market segment.

As we have seen, variability and imprecision exist around the perception of both price and benefits. The value equivalence *line* on value maps might be taken to imply that any price movement—no matter how small—might change a supplier's value position and affect customer choice. This is seldom the case. In fact, a range of prices—a *zone of indifference*—usually exists in which a customer will buy a given product. Depending on a host of factors, the zone of indifference can be narrow (for instance, less than plus or minus 1 percent) or wide (plus or minus 5 percent or more). It varies by customer segment and even by individual supplier. When price elasticity research is conducted, it should be explicitly designed to measure the magnitude of the existing zone of indifference. Increasing list prices or base prices within this zone of indifference can be one of the most risk-free ways of quickly improving price and boosting profits.

PRICE ELASTICITY—NOT AS SIMPLE AS IT SEEMS

Although the concept is straightforward (elasticity shows how price changes affect volume sold), elasticity is complex in practice and care must be taken not to misuse or over-rely on simple elasticity numbers for pricing decisions. A variety of issues that complicate the simple application of elasticity research results are listed below.

- *The zone of indifference.* Within the zone of indifference, price elasticity can be thought of as zero. For items within this zone, pricing moves—sometimes small, often larger than expected—do not impact volume purchased. This indifference may be due to low pricing visibility, increased hassles, or real switching costs.
- *Nonlinear nature of elasticity.* Price elasticity is rarely linear; as the price gap to alternatives gets progressively larger, elasticity changes. As a result, blanket statements like "the elasticity in this market is –1.7," which ignore this nonlinearity, oversimplify the true nature of elasticity.
- *Variance by segment.* Just as different types of customers have different needs and benefits perceptions, they also have varying levels of price sensitivity. Companies must be careful and avoid generalizing price elasticities blindly *across* customer segments.
- *Variance by occasion.* The context in which we buy a product can influence elasticity dramatically. For instance, a soft drink purchased in a vending machine for immediate consumption can have different price elasticity than in-store purchases for future consumption.
- *Variance over time.* As time passes, markets evolve and customer needs and preferences change. Customers become more comfortable with existing offerings and inevitability push for new products

and more benefits. To meet this demand and price for profitability, companies must continually reevaluate their elasticity research to make sure it is up-to-date.

- *Variance by price communication method.* How price is communicated—for instance, as a daily rate, monthly rate, or yearly rate—can have a surprisingly strong effect on how sensitive customer segments are to the same net change in price.

- *Variance by waterfall element.* As we saw in Chapter 3, "Transactions," the final pocket price is derived from a series of waterfall elements, each of which drives different behaviors. Even if the pocket price remains constant, different customers will be more or less sensitive to changes in different waterfall elements.

MAKING MOVES ON THE VALUE MAP

Understanding the benefit and price levels customers perceive and seeing where those views position a product relative to the competition on a value map are fundamental components to making customer value tradeoffs. But in truth they are just the beginning.

So far, we have only looked at value in a stable environment. The real competitive world is dynamic. New features and benefits are constantly being introduced, cost-cutting and efficiency programs often lead to lower prices, and new players are always watching for opportunities to enter the market. Shifts in customer needs and desires keep the demand side in flux. A new technology such as 3G telecommunications networks can increase the demand for related products such as multimedia mobile phones.

As a result, value maps are constantly changing in important, often predictable ways. It is essential for a company to manage its value position continually and proactively. Managers should understand exactly how they want their value map to evolve, plan carefully where they want to position current and new products for optimal returns, and be ready to capitalize on economic swings and market cycles.

THE DYNAMIC VALUE MAP

Any change in value positioning by one competitor—a price cut or feature improvement, for instance—will cause other players to react, either to preempt shifts in market share or to adjust to them. *Dynamic value management* is the discipline of managing price/benefit positioning in light of likely changes in the value positions of competing products and in the benefits perceptions of customers.

The case of an electric motors company shows how misjudging these dynamics can destroy earnings. Sure Motors made motors for heavy-duty industrial applications, such as machine tools that are often exposed to corrosives or extreme environments. The company's products were high quality and durable, and the company had broad application expertise. Sure Motors and its three primary competitors were each positioned along the VEL in a stable market.

Industry dynamics changed drastically when Sure Motors released a new line of motors that was a little more durable than the previous model and carried a slightly better warranty. Managers at Sure Motors, under pressure from their large customers to deliver increased value in a very competitive market, decided to hold prices steady, especially as manufacturing costs were roughly the same for both models. As shown in Exhibit 4-7, this strategy shifted Sure Motors into a value-advantaged position; as customers began recognizing the new value position, the company started to pick up volume.

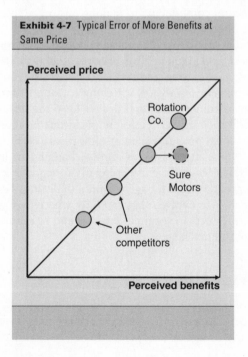

Exhibit 4-7 Typical Error of More Benefits at Same Price

Because the total market for electric motors did not expand, the increased volume came at the expense of Sure Motor's competitors, particularly Rotation Co., the premium player in the market. At first the strategy seemed promising and Sure Motors gained market share, but soon competitors started to protect their share positions. Rotation faced the most immediate threat because the benefit gap between Rotation and Sure Motors had closed; Rotation responded by improving its own warranty and lowering prices. Other suppliers did not have the expertise or resources to match the increased benefits. Faced with falling sales, the suppliers reached for the only lever available: lower prices.

As shown in Exhibit 4-8, Sure Motors' strategy triggered a series of moves across the market that pushed the VEL lower. Overall prices fell, while each player's market share remained for the most part unchanged. The collective actions of these companies essentially nullified Sure Motors' value-advantaged position. The lowered VEL was good for customers because they got more for their money, but the suppliers got less for their products. The final effect was a wholesale transfer of economic surplus from suppliers to customers.

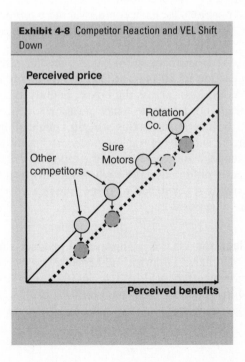

Exhibit 4-8 Competitor Reaction and VEL Shift Down

Could Sure Motors have managed the value dynamics of this situation better? Possibly. If Sure Motors had raised the prices of its new motors to match the increased benefits being offered (and stayed on the original VEL), it would probably have held its traditional share, but at the higher price. In this scenario competitors would not have lost market share and might not have reacted at all. As a result, industry prices generally would have remained stable, while Sure Motors' profit would have increased significantly.

TWO MOVEMENT OPTIONS

Whether improving customer benefit perception, adjusting price perception, or some combination of these, marketing managers have two basic options: repositioning along the VEL or moving off it, usually into value-advantaged territory. It is vital that a company understand these choices, because each may lead to a significantly different outcome—different competitor and customer reactions, prices, volume, profit, and risk.

As companies design moves on the value map, they need to address a central question: how do they want the value map to look in the future? A business with *the price advantage* will often look years down the road and determine its desired future value map, showing its own preferred position and the preferred positions for each competitor. The company can then use that map to develop a strategy to position itself and influence its competitors over time.

For instance, say a new competitor enters a stable market with a stated market share aspiration of 10 percent. The savvy incumbent, rather than fighting the new competitor across the board, might project the value map for five years ahead and determine which position for the new competitor would be best for the incumbent. In this case, they might allow the new player to take its 10 percent share from the low price/low benefit territory, and, in the process, prevent a wholesale drop in the industry VEL. To accomplish this, the incumbent would undertake a whole set of customer-targeting and benefit-creation initiatives designed to corner the new entrant into the low price/low benefit value position.

Repositioning Along the VEL   Repositioning a product along the VEL requires simultaneous changes in price and benefits. It is usually a less aggressive move than moving off the VEL and carries less risk of strong competitive response. Such shifts generally focus on increasing profits, rather than market share, although they may increase share depending on where customer clusters and competitors are located.

In moving along the VEL, a company can remain within the price/ benefit boundaries set by its current competitive positioning or it can move to a position beyond the two extremes (represented by the high- and low-end players). Staying within the current landscape can succeed if the new location represents a more attractive customer cluster and the company's product can stand out from its competitors. This type of move is unlikely to expand the overall market, so as market shares shift, competitors faced with declining sales will probably react. If that reaction is likely to be a price cut, which is often the case, a company should consider its strategy carefully to avoid touching off a downward price spiral. (See Chapter 8, "Price Wars.")

By contrast, adopting a new position outside the prevailing boundaries could expand the market by tapping into latent consumer demand at the high end or the low end of the market. Because the company is moving into new territory, other players are typically less threatened and less likely to retaliate immediately. If the move is successful, others might try to follow suit. Success can bring significant returns, but the company must first accurately identify and quantify a pocket of unmet demand. This can be difficult because consumers may not know what they want or how much they would pay for it until the product and its price tag are in front of them. (See New Products section in Chapter 13, "Tailored Value.")

Whatever repositioning a company decides to adopt, it must understand the risks and opportunities it faces when moving a product along the VEL. When a product moves, it will undoubtedly lose some customers who preferred the old positioning and gain customers who prefer the new positioning. The goal is to gain more customers than are lost—and more attractive, profitable ones; however, companies need to carefully assess the tradeoffs between the various customers in the different value map positions.

With any change in benefits, a corresponding change in price should be considered. As seen in the Sure Motors case, not increasing the price to match the added benefits will often force competitors to react, generally by cutting prices. In contrast, raising the price higher than justified by the benefits improvement will lead to a loss in sales volume. The market research tools noted earlier in this chapter can help companies find the appropriate price for a change in benefits.

Companies moving up or down along the VEL should also be aware of hidden traps that go beyond unilaterally adjusting prices and benefits. A company moving up the VEL into a higher-end market may find that customers in the new region expect a different range of benefits than the company is willing or able to offer. Though a company can charge higher prices, the costs to serve these customers may also be higher. For example, moving into a completely natural or organic category in the grocery market will allow a company to charge premium prices, but the move would also bring increased costs for storage and packaging.

Similarly, moving down-market can cause unexpected problems. All too often, a supplier is unable or unwilling to reduce service levels on lower-priced products. For example, a company's brand might be tarnished if it provides lower service levels even for a lower-priced product. If it does reduce the service levels, a down-market option may hurt the relationship benefits associated with the brand. On the other hand, if the down-market offer is good enough, the company risks cannibalizing its higher-end business. In addition, companies moving down the VEL often find it difficult to create a competitive cost position for the low-end market. As a result, margins will be tight and the return on investment (ROI) may not be enough to justify the move.

Moving Off the VEL A move off the VEL into value-advantaged territory might seem attractive initially, but such moves require a much deeper under-standing of the dynamics and risks of the market than does a move along the VEL. Although repositioning along the VEL often threatens only one or two competitors, a move off can often force every industry player to reconsider its own position and eventually produce a new, lower VEL.

Moving the VEL upward is more difficult and less common. Customers must accept an across-the-board lower level of value and most suppliers move in the same direction. Typically, the VEL shifts upward only when structural changes occur in an industry, such as dramatic increases in raw material or production costs or new regulations that increase costs. Compa-nies need to answer two basic questions—how and how far—when moving off the VEL. They can change benefits, price, or both; but they must be clear on which attributes and what price levels actually influence customer behav-ior. The answer to "how far to move" depends on several factors, including how aggressively it wants to increase market share, how much competitor retaliation it is willing to risk, how long it can wait for results, and how sensitive the market is to changes in value.

When a product is repositioned below the VEL, its "horizon" of po-tential customers grows, as shown in Exhibit 4-9. The new positioning continues to appeal to old customers, who are now offered higher benefits at a lower price (unless the new benefits exceed the needs of some clusters). At the same time, it can attract two new customer groups: those who were paying more for a set of benefits similar to the product's new positioning, and those who were getting less benefit at the same new price.

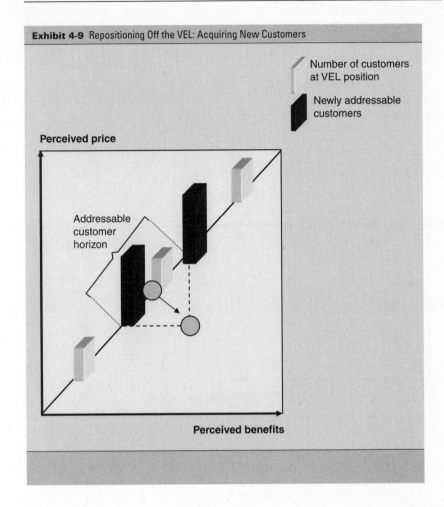

Exhibit 4-9 Repositioning Off the VEL: Acquiring New Customers

Number of customers at VEL position

Newly addressable customers

Perceived price

Addressable customer horizon

Perceived benefits

But moving off the VEL to expand the customer base does not guarantee success. First, market research must establish that the expanded horizon includes new, viable customers. Exhibit 4-10 shows how, for example, a premium supplier might try to cut its price in order to increase its market share. Unfortunately, the new price is not low enough to pull in a new group of customers. The next addressable cluster of customers is satisfied with the benefits it is receiving and has no desire to pay more, even for an increase in benefits. As a result, the premium supplier does not gain market share, but faces a substantial loss of profit under the new prices. The same effect can happen anywhere along the VEL.

Exhibit 4-10 Repositioning Off the VEL: Moving to Empty Space

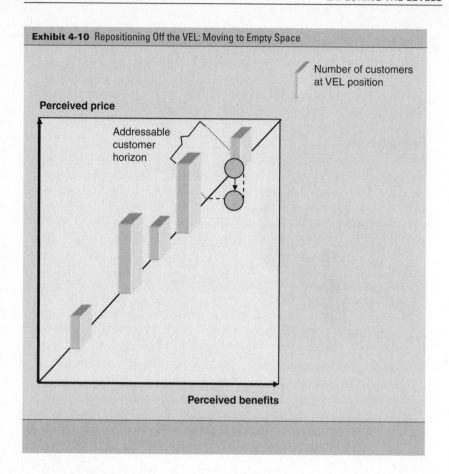

In a consumer dental hygiene product example, a private label attacker tried to grab market share in a particular line with an aggressive, low-priced move against a dominant branded incumbent. The incumbent's immediate reaction was to consider a defensive price cut, but before making a move it researched the market. It found that only a small portion of the market was price sensitive and likely to switch. In addition, the research showed the incumbent had high customer satisfaction ratings. Using the market discontinuity as an opportunity to adjust its offerings, the incumbent released several new varieties of the product and raised prices across the board. Volume loss was much less than originally feared, and the higher prices drastically increased the profitability of the category.

Companies must also be sure that their move off the VEL is large enough for customers to notice. Marginal moves often backfire, as consumers do not see enough difference to make them switch suppliers. In essence, the move keeps prices within the zone of indifference. A company contemplating a move off the VEL must also have a solid appreciation of its competitors' positions and strategies. Competitors monitor such moves closely and will rarely stand by and watch volume or market share drop. They usually improve the attributes of their own products, cut their prices, or both. If they do these things, the VEL can drop while market shares remain stable, as we have previously shown. Careful consideration should therefore be given to how competitors can and will respond.

Often competitors will react by matching the change that triggered the shift in market share. If a company cuts price, rivals are likely to follow suit; if it increases services, they will probably try to do the same. With this in mind, the less damaging move off the VEL is often a repositioning along the benefits axis, rather than the price axis, because it usually takes longer for competitors to mount an equivalent response. It is also easier to retract benefits that are rejected by the market or cannot be provided economically, than to try to raise prices after a round of reductions. As we have seen, however, a shift in benefits does not always prevent a wave of price cuts. If others in the industry cannot match the improved attributes, they are likely to lower prices.

ESTIMATING COMPETITOR RESPONSE

Over time, businesses usually respond predictably—although sometimes appearing irrational—to events in their marketplace. Past behavior and recent strategic steps can offer useful clues to a company's likely response to a price move you make. Several factors to watch for include:

- *Strategic intent.* Companies can appear to respond irrationally from a profit perspective when core markets are threatened. This behavior often occurs if the organization has a product that is a strong profit generator in the market or has made a public announcement that it is targeting a specific market. If the firm is looking to exit the market, it is less likely to fight for the market.
- *Recent investments.* Companies that have recently invested in capacity expansion or in an expensive marketing campaign are

(Continued)

ESTIMATING COMPETITOR RESPONSE (*Continued*)

unlikely to give up without a fight, even if their products are based on older technology or are otherwise inferior.

- *Range of options.* Competitors may not have the ability to match the new features or other benefits delivered by a product. On the other hand, their cost structure might preclude a defensive price cut. Understanding key competitors' range of likely response options should always inform your own moves on the value map.

- *Level of threat.* Not all competitors will react with the same intensity. The strongest reaction, whether it is a benefits or price move, is likely to come from the competitors closest to your product on the value map. Competitors who feel distant from your product on either price or benefits may choose not to react.

- *Market position.* Players already in a value-advantaged position usually respond less aggressively than those that are or become value-disadvantaged.

- *Financial health.* Robust income statements and balance sheets can give the luxury of patience, buying more time to gauge the true effect of a rival's move on the value map.

- *Maturity.* Companies that have survived multiple business cycles and learned the risks of reacting too quickly or too strongly are likely to weigh their response to a rival's price move more carefully.

- *Industry tradition.* Past patterns are often repeated: for example, matching innovation with innovation or avoiding price wars; the same applies to aggressively defending share.

If pricing behavior moves the VEL downward, customer clusters may also shift. As the line shifts through different combinations of price and benefits, customers distributed along the VEL could break up into smaller clusters, as illustrated in Exhibit 4-11. Some customers might not want additional benefits, while others might use the changes to rethink their price/benefit tradeoffs. New offers could stimulate latent demand.

A move off the VEL can bring increased profits if it taps into a valuable customer cluster and can be sustained amid aggressive competitive reactions. In many cases, however, the move is made blindly with little notion of what customers really want, how competitors will react, and how demand patterns might change in the new landscape. Such shortsightedness can kill profitability, as well as the high hopes that were behind the decisions.

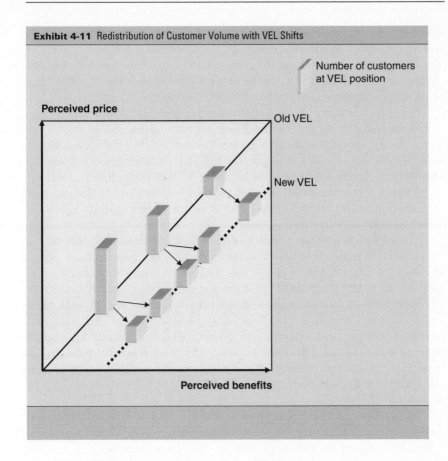

Exhibit 4-11 Redistribution of Customer Volume with VEL Shifts

PUTTING CUSTOMERS ON THE VALUE MAP

All positions along the VEL are not created equal. Even on a value map that describes a well-defined customer segment, customers are not spread evenly along the line. Instead, they typically cluster at various points, with higher volume at some positions than others.

One reason that clusters form is that many customers can be *benefit-bracketed*. They will not accept or consider any products with benefits below some minimum level—nor will they consider any product with benefits exceeding some maximum level. The bottom of a benefit bracket represents the minimum requirements of a buyer. Some automotive component buyers will not accept delivery reliability below a certain level no matter how advantageous the price. On the other hand, benefit ceilings usually show the maximum level of benefits for which a customer is willing to pay. Some computer buyers know how much memory would satisfy their needs and will simply not pay for any more. At times, additional benefits, even at the same price, can even alienate customers. A corporate purchaser might choose a bland ballpoint pen over an elegantly styled alternative at the same price, simply to avoid the impression of extravagance.

Clusters also form because customers are *price-capped*. They are unwilling to spend more than a fixed amount for a particular product. For many, the caps are formed by budgetary constraints, but there can also be psychological aspects. For example, the price of the average home personal computer in the United States held at about $1,000 for well over a decade even though performance improved sharply during the period. This suggests price-capped customers at this level who were unwilling to spend more, even if they could get additional features.

Nuances of benefit perceptions can also lead to clusters. Order of entry can play a major role, particularly in sectors like telecommunications and utilities. Even if a new player meets or exceeds an incumbent's value proposition in terms of "hard" benefits such as product quality or service offerings, it could face an insurmountable challenge as it tries to grab market share. This is because "soft" benefits—those linked to lower risk and increased comfort—are often tied to historic relationships and are almost impossible to replicate. Distorted impressions of how much it would cost to switch to a new supplier, whether in terms of actual expense or hassle, can also contribute to customer inertia, even if the added value of a new supplier is obvious.

Just as there are customers who fall into these various benefit-bracketed or price-capped categories, there are others who do not. These buyers are willing to consider the full range of tradeoffs along the VEL. In corporate environments, as long as the ROI is positive and better than a lower-priced alternative, price is only one of many factors considered, and the entire range of offerings is on the table. Even in certain consumer markets, in areas ranging from treats (coffee or ice cream) to luxuries (perfume or designer clothes) to necessities (life-saving medical procedures), price can be no object.

Understanding customer cluster volume distribution along the VEL is crucial to making intelligent decisions about product position. In many cases, however, volume distribution is poorly understood, which leads to bad positioning decisions. Companies tend to make two typical mistakes:

1. *Blank space.* An otherwise competitive product could be positioned amid blank space on the VEL where there is no customer volume. A maker of metal-coating machinery positioned a new product halfway between two competing products, hoping to pull in customers not entirely satisfied by either. Unfortunately, the company did not realize

there was no significant customer volume that was willing to buy at that intermediate price/benefit point. Each machine offered a specific speed required by customers, and there was no demand for an intermediate speed. Even though the new coating machinery was competitive based on technical specifications and price, the manufacturer could not attract the sales volume it expected. Failing to understand customer volume distribution along the VEL forced it to take a multimillion-dollar write-off.

2. *Cutting off customers.* Pushing beyond the extremes of the VEL can inadvertently exclude a large portion of price-capped or benefit-bracketed customers. A quality and price leader might strive for continuous improvements and unknowingly move into blank space at the top of the VEL. A low-cost producer could bring prices so low that customers find any benefit proposition incredible. A cheap car might be marketable, but a model could become so cheap that buyers doubt its safety.

VALUE PROFILING

While basic value maps can help diagnose problems and uncover market opportunities, an additional level of insight can be achieved with a technique we call *value profiling*. Price and benefit perceptions can vary significantly within a market, and making a detailed profile of how the market sees a product's value can uncover misalignments between a company's desired value positioning and its actual positioning. With this information as a starting point, a company can pinpoint the problem—for instance, ineffective benefits communications, inappropriate discretionary discounting, or benefits delivery problems—and design a solution.

Thorough analysis of perceived benefits, perceived pricing, and the zone of indifference allows a company to portray the shape of a product's positioning on the value map as an ellipse rather than a point, as shown in Exhibit 4-12. The height of the ellipse from its center point is determined by the standard deviation of price responses from the research, while the width is set by the standard deviation of the benefits responses. As with earlier value maps, the ellipse can fall within the zone of indifference or in the value-advantaged or -disadvantaged areas, as shown in Exhibit 4-13.

The complete picture formed by value profiling can be the basis for sound pricing decisions. The shape of the ellipse can bring additional insight, especially when the variance of price or benefit perception is larger than expected. Typically, misshapen ellipses suggest that the market is not clear on a product's price or benefit position—or perhaps both. Exhibit 4-14 shows three typical problems. In the first value map, product A's benefits perception

Exhibit 4-12 Standard Value Profile

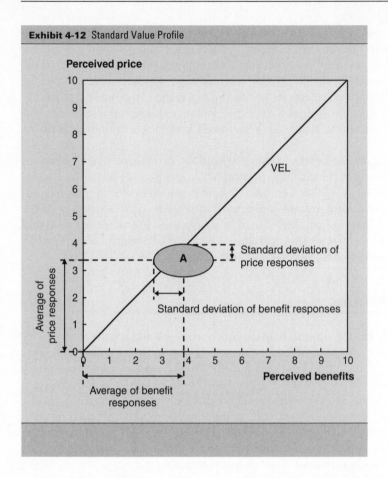

varies widely; in the second, its price perception is the problem; and in the third, both price and benefit perceptions show significant variation. Failure to understand what forces are shaping these ellipses can lead to erroneous pricing decisions; unearthing the causes and acting on them can capture significant opportunities.

Misalignment often occurs when a company has inadvertently combined multiple market segments into the same pool. Consequently, when an identical offer is communicated the same way, some customers may view it as too expensive, others as a great deal; similarly some could view it as rich in benefits, others as insufficient. The challenge here is to develop different communication or go-to-market approaches by segment, or, in more severe cases, to develop differentiated offerings that better align with the specific needs of the corresponding segments.

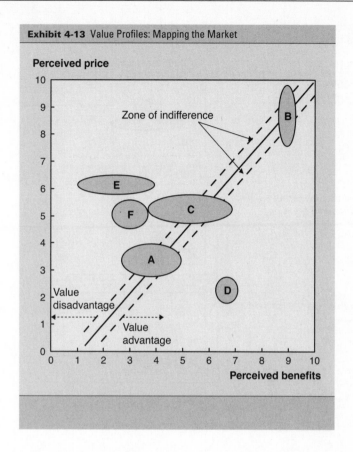

Exhibit 4-13 Value Profiles: Mapping the Market

The problem of segment pooling could also explain differences in either price or benefit perception alone. Assuming that the value profiles accurately reflect the views of a discrete market segment, let us look at again at Exhibit 4-14.

In the first case, the market has a consistent view of a company's price position, but customers perceive a broad spectrum of benefits delivered. Two explanations present themselves. First, the physical delivery of the value proposition may vary significantly by customer—for instance, because of a product changeover, quality problems, or differences in local support capabilities. Second, there may be inconsistencies in the company's ability to communicate the benefits. This could be due to the complexity of the offering, inadequate marketing support, or inconsistent sales skills, and it may suggest that a more effective marketing and sales communication strategy is needed.

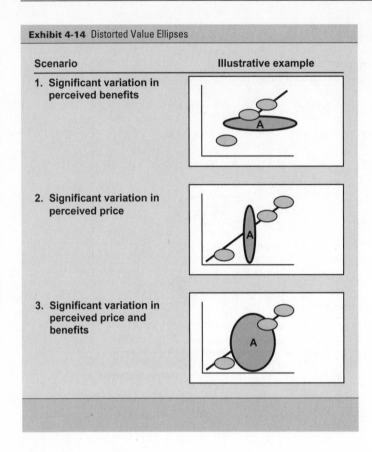

Exhibit 4-14 Distorted Value Ellipses

Scenario	Illustrative example
1. Significant variation in perceived benefits	
2. Significant variation in perceived price	
3. Significant variation in perceived price and benefits	

In the second situation, the market perceives a common benefits level, but perception of price varies widely. Lack of pricing discipline is a frequent explanation. As the range of pocket prices is allowed to spread outside of acceptable limits, different customers may begin to see huge price variances for essentially the same offer.

In the third situation, the offering's perceived value position is simply unclear. In essence, this is a combination of the two previous situations. This case requires careful consideration because the problem could be driven by a combination of benefits miscommunication, lack of pricing discipline, or failure to recognize multiple segments.

* * *

The Customer Value level of price management is centered entirely on the customer perception of price and benefits. The primary issue here is how to determine and manage your offering's price/benefit positioning relative to competitors—to come up with list prices or base prices that reflect, for each market segment, the best value position for a company's products over time. The value map is a core tool to help understand how the critical price/benefit tradeoff works and drives customers' selection of suppliers.

Businesses that excel at the Customer Value level are obsessed with understanding their customers. They regularly invest in research to comprehend in detail the benefit attributes that influence customers' buying behavior and choice of supplier. They understand the current and changing importance of each attribute and their own performance against those attributes, as well as the performance of key competitors. They sustain an equally well-informed perspective on customers' perception of their own and their competitors' price levels. For their most important products and segments, they maintain current value maps—showing the value positions of their own offerings and those of competitors—that are updated whenever significant market events occur.

These businesses use these value maps to guide strategy—for instance to adjust list prices and benefit offerings, to react to competitive repositioning of price and benefits, or to determine the price positioning of new products. Beyond static management of value position, they use these current value maps to understand market dynamics—to anticipate competitor reactions to their own and others' value moves. They look into the future, create target value maps of desired competitive value positions, and then take the necessary actions over time to move themselves and to influence their competitors' movements toward those target positions.

Without this level of rich understanding of customers and competitors and this level of thoughtful price and market strategy based on that understanding, no company can truly claim *the price advantage* as its own.

CHAPTER 5

Market Strategy

The Market Strategy level is the broadest and most general level of price management. It is informed by the overall business strategy and context (e.g., share/volume growth aspirations, desire to penetrate new markets, need to improve profitability) and in turn sets the stage for the remaining components of *the price advantage*. Market price levels are the critical issue here—knowing them, predicting them better, and, if possible, independently influencing them in a positive direction. Failure here can, at the least, create unnecessary downward pressure on industry prices; at worst, it can lead to destructive price wars. Managers who overlook market strategy risk seeing falling industry prices wipe out all of their hard-fought pricing gains at the Transactions and Customer Value levels. By contrast, success can produce positive industry-wide pricing conduct. Such wins occur not when prices outstrip the benefits delivered to customers but rather when prices are justified by the benefits customers receive.

Companies that excel here understand better the supply, demand, cost, and other trends that affect overall industry prices and the factors that drive these trends. They independently, unilaterally, and proactively face and encourage the trends that benefit the industry, rather than passively accepting the market's invisible hand. Using their superior understanding of microeconomics, they are able to adjust their tactics ahead of—and therefore outperform—the market. For instance, they may avoid long-term, fixed-price deals just before an expected upturn, or add new capacity to match expected increases in overall demand.[1]

---

[1] It is important to note that although the approaches outlined in this chapter are not intended to contravene any applicable laws, company executives should always seek appropriate legal counsel before taking action. We have made all reasonable efforts to ensure that the actions suggested here are legally permissible, but the nature of the issues makes collective actions by industry participants legally sensitive.

It is crucial to note that prices do *not* automatically rise along with positive changes in industry microeconomics. While a clear understanding of microeconomics may suggest when and how much prices might change, each company must decide when and how much to change its prices. An environment of good pricing conduct is often required to trigger such price moves. A market strategy that fosters good pricing conduct initiates upward price moves when conditions are appropriate and supports competitors' independent decisions to follow.

Promoting good industry pricing conduct within the letter and spirit of the law is a legitimate and legal strategy. It includes, among other aspects, shunning actions that could fuel destructive price wars, being legally transparent in pricing actions and motives, promoting a longer-term view of industry profitability, and recognizing when the conditions are right to try to move prices higher. Companies that excel at this level of pricing can independently influence industry economics and shepherd prices to their appropriate levels.

Many companies miss opportunities at the Market Strategy level. First, many firms' unrelenting focus on immediate shareholder value has increased competitive rivalry and produced a tunnel-vision view of near-term volume and market share—one that leaves out longer-term price and profit improvement. Second, few have anyone assigned to maintain an overview of industry pricing (e.g., systematically looking for patterns of competitive behavior that suggest a price increase opportunity). Third, many companies overlook the range of tools available to forecast industry trends. Lastly, small- and medium-size companies may underestimate how much they can influence market prices—for instance, by adding marginal capacity or positioning themselves as the market's low-price alternative. Many other companies also underestimate their legal degrees of freedom for taking pricing actions at this level.

These factors regularly cause companies to miss the intricate yet promising opportunities a well-designed market strategy can offer. But companies also miss low-hanging fruit simply because they are not looking for it. One specialty chemicals company failed to spot two price increases announced by a competitor over five years. Because no other companies followed its increases, the competitor rolled back prices each time, and everyone missed an opportunity to turn around declining industry profits. Because the company was not even watching for such price moves, it never even had the internal discussion about whether to follow the move. We have seen numerous cases in which companies have missed similar opportunities because they overlooked favorable conditions they should have easily recognized.

The rest of this chapter covers a number of opportunity areas at the Market Strategy level, including profiting from better price predictions, planning for an expected price change, adjusting production to influence market prices, and improving pricing conduct.

PROFITING FROM BETTER PRICE PREDICTIONS

Companies that are better at predicting industry price changes can capture substantial rewards from this knowledge. This is particularly true for cyclical products, such as commodities, and those with short life cycles, such as high tech. At one consumer electronics company, a two-week delay in dropping prices at the end of a product's lifecycle could have increased its annual profit by as much as 17 percent.

At the root of better price prediction is a more complete understanding of the industry factors at play. Every company in the industry experiences these factors and should incorporate them into pricing decisions. A complete discussion about how to model industry supply and demand, cost curves, and other essential tools is available from several sources,[2] and so is not covered here. Generally speaking, however, managers need to watch three areas constantly for indications of a shift in industry price levels:

1. *Cost changes,* which may be triggered by an abundance or shortage of key raw materials, new manufacturing or distribution approaches, or improved technology.
2. *Supply changes,* which may be triggered by events such as new capacity coming online, patents expiring, or plant closures.
3. *Demand changes,* which may be triggered by market shifts for supplemental or complementary products, changes in consumer tastes, new benefits that uncover latent demand, or new regulations.

Although high-level analysis is necessary for all of these elements, it can be beneficial to take the pulse of the market by gathering information from the frontline sales force, industry analysts, and customer surveys when examining market balance changes. Anecdotes from the field must be assessed carefully and corroborating information sought to ensure that the information is accurate. For example, a report that a competitor is experiencing supply problems may be accurate, a false rumor, outdated information, or simply incomplete.

---

[2]One excellent book is by Kent B. Monroe, *Pricing: Making Profitable Decisions* (New York: McGraw-Hill/Irwin, 2003). Another is by David Besanko and Ronald R. Braeutigam, *Microeconomics* (Hoboken, NJ: John Wiley & Sons, 2005).

Anticipating these microeconomic changes in cost, supply, and demand requires not only an in-depth awareness of events within a company's own industry, but also familiarity with the events in its suppliers' and customers' markets. For example, labor problems may trigger a disruption in suppliers' operations, leading to higher costs throughout your industry; regulatory changes that affect your customers' operations may impact their purchases from your industry. Understanding what drives your industry prices can give managers additional confidence, assist them in communicating with customers, and cut the time you spend investigating recent price movements. But the greatest value from improved industry price forecasting comes from two fronts—proactively preparing for an expected price change and fine-tuning production levels.

PLANNING FOR AN EXPECTED PRICE CHANGE

A company that anticipates a price change can prepare for the shift and respond more quickly when it takes place. In the U.S. styrene industry, as in many other markets, prices soar when demand pushes production capacity to its limits. As Exhibit 5-1 shows, the fly-up in spot prices and the accompanying margins can be significant. But the price shift usually lags the move toward full capacity because customers pressure their suppliers to keep the old prices as long as possible. (There is usually no similar lag when prices drop.)

If a major producer carefully tracks industry utilization and realizes that spot price increases portend a longer-term structural increase in industry prices, rather than a temporary aberration, it can use this knowledge to drive and justify earlier and higher increases in contract prices (e.g., by sharing the facts on industry price trends with customers). It might also build inventory beyond current demand, to sell once prices rise. Such an approach could allow a company to gain an extra five to seven cents a pound for styrene over three months during a fly-up year. For a typical styrene company producing about 2 billion pounds a year, this would bring $2 to $3 million in additional operating profit.

The same type of rapid response to unanticipated supply changes can also bring a substantial payoff. One electronics supplier increased annual profit by an estimated $25 million when it reacted more quickly than others to the temporary market shortages for a key component—shortages caused by a major supply interruption.

Companies benefit from superior industry price predictions in other ways as well. Ahead of an upward price trend, companies can shorten the term of new contracts to avoid being locked into the lower price well after industry prices have moved upward. If the price increase is driven by

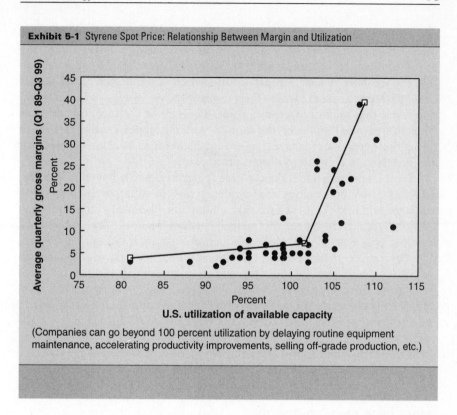

Exhibit 5-1 Styrene Spot Price: Relationship Between Margin and Utilization

increased input costs, a supplier might push hard to insert a clause into the contract that allows it to pass such increases on to its customer if they occur.

And if industry prices are expected to drop? A company could profit by taking the opposite tack, for example, pushing for longer-term contracts or eliminating input-cost clauses. Some pharmaceutical companies have offered discounts to customers if they sign longer-term purchase commitments just as a patent is due to expire. Although these discounts might hurt short-term profits, in the longer term the supplier maintains relatively stable earnings in the face of increased competition and keeps the medication's presence in the market.

MAINTAINING OPTIMAL PRODUCTION AND CAPACITY

In industries where prices are sensitive to changes in supply—for instance, those with steep cost curves at the current price levels—companies should be particularly careful that their capacity decisions do not spark unnecessary price declines. Producers with low or moderate relative costs will usually run at full capacity to maximize profits. But if microeconomic analysis shows that the industry is near a break point—where a small increase in supply could push prices much lower—these companies may want to avoid production levels that might breach this point. This can be the case, for instance, when the marginal producer (the supplier with the highest costs that is still in the market), has costs that are significantly higher than its closest competitor and just enough demand to keep it profitable.

Some companies have taken on creative strategies to help maintain prices at an attractive point along the supply curve—for example, by discouraging large additions of new capacity. One major chemical company began auctioning capacity shares in "virtual ethylene plants." The company, a low-cost producer, had ethylene production capacity it did not need for its own derivatives manufacturing operations. Other players, who did not always have the ethylene production capacity to meet their own needs, would often go to this company in a pinch. To discourage the other players from adding ethylene capacity in an effort to become completely self-sufficient, the company offered these virtual shares. The buyers benefited from the company's low-cost position, which they probably could not replicate, and an assured ethylene supply. The company's efforts also helped the industry maintain relatively high utilization and stable margins.

IMPROVING PRICING CONDUCT

A profound understanding of the microeconomics of an industry can lead to quick wins, such as taking supply/demand–driven price increases sooner or fine-tuning contract terms to take advantage of expected industry price movement. Beyond the microeconomic opportunities is another related but largely overlooked market strategy opportunity—the pursuit of improved pricing conduct. Through effectively inspiring good pricing conduct throughout an industry—avoiding price wars, maintaining regular price increases, and capturing the full value of innovation—and knowing when the time is right and how best to move prices higher, a company can unilaterally contribute to increased industry profitability.

Improved pricing conduct, at a high level, means that the company designs a sound pricing strategy that does not overestimate customer price sensitivity and that takes into account the potential that competitors may follow a price move, rather than undercut it. It includes clear, consistent, legal communication of a company's pricing strategy, its rationale, and value. Pricers use specific approaches to discourage other players (resellers, customers, and competitors) from undermining their pricing strategy. In markets where improved pricing conduct has evolved (e.g., select consumer durable goods, chemical, package delivery companies), industry return on sales (ROS) has risen by 2 to 7 percentage points.

Some fundamental misconceptions shroud the pricing conduct opportunity for many companies, making it difficult for companies to capture this potential. First, companies believe it is illegal. Indeed, a pricing conduct improvement strategy requires careful attention to laws that prohibit collusive action among competitors. But important, substantial distinctions exist between pricing conduct improvement and unlawful activities:

- Pricing conduct improvement is about being aware of competitive pricing intentions, not reaching any agreement with competitors.
- It is about communicating pricing and pricing information to a wide range of stakeholders for legally legitimate purposes (e.g., to help a customer plan for future price list changes), not using price statements to signal competitors unlawfully.
- It is about watching out for destructive pricing, not using price and market power to push competitors out of business.
- Finally, it is about unilateral resale price policies, not agreements with resellers or coercion to get them to set a certain price.

For a fuller survey of legal considerations, see Chapter 9, "Legal Degrees of Freedom."

The second misconception is that many managers think price increases can happen only in limited circumstances. For example, they assume such changes can be effectively done only by an industry's low-cost or market-share leader. Managers also believe they can try to improve pricing conduct only when a new product is released. Managers worry that seemingly irrational competitor behavior would preclude price increases. Finally, managers feel their hands are tied; industry prices are like the weather—they cannot do much about either. All of these beliefs are generally misguided. Any company that recognizes the opportunity has a chance to contribute to pricing conduct improvement, either by being the first to raise prices or by quickly following other players in the industry.

So what underpins successful pricing conduct improvement? We have found three basic requirements. First, *visibility* of pricing must exist across the industry. It is hard for a company to move upward comfortably if prices are hidden and it does not know how other players are acting. Second, companies must share a *common motivation* that centers on growing profits through better pricing rather than on aggressive volume gains. Major competitors have to be independently playing a similar game. Third, firms need the internal *resolve* to pursue pricing conduct improvement persistently. Improving pricing conduct requires tough choices, be it walking away from an account that could add incremental volume, instituting greater controls over frontline price decisions, or taking a visible position with customers regarding raising prices.

INFLUENCING THE ELEMENTS OF PRICING CONDUCT

Structural industry conditions (Exhibit 5-2) can set the stage for effective pricing conduct improvement, but alone these conditions will not bring about higher prices. Successful pricers understand that they can influence and use the three essential elements—visibility, common motivation, and resolve—to increase the likelihood that a pricing conduct improvement initiative will succeed. For each element, there are several practical tools readily at hand to move toward this goal.

VISIBILITY

Companies that aspire to improve pricing conduct take pains to assure that their own pricing actions are visible and not misinterpreted by customers and

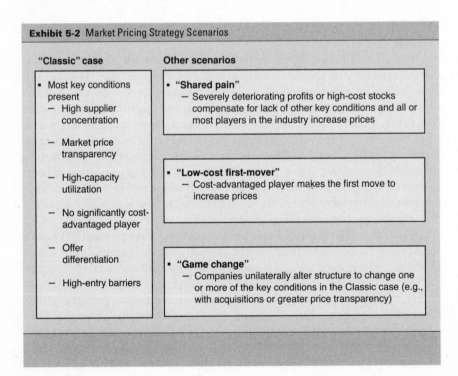

Exhibit 5-2 Market Pricing Strategy Scenarios

"Classic" case

- Most key conditions present
  - High supplier concentration

  - Market price transparency

  - High-capacity utilization

  - No significantly cost-advantaged player

  - Offer differentiation

  - High-entry barriers

Other scenarios

- **"Shared pain"**
  - Severely deteriorating profits or high-cost stocks compensate for lack of other key conditions and all or most players in the industry increase prices

- **"Low-cost first-mover"**
  - Cost-advantaged player makes the first move to increase prices

- **"Game change"**
  - Companies unilaterally alter structure to change one or more of the key conditions in the Classic case (e.g., with acquisitions or greater price transparency)

the market. Generally, good pricers at this level strive for transparency in two areas: price and rationale. Although these two areas are often interwoven in execution—a single announcement may feature a new price list and the reasoning behind it—they address different issues.

Transparent Prices In many industries, there is no accurate barometer for prices. Deals are negotiated individually and the only information about market prices may be hearsay. Even if the information is accurate, it could easily be outdated. In these conditions, gauging industry price trends can be excruciatingly difficult.

In such industries, pricers can increase price transparency by encouraging an independent source, often a trade magazine or association, to develop and publish a standardized price index. This approach has worked in many sectors, including the chemicals industry. Price indices help buyers peg prices to the industry, ensuring that they are not paying more than their competitors are for a key manufacturing input. For suppliers, these indices provide needed visibility for overall price trends in a market. For these indices to succeed, major players would have to cooperate with the index producer while ensuring that their specific price levels are not disclosed to third parties.

There are other ways, some quite creative, to increase price transparency. Prices in the elevator industry had historically been opaque. Each order was as unique as the building it would occupy, and the price depended on a combination of various features: for example, the number of floors serviced, elevator size, desired speed, and interior features. Each feature had numerous options, opening the door for an infinite number of configurations and prices. Closed bids were the market norm, creating an environment where it was difficult for customers and the market to discern general price trends. In the early 1990s, one company decided to change this. The company created a "building designers' elevator guide" that detailed three "standard elevators"—hypothetical models that would never be built—and published a price for each. This guide gave designers, for planning purposes, a rough estimate of approximate elevator costs for a new building. Actual prices for an elevator installation would be built up from these standard prices based on the customized features needed for each project. These hypothetical units became an effective tool to bring visibility to price trends in the market. Whenever the company thought the time was right to take prices up by 2 percent, for example, it would simply republish its guide, with the prices for the hypothetical standard models increased by two percent.

But it is not enough for a company to improve its own price transparency. The company must also actively look for and understand moves made by others in the industry. Even the clearest pricing action can be missed if no one is watching. A distilled spirits company had a policy of maintaining a routine price premium over a specific competitor in selected markets. Despite this policy, close analysis of resale prices revealed that the specific competitor had brought its prices up over the course of two years, at one point reaching parity with the brand that had traditionally been premium priced. The spirits company had failed to track competitive pricing at the local market level and missed an opportunity to increase prices. In contrast, successful pricers at the Market Strategy level systematically monitor competitive pricing, generally and for specific markets, and closely track public announcements by others in the market to keep abreast of any changes in the industry landscape.

Transparent Rationale   In addition to price transparency, a company must also be sure that the rationale behind a price move is clearly stated to avoid misinterpretation by customers and other stakeholders. A clear rationale can set the right expectations for customers and other stakeholders—particularly in the wake of a price decrease. Without an explanation, the market is likely to interpret a price cut as an aggressive move to gain market share, while the true motivation could be much more benign, such as the need to clear obsolete inventory. In the case of an increase in prices, a clear rationale can help customers, investors, and other stakeholders evaluate and develop their responses better. As covered in Chapter 9, "Legal Degrees of Freedom," it is important that legal counsel be brought in to ensure that there is a clear customer reason for any external communication surrounding a price increase and that these actions are not misconstrued as an attempt to signal to competitors.

The method of communicating a price change to customers can also indicate the motive and commitment behind a price move; here, too, companies must be careful to avoid misinterpretation. The way the pricing move is done, when it is done, how it is announced, who announces it . . . the list goes on and on. Each component can increase or decrease the impact of the message. For example, a company can follow precedent and put a price change into effect on a specific date, such as January 1, or it can send a stronger message by picking an effective date that breaks precedent. The announcement can either be buried in a press release or be a key point in a speech by the CEO.

Many companies try to minimize communication around price increases, believing that sneaking an increase through will minimize resistance. But pricers trying to improve conduct understand how to communicate that message clearly and carefully to customers to maximize the outcome of their price increase initiative. As Exhibit 5-3 outlines, managers have many options for using their price increase approach for delivering a high-impact message of improved pricing conduct.

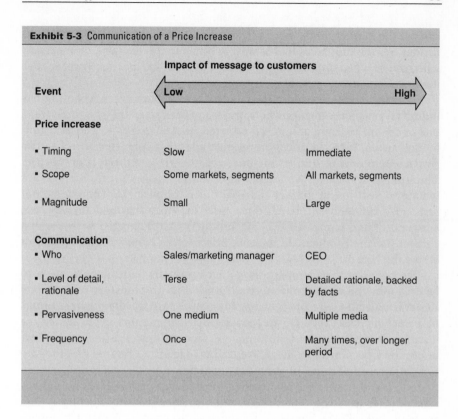

Exhibit 5-3 Communication of a Price Increase

Event	Impact of message to customers	
	Low	High
Price increase		
• Timing	Slow	Immediate
• Scope	Some markets, segments	All markets, segments
• Magnitude	Small	Large
Communication		
• Who	Sales/marketing manager	CEO
• Level of detail, rationale	Terse	Detailed rationale, backed by facts
• Pervasiveness	One medium	Multiple media
• Frequency	Once	Many times, over longer period

COMMON MOTIVATION

Behind every act of business, there is motivation. Companies excelling in pricing conduct realize that to have price increases stick, the market in general must have a common general motive (e.g., profit growth). If a significant player is intent on share growth, it will be much more difficult for prices to move up. In such cases, pricing conduct improvement efforts must first focus primarily on convincing stakeholders on the benefits of profit growth as a motive. Successful pricers at the Market Strategy level encourage movement away from a fixation on share and low prices and toward a focus on profit and price increases. One building products company issued a "state of the industry" letter to customers with detailed rationale behind its pricing and capacity actions. It laid out the argument as to why more stable prices were better for customers (e.g., increasing the chance that supply will always be available at a fair price instead of largely fluctuating prices and frequent industry shortages). By announcing its own motives to customers, a company can tell the market that it has analyzed the situation and concluded that its actions are the most reasonable way to attain a specific goal. Competitors who have reached different conclusions will often independently reexamine their own situation.

In many situations, actions can indeed speak louder than words. In one industrial products category where prices had been stagnant over three years, one of the major companies used targeted price increases to trigger a shift in motivation. It raised prices on product lines that competed with its main rival's core products, but left the prices of its own core product untouched. The strategy was clear: We are not after market share, but we are also not willing to risk losing market share in our core business. The competitor responded rationally. It matched the price increases that had already been announced, and it raised prices on products that competed with the first company's core products. In the end, prices in the industry were up almost across the board.

Recognizing that competitors *do* act rationally and they are likely to be driven by the same profit motive (rather than an obsession with market share) is crucial. Quite often, when companies forecast the possible results of a price increase, they fail to consider that competitors might match the increase. When potential followership is factored into the analysis, bolder price moves become more attractive, and managers are assured that they are evaluating the full range of potential outcomes.

Successful pricers are also willing to challenge assumptions about customers' price sensitivity. Internal estimates of price elasticity can be less than rigorous and reflect a conservative approach to change. A major tire manufacturer under constant pressure by retailers to keep prices low decided to research demand elasticity for its products and cross-elasticity with competitors' products to understand its true risks, as well as the risks faced by its retailers. The project revealed that the company and its retailers had erred in their high-elasticity estimates. Customers were much less sensitive to price than the companies thought, and the likely effect of a price increase would be greater profit, rather than a significant loss in volume. Armed with that information, the company gained a clearer picture of the potential advantages of pricing conduct improvement: Even if competitors did not follow, they would make much more money with little share loss. Unfortunately, too many companies fail to invest the time to get a true handle on the risks and rewards of pricing conduct improvement.

RESOLVE

Organizational resolve is vital for pricing conduct improvement because its full rewards are rarely immediate. Price increases may succeed in the near term, but successful pricing conduct improvement is a long-term strategy and must be backed by internal commitment to see it through over time, as well as by an industry-wide belief that success will bring long-term benefits for all players. This resolve must be behind every move, because customers and the market will judge you by your worst pricing behavior. Ninety-nine out of a hundred contracts may be consistent with a pricing conduct improvement strategy, but the hundredth, which gave away lower prices, will be the one the market talks about and remembers. Invariably, such a lapse will be misread as an indication of your true pricing intentions.

Companies create resolve in four important ways: strong internal controls, continual and consistent communication, active monitoring of competitive action (and appropriate responses when necessary), and specific tools to influence resellers to support their pricing strategy.

Internal Controls   Resolve is founded on a belief that success is attainable and worthwhile. The entire organization must support the goals of pricing conduct improvement. Many of the transactional pricing tools discussed in Chapter 3, "Transactions" can help make this happen: sales incentives focused on profitability, strong management controls, and organizational alignment around the strategy. Top managers must also exercise self-control, because field reps will take their cues from executives before risking their careers by holding tough during a critical negotiation.

Such behaviors and policies are essential. A company that was trying to maintain a price increase barely avoided a major, visible discrepancy. Its top sales rep was using large discounts as an incentive to close a major deal with a highly visible customer. Luckily, a manager caught the incongruity; otherwise, the prices and discounts would have undermined the company's extensive efforts to support the price increase.

Communication   If pricing conduct improvement is seen as nothing more than a one-time tactic, commitment will be weakened. Messages must be repeated to each important stakeholder and reinforced with actions if the company wants to build credibility and understanding. One consumer durables firm shared a detailed "pricing conduct improvement communication plan" with employees on how to explain its strategy, including a price increase, to customers, shareholders, market analysts, employees, trade press, and retailers. As Exhibit 5-4 outlines, the company did not launch all of these efforts at once. In an effort to be clear in its resolve, it designed the plan to make sure that stakeholders would receive many mutually reinforcing messages during the launch phase and beyond.

Monitoring   As a company moves toward improved pricing conduct, pricers must continually monitor the situation and be ready to act appropriately to reinforce the benefits of resolve. Occasionally, this may also mean taking

Exhibit 5-4 Consistent Message Reinforcement

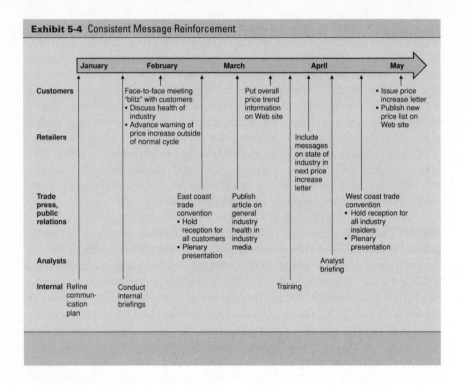

steps to counter disruptive behavior. Pricing conduct improvement seemed to be working in the U.S. beer industry, with two of the larger breweries taking prices up in most markets. But when one player saw the other attacking one of its strongholds by offering discounts, it responded with its own aggressive price promotion in that market. The detractor relented, and prices turned back upward. Other moves that can reinforce pricing resolve include writing contract stipulations such as meet-the-competition clauses, in which a company agrees to match lower prices offered by competitors to the customer; and most-favored-customer clauses, in which a company agrees to match lower prices offered by it to other customers.[3]

Resellers In multitiered distribution environments, a successful conduct improvement strategy depends heavily on resellers supporting the effort or, at least, not derailing it. But retailers, who are becoming increasingly powerful, may not have the same market perspective, information, or agendas

---

[3]Meet-the-competition and most-favored customer clauses can be legally problematic in concentrated industries in some jurisdictions.

as the supplier; in fact, their agendas may actually conflict with those of the suppliers. Rather than raising their hands in surrender, suppliers can use a range of tools to influence their resale channels. These tools include promotional allowances for advertising a product at a certain price level or end-of-year rebates tied to meeting specific average retail price targets. Market knowledge can often be the most powerful tool, as one home appliance maker found.

Catering to the low-end market, this supplier had once commanded healthy margins on its appliances. But the market changed when a low-priced competitor that could match its performance standards entered. For seven years, the appliance supplier did not raise its prices once. Meanwhile, as raw materials costs rose, the company began losing money.

To combat this trend, the company took a closer look at its customers and their behavior. Consumer pricing research revealed two attention-grabbing insights. First, even though the two low-cost brands were technically similar, the original maker's products had quite strong brand equity—enough to raise prices 10 to 15 percent before its customers began switching. Just as interesting, the research showed that if retailers rebelled against a price hike and dropped the brand, most of their customers would trade up to more expensive models that were less profitable for the retailers. The supplier shared this information with its retail outlets and announced a 10 percent price increase. It also suggested to its retailers that they could raise their prices by 12 to 15 percent without risking volume. The choice was simple: Go along and make more money, or drop the brand and lose money. No retailer opted to drop the brand.

A WORD ON FOLLOWERSHIP

In almost all of the successful cases of pricing conduct improvement we have seen, one of the top three players in a market was the first company to initiate a price move. However, in each case, a key to success was that other companies, large and small, were good followers. These companies played key supporting roles that were essential to overall good pricing conduct. In one case, a company matched the first mover's price increase within days with an announcement of a price increase that explained its rationale in similar detail. In other cases, followers were the first to rein in their sales force's discounting discretion or change their objectives from aggressively capturing share to increasing profits.

Not everybody can be a first mover, but everybody can independently decide whether it makes sense to follow moves by others in the industry. A story from the electronics components industry shows how important

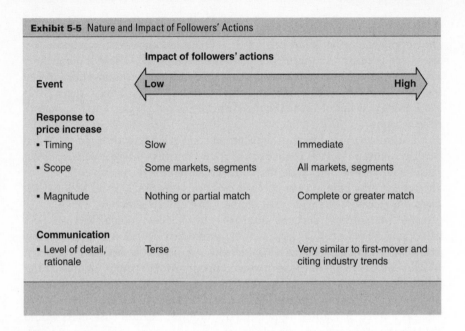

Exhibit 5-5 Nature and Impact of Followers' Actions

Impact of followers' actions

Event	Low	High
Response to price increase		
▪ Timing	Slow	Immediate
▪ Scope	Some markets, segments	All markets, segments
▪ Magnitude	Nothing or partial match	Complete or greater match
Communication		
▪ Level of detail, rationale	Terse	Very similar to first-mover and citing industry trends

faithful followers are. In a sector plagued by low profitability for several years, one supplier took a brave step and announced a bold 4 percent price increase. Then the supplier waited, and waited—for two weeks. Nothing happened. It decided the move was too risky and rescinded the price increase.

Unfortunately, the reason there was no reaction was the competitor's president, who had the final word on raising prices, was on vacation and so no decision could be made. The president returned and was about to authorize a price increase when word arrived that the first company had taken back its own price hike. Eventually industry prices were raised, but the companies lost about six months' of increased revenue and higher profits because of the miscue.

Obviously, price followers can support a first mover by acting in their own economic self-interest and matching the first mover's pricing moves. But as Exhibit 5-5 shows, there are many other ways to follow, some with more impact than others. For example, a company that follows slowly or hesitantly can stymie the first mover's motivation and commitment.

In addition to following the price move itself, followers can support pricing initiatives internally by maintaining transactional discipline and making sure that sales reps are not attempting to poach accounts aggressively when a competitor may be most vulnerable.

* * *

Market Strategy excellence is an essential part of *the price advantage*. It can yield multiple percentage points of price increases. Furthermore, it decreases the risk of destructive competitive pricing actions and creates an environment where pricing gains generated at the Transactions and Customer Value levels can be sustained.

The central issues at this level are predicting industry price trends more accurately; responding to them effectively; and, where possible, influencing them positively. A number of well-documented microeconomic frameworks like industry cost curves and demand analysis can help companies predict price shifts related to structural changes in an industry.

Companies that are distinctive at the Market Strategy level deliberately invest in gaining deep understanding of the underlying drivers of industry price trends—supply, demand, regulations, costs, and competitors, among others. As a result, companies predict price shifts better, react to them to their greater advantage, and influence them where possible. However, *the price advantage* at this level is more than just mastery of market structure dynamics. It also entails, as we have shown, being clear on when to increase prices. Excellence here requires the creation and support of legally permissible price visibility, common motivation across the market, and organizational resolve. It also demands orchestration throughout the entire organization to ensure that its actions are consistent and that the market sees it as an unambiguous price first mover or a rational price follower.

CHAPTER 6

Pricing Infrastructure

Pricing infrastructure underlies pricing excellence and its three levels of price management—Market Strategy, Customer Value, and Transactions. Without it, most of the pricing opportunities identified within and across the three levels would not be fully realized. It is also what enables the best companies to sustain their performance and avoid returning to the status quo after an initial improvement; recognizing the size of the payoff, the companies invest in the infrastructure needed to achieve *the price advantage* over the long term.

So what is pricing infrastructure? It includes the processes, organization, performance management, and systems and tools necessary to support the pricing function within a business. It addresses questions like: What should the processes for pricing decision making be? How should the pricing organization (i.e., function) be structured and what skills are required? How should pricing excellence be recognized and rewarded? What tools are required to support pricing excellence?

Price advantaged companies often treat their pricing function as a significant *profit center* within their business. Such companies invest in it and ensure that it has the leadership, management focus, talent, and systems it needs to drive results. Simple math makes the reason very clear: we know from Chapter 1, "Introduction," that a 1 percentage point improvement in return on sales (ROS) leads to an 8.7 percent increase in operating profit for the typical Global 1200 company (Exhibit 1-2). Based on our work with thousands of companies on pricing programs, it is common for a well-executed pricing improvement program to yield 2 to 7 (or more) percentage point increases in ROS. The implication? For the typical Global 1200 company, *getting this improvement and sustaining the price advantage on a long-term basis could represent roughly 15 to 40 percent of the total profits generated by the business* (relative to the increased profit base).[1] Need we say more?

While the upside is clear, so is the danger. Failing to address gaps in pricing infrastructure can allow percentage points of price improvement to slip through companies' fingers. Unfortunately, infrastructure is one of the most frequently overlooked ingredients of *the price advantage*. Companies often try to get by with minimal investments in this area, concentrating instead on the three other components of pricing excellence. Our experience, however, shows that this approach is not only unable to sustain impact but rarely secures even short-term results.

In addition, companies often think that ongoing attention to pricing infrastructure is unnecessary. A diagnostic scan, for instance, might reveal significant pricing improvement opportunities, leading to a subsequent set of "quick hits" that generate bottom-line improvements quickly and with relative ease. Unfortunately, businesses then tend to declare victory prematurely on the pricing front and move on to focus time, energy, and talent elsewhere—with the unsurprising result that the actual impact realized diminishes over time and falls far short of the full pricing potential. In many cases, the company rapidly returns to its prior status quo with no remaining performance lift.

Successful companies build a strong pricing infrastructure—one that creates and enables the functional capabilities and processes that underlie and sustain pricing excellence. In these cases, the story plays out differently, as the pricing infrastructure helps maintain pricing focus and momentum. As mentioned earlier, hallmarks of top-notch pricing infrastructures include:

- **Well-defined pricing processes** where process steps, owners, inputs, and outputs are clearly defined and followed (examples include analyzing pricing performance data, assessing competitor pricing, supporting deals, and actively managing price levels and discount structures).
- **High-caliber organizational elements** in which pricing roles, responsibilities, decision rights, and accountability are explicitly assigned.
- **Performance management systems** with metrics and incentives (both financial and nonfinancial) aligned to reinforce pricing execution at the business and individual level.
- **Pricing systems and tools** that provide visibility into ongoing pricing performance, support for negotiations, and insights into new opportunities.

---

[1] Even if the pricing impact applied to only 50 percent of sales, the share of profit creation would still make the pricing function a significant profit center in the context of the whole business.

Together, these elements increase the likelihood of enduring impact. Moreover, the essential ingredients provide benefits in other critical ways, like raising pricing's profile in a business or shifting the culture from passive price takers to active price shapers. Building a strong pricing infrastructure can be one of the most rewarding—and challenging—elements of *the price advantage*.

Best-in-class pricers deliberately focus on all four elements of pricing infrastructure: processes, organization, performance management, and systems and tools. They also tend to do it in that order; they follow the maxim that "strategy drives structure." Managers start with the most critical pricing processes, those that support the overall business strategy. After identifying these processes, the next most important step involves the organization—who is going to own and drive the pricing profit center? What talent, skills, and roles are needed to execute the pricing processes? Performance management comes after that; it ensures that the business constantly focuses on pricing, strongly motivates people to increase pricing performance (in the context of the overall business strategy), and holds people accountable to meet or exceed expectations. Finally, systems and tools enable pricing processes, equip people in the pricing organization, and support performance management.

PROCESSES—WHAT ARE THE MOST CRITICAL TYPES OF PRICING DECISIONS FOR YOUR BUSINESS?

Pricing processes, which govern decision making and core pricing activities, lie at the heart of pricing infrastructure. Companies must first determine which specific pricing decisions are critical to their success and then build up robust processes around those decisions. One way to identify the essential decisions is to answer the following question for each of the three components of pricing excellence: "What must we get right for this component?"

The most vital pricing decisions and therefore the most critical pricing processes will differ dramatically based on industry. A chemical company might focus heavily on the Market Strategy level (e.g., keeping up-to-date on production capacity and cost curve information that is critical to understanding overall market price levels). A consumer electronics manufacturer may concentrate more on the Customer Value level, using consumer focus groups and next-best alternative pricing information to set and adjust their products' list prices. Finally, an industrial parts original equipment manufacturer (OEM) that sells to businesses might primarily focus on the

Transactions level, putting rules and policies in place that govern discounts for different products and volumes. In general, businesses should manage across all three levels of price management, though one or two will often be especially relevant. The question for you is: Which pricing decisions should *your* business focus on?

Companies frequently identify the following partial list of pricing processes as critical (though many other processes can be important):

1. **Setting and managing list and target prices**—establishing list price levels for new offerings and adjusting list prices for existing offerings (including those at or near late-life).
2. **Establishing pricing architecture**—reengineering the pocket margin waterfall or determining the mechanism by which a product or service will be priced (e.g., one-time charge, annual subscription, usage-based pricing, "razor/razor blades" model).
3. **Setting allowed terms and conditions**—establishing standard terms and conditions (e.g., payment terms), allowed exceptions, and the workflow for approving nonprice exceptions.
4. **Managing special price requests**—limiting authority to allow nonstandard pricing; designing the workflow for approving/denying special price requests.
5. **Monitoring pricing activities and impact**—determining what and how to monitor pricing performance, how often to update data, and how to disseminate summary reports to managers and other pricing decision makers.
6. **Gathering competitive and market price intelligence**—establishing the methods and means for collecting, synthesizing, and distributing information about market pricing trends and competitive pricing tactics.
7. **Communicating pricing**—defining goals, rationale, and tactics for both internal and external audiences; crafting messages about a company's pricing strategy.

These processes will add value to the business only if they function smoothly; that requires clear ownership and accountability throughout the process. Few companies achieve this. Too many try to get by with an ad hoc or management-by-committee approach with no clear owner, where the process itself occurs only when absolutely necessary.

A high-tech company suffered from this type of breakdown in their new product pricing process. The engineering and product development groups worked on a new product for more than a year. A prototype existed and marketing was already working on a launch campaign. The launch date was only six weeks away when management realized no one had thought about pricing. Product marketing panicked and asked the pricing group for advice. A mad scramble ensued to set the product price and the discounting ranges. To this day, management believes that millions of dollars of uncaptured value were lost because insufficient research was done to price the product appropriately for the benefit being delivered. The lack of clear ownership and accountability for new product pricing, which formed a striking contrast to the disciplined process for product development, resulted in this lost revenue. So whatever pricing processes matter to your company, ensure that they run smoothly with clear ownership and accountability; otherwise, much of the pricing potential may be left behind.

WHEN IS AN EXCEPTION REALLY AN EXCEPTION?

One of the important processes listed above—*managing special price requests*—deals with handling exceptions. The situation at one distribution company illustrates how far things can go astray when businesses are not careful. Internally, this distribution company used the phrases "exception pricing" or "nonexception pricing" to describe all their deals with customers—"standard pricing" was not in their vocabulary. Exceptions were so common that they represented well over half of sales, meaning that exceptions were truly the standard!

One common cause of runaway exception pricing is the seller's perception, which may be real, that it is easier to negotiate pricing *internally*, with those who can grant price relief, than *externally* with customers. To better manage and control such abuses, many companies employ a "deal" or "bid" desk that reviews and potentially refines pricing requests that fall outside normal discount guidelines. The desk has several purposes (Exhibit 6-1):

- Approve or deny special pricing requests initiated by sellers (i.e., outside sales reps, inside sales, or business partners).
- Provide pricing guidance to sellers in deals where they may not know what a winning price is (e.g., highly competitive deals; deals with products the seller is unfamiliar with).
- Analyze special pricing requests to develop competitive and market intelligence (e.g., Competitor A is targeting mid-size accounts in the South with low prices).

The desk should track the number of times it denies special pricing requests; a very rough rule of thumb is that 10 to 20 percent of exception pricing requests should be denied or modified. Ensuring that special pricing requests are actually rejected from time to time will make exception pricing truly the exception. With the appropriate approval process and

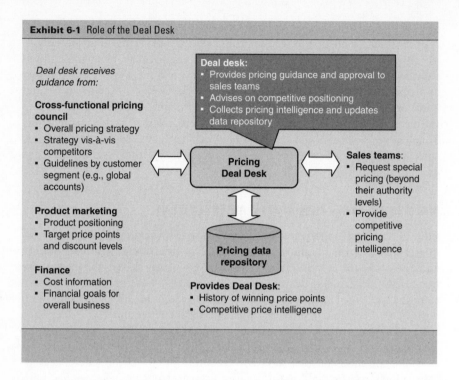

Exhibit 6-1 Role of the Deal Desk

Deal desk receives guidance from:

Cross-functional pricing council
- Overall pricing strategy
- Strategy vis-à-vis competitors
- Guidelines by customer segment (e.g., global accounts)

Product marketing
- Product positioning
- Target price points and discount levels

Finance
- Cost information
- Financial goals for overall business

Deal desk:
- Provides pricing guidance and approval to sales teams
- Advises on competitive positioning
- Collects pricing intelligence and updates data repository

Pricing Deal Desk

Sales teams:
- Request special pricing (beyond their authority levels)
- Provide competitive pricing intelligence

Pricing data repository

Provides Deal Desk:
- History of winning price points
- Competitive price intelligence

supporting tools and data, a deal desk can provide exceptional value to sellers, act as a guardian of margin for the business, and even discern market-pricing trends.

Companies should also try to make sure that the amount of revenue flowing through the desk is limited. In another example, the deal desk manager at one high-tech manufacturer repeatedly requested additional resources to staff the desk. When senior management investigated, they learned that more than 90 percent of all deals were going through exception pricing. Clearly something was broken; in this case the company had not adjusted list prices and discount authority levels for several years. Because market prices had fallen, both had to be reset. A good guideline for high-transaction businesses with mostly standard offerings is that no more than 50 percent of revenue (and usually a much lower percentage of transactions) should go through exception pricing; indeed, 20 to 30 percent is closer to best in class (Exhibit 6-2).[2]

---

[2]The frequency of exception pricing will depend on the fraction of the business that is related to complex deals with highly customized product/service offerings and complicated contract negotiations.

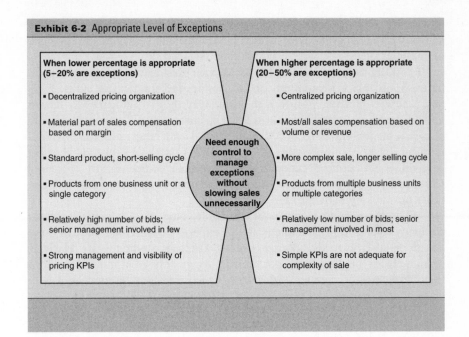

Exhibit 6-2 Appropriate Level of Exceptions

When lower percentage is appropriate (5–20% are exceptions)

- Decentralized pricing organization

- Material part of sales compensation based on margin

- Standard product, short-selling cycle

- Products from one business unit or a single category

- Relatively high number of bids; senior management involved in few

- Strong management and visibility of pricing KPIs

Need enough control to manage exceptions without slowing sales unnecessarily

When higher percentage is appropriate (20–50% are exceptions)

- Centralized pricing organization

- Most/all sales compensation based on volume or revenue

- More complex sale, longer selling cycle

- Products from multiple business units or multiple categories

- Relatively low number of bids; senior management involved in most

- Simple KPIs are not adequate for complexity of sale

ORGANIZATION—WHO IS RUNNING THE PRICING PROFIT CENTER?

Earlier we demonstrated pricing's substantial top- and bottom-line impact. Why is it, then, that so many companies woefully under-staff the pricing function? One common misconception is that dedicated personnel are not required for pricing; rather, companies believe that pricing responsibilities can be effectively spread across multiple personnel with other day jobs (e.g., sales, marketing, and product management). In these arrangements we inevitably find pricing neglected as the other responsibilities come first. If 15 to 40 percent of your profits could be directly attributed to pricing, would you staff the pricing function differently—and in proportion to its role as a profit center?

ORIENTATION—TREAT THE PRICING ORGANIZATION AS A PROFIT CENTER

Staffing an organization responsible for a significant portion of a company's profits requires a deliberate recruiting strategy, commensurate compensation, and clarity on the types of skills and attitudes required for each role. Typical roles in a pricing organization range from a senior vice president of pricing who regularly interacts with C-level executives to pricing analysts who are comfortable crunching numbers and carrying out a variety of analytics.

For more senior roles, like the senior vice president of pricing, the company should place a premium on leadership and influencing skills. Businesses should fill these positions the same way they would carefully recruit and interview an executive to run a large business unit. The executive should possess a demonstrated record of inspirational leadership and excellent communication skills and presence, allowing them to act as a peer to C-level executives. Senior pricing leaders should have their compensation structured to reward pricing performance and specific goal attainment—just like any other business unit (BU) leader.

When it comes to recruiting it sometimes pays to look outside of your company to recruit pricing talent. In our experience external hires can bring a fresh perspective to all aspects of pricing. External candidates are relatively immune from the "but that's not the way we've done it" argument, and for many industries it is easier to get up to speed on the industry than it is to learn how to be a good pricer.

Pricing analysts, not surprisingly, need to be comfortable with quantitative thinking; they will interpret historical market, sales, and pricing data. However, the most effective pricing analysts also possess excellent people skills. They are persuasive with the facts at hand and are not afraid to go toe-to-toe with sales teams that may be demanding price relief.

ACTIVISM—ASPIRE TO BE AN ACTIVE VERSUS PASSIVE PRICING ORGANIZATION

If pricing is a profit center, then an approach that actively manages pricing will achieve, over time, superior returns over an approach that treats pricing passively. This difference between active and passive is what separates a great pricing function from a good one. Far too frequently, pricing organizations take a passive approach where they only respond to the business (e.g., provide reports and support deals). Passive pricing organizations do not drive continuous improvement.

By contrast, high-performing pricing organizations take an activist approach (Exhibit 6-3). These organizations identify additional pricing improvement opportunities and regularly engage senior leaders to help raise pricing performance. They help design and deliver training related to pricing and offer substantial input into other areas (e.g., creating value-based selling materials). They also support day-to-day pricing activities (e.g., reporting and deal support), but it is the proactive, continuous improvement mindset that separates the great from the good pricers.

Exhibit 6-3 Active versus Passive Pricing Organization

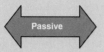

"Continuous improvement mindset"

- Fails to engender top management awareness and support for pricing

- Focuses on day-to-day pricing execution, not capability building
- Fails to set aggressive margin goals
- Reports rather than drives performance (e.g., general pricing reporting)

- Allows field to drive most margin opportunities, regularly deferring to them and seldom pushing back

- Enjoys explicit senior management support

- Raises pricing to core capability status
- Drives continuous stream of margin improvement ideas
- Exerts steady upward pressure on price across entire organization
- Facilitates cross-functional dialogue on pricing strategy

- Routinely pushes field on margin management
- Creates reliable pricing metrics and stretch targets
- Creates tools for field to identify/capture margin opportunities

REPORTING PATH—WHERE SHOULD I PUT MY PRICING PROFIT CENTER?

One of the most frequently asked questions about the pricing organization is "Where should the pricing function sit in the company?" There is no one right answer. Many factors come into play: where the primary profit and loss (P&L) responsibility resides; the degree of centralization in the company; the pace of new product introductions; and the frequency and degree to which transactions are negotiated.

It is generally a good idea to separate the pricing group from those responsible for negotiating prices with customers. Pricing is almost always separate from sales. This division creates a healthy tension between price negotiators and price managers and eliminates the problem of the fox guarding the hen house—that is, if pricing were in sales, the temptation would be great to reduce price in order to make selling volume (not value) easier. To achieve this separation, the pricing group might report up through finance (e.g., a large high-tech company) or product management (e.g., a Fortune 500 medical products company). We have also seen pricing organizations work well when they report directly to a BU head or strategy group.

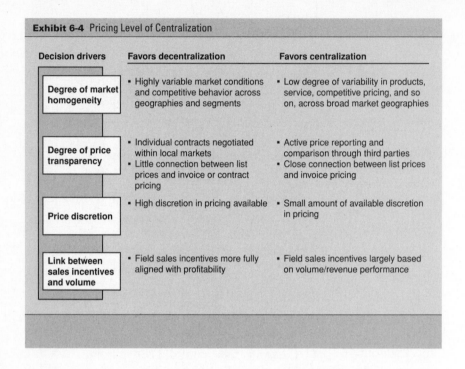

Exhibit 6-4 Pricing Level of Centralization

Decision drivers	Favors decentralization	Favors centralization
Degree of market homogeneity	• Highly variable market conditions and competitive behavior across geographies and segments	• Low degree of variability in products, service, competitive pricing, and so on, across broad market geographies
Degree of price transparency	• Individual contracts negotiated within local markets • Little connection between list prices and invoice or contract pricing	• Active price reporting and comparison through third parties • Close connection between list prices and invoice pricing
Price discretion	• High discretion in pricing available	• Small amount of available discretion in pricing
Link between sales incentives and volume	• Field sales incentives more fully aligned with profitability	• Field sales incentives largely based on volume/revenue performance

Many companies also struggle with the fundamental question: "What is the right balance between central control over pricing and speed of execution for the customer?" Although many elements affect this decision, four drivers can help companies reach preliminary decisions about the balance between central and decentralized pricing governance (Exhibit 6-4).

When a large number of transactions involve special price negotiation, it often makes sense to have pricers close to the field so that they can quickly respond to requests for support and stay in tune with local market dynamics. In one large industrial equipment firm, major pricing policy decisions are made centrally but execution is driven locally within each geographic theater (e.g., North America, Western Europe, and Asia). Each theater has a separate pricing team (manager and analysts) that regularly interacts with the business managers and supports the sales division.

HEALTH AND VITALITY—HOW DO I KNOW IF EVERYTHING IS WORKING?

Every high-performing organization takes time to regularly evaluate its overall health and vitality. Pricing should be no different. Our experience shows that three good practices will help keep the overall organization on track and fulfilling its mission.

1. *Well-defined career path.* Employees should see the pricing organization as an excellent stepping-stone on the path of career advancement. Key roles within the pricing organization should have a clear road upward. Defining and making these roles known will help attract high performers and retain them in the pricing organization.
2. *360-degree feedback for key roles.* Because the pricing organization has to interact well with so many other groups, gathering feedback from them on pricing leadership's performance is essential. We recommend investing in this process for the most visible, senior pricing roles (e.g., senior vice president of pricing).
3. *Health metrics.* A few easily tracked health metrics (e.g., rate of employee turnover, job satisfaction scores) will help managers spot trouble early and address it.

PERFORMANCE MANAGEMENT—HOW SHOULD WE RECOGNIZE AND REWARD PRICING PERFORMANCE?

Performance management is the process that regularly measures pricing's impact on the business and uses rewards and consequences to reinforce or correct behaviors and refine direction. It can support any of the three levels of price management.

While financial incentives are the most common tool in pricing performance management, our research shows that best-in-class pricers use three others that are just as important: performance metrics; nonfinancial incentives; and regular dialogues and evaluations. Together, these four reinforce one another. For example, many companies base some portion of sales manager compensation on margin attainment. While much better than purely volume-based compensation, this step is still usually insufficient to guarantee good pricing performance. Cost-reduction improvements (e.g., better procurement or lower cost design) are still passed along to the customer in the form of lower prices unless margin goals are adjusted. Managers who have fewer price-sensitive customers or more customers that buy a higher margin mix of products will end up being paid well, independent of whether they are good pricers.

Best-practice companies go much further. They reinforce financial incentives with regular performance reviews that focus on a set of pricing metrics and nonfinancial incentives that act on the competitive psyche of employees typically responsible for pricing (e.g., sales).

PERFORMANCE METRICS—WHAT TO MEASURE AND WHY

Every company should have a set of pricing metrics that measures the health of pricing across the business. Metrics should cover both financial and operational aspects.

- Financial examples include average selling price, discount, and margin for key products; percentage of revenue occurring at each discount tier or breakpoint; change in waterfall elements; average discount compared to peer transactions; and average margin by sales channel and customer segment.
- Operational examples include number of pricing exceptions; win/loss percentages; tool adoption and usage; and percentage of sales people completing pricing training.

Many companies also create special metrics to track the progress and impact of specific pricing initiatives (e.g., an effort to improve pricing of low margin stock-keeping units [SKUs] or low margin accounts).

Best practice companies create cascading dashboards and deploy them across the business. Each dashboard covers the same core metrics (e.g., average selling price) so management can compare and discuss the same measures and focus on the same priorities. Individual dashboards display the values appropriate to the manager using them. The word "cascading" refers to how the same set of metrics can roll up or down to the appropriate level for the manager viewing a specific dashboard (Exhibit 6-5). For instance, the manager of a single product line might only see the metrics for her product, while the general manager of a business unit might first see the metrics for the entire operation but be able to drill down to the individual product level to understand the root causes of pricing performance.

The nature of the business determines how frequently dashboards need to be updated. A packaged goods or consumer electronics retailer may need to monitor prices daily, but a capital equipment maker might get by with monthly updates.

Companies should also connect pricing metrics to financial incentives. For example, individual managers' performance bonuses should be linked to specific metrics (e.g., percent difference from target price) to reinforce the importance of managing the metrics. Without tight connections to individual performance management, most metrics quickly become irrelevant.

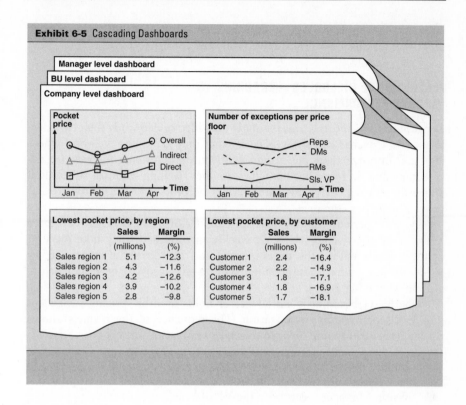

Exhibit 6-5 Cascading Dashboards

NONFINANCIAL INCENTIVES—A POWERFUL FORM OF MOTIVATION

Although often overlooked, nonmonetary incentives can be extremely valuable. One of the simplest and most effective is publishing a stack ranking of salespeople by margin or discounting performance (possibly after normalizing for variables such as account size and product mix). This move appeals to the competitive psyche of salespeople and creates a healthy dynamic among peers; those on top of the ranking want to stay there and those near the bottom aspire to move up!

Multiple types of successful nonfinancial incentives exist. Recognition for exceptional performance by your peers and manager (e.g., annual awards or more frequent ones) can provide immediate reinforcement. Under the right circumstances, leadership may also reward people for behavior that is counterintuitive (e.g., walking away from deals as part of an initiative to shed unprofitable business). Making specific measures of pricing skills key inputs into promotions (e.g., within the sales force) sends a strong message that pricing skills are a "must have," not just a "nice to have."

PERFORMANCE DIALOGUES—COACHING TO IMPROVE PERFORMANCE

Top athletes and sports teams regularly use videotape to study their own performance. Coaches can show players what they are doing well and where they can improve their performance. In business, pricing metrics are the videotape and performance dialogues are the coaching sessions. When used diligently and regularly, this combination becomes a powerful tool to improve pricing performance.

In our experience, high-impact pricing performance dialogues do three things: they occur regularly (e.g., weekly or monthly); they take place at multiple levels within the organization; and they cover a specific set of questions (e.g., what is happening, why, what needs to be done) before dealing with other issues.

One heavy equipment manufacturer holds monthly pricing reviews at four levels of its sales organization. The sequence of the reviews allows pricing issues to cascade upward to senior managers:

1. Sales Rep meets with Sales Manager.
2. Sales Manager meets with Division Manager.
3. Division Manager meets with the VP of Sales.
4. Monthly business review occurs with leaders from all major functions (President, CFO, VP Sales, Product GMs, Supply Chain, et al.).

Managers use a set of probing questions tailored to each pricing review to gain a quick sense of what is happening (e.g., gap to target?), the root causes (i.e., why the gap?), and a path to address the issue (i.e., what can be done?). After the company started using this approach, pricing performance improved and has been sustained over several years despite the influx of new salespeople.

FINANCIAL INCENTIVES AND COMPENSATION—ENSURING ALIGNMENT WITH BUSINESS OBJECTIVES

Finally, a brief word about linking financial compensation to pricing performance. Financial incentives are often the primary mechanism that drives behavior in individuals. Managers who want to create good pricing performance should design an incentive plan that strikes a balance between increasing revenue and achieving healthy margins and/or low discounts. Individual plans should vary according to the individual's influence over pricing. For example, a frontline salesperson with little ability to influence price may have only a small portion of pricing-based compensation. However, it is important to recognize that even if a salesperson's range of discount authority is narrow, he still plays a crucial role in communicating benefits and convincing customers to accept appropriate pricing. And for this, skillful salespeople should be rewarded to some degree. In contrast, a senior sales manager with a wide range of discounting authority should have a significant portion of her compensation tied to margin or discount performance.

Much more has been written about designing sales and other compensation packages;[3] what the reader should take away here is that pricing performance management is much more than just a paycheck tied to pricing.

SYSTEMS AND TOOLS—NO MAGIC BULLET EXISTS

Pricing excellence demands accurate and current pricing data, tools to turn that data into information, and a business willing to invest in systems to collect that data. What it does *not* require is overly expensive systems. Unfortunately, most companies do not have the tools and systems they need. Organizations tend to fall short either because they do not understand why they should invest or because they overspend on unnecessarily complex systems that do not match their pricing needs.

Many under-investors do not recognize the importance of good pricing information for decision making and pricing performance management. Even when they do, they are scared off by what they believe is the herculean, hideously expensive task of seamlessly connecting data from multiple databases, data warehouses, and financial systems.

Over-spenders fall into the trap of spending on IT as if it were a magic bullet and rushing in before truly understanding what they really need to serve their business needs. They invest significant time and money (often in the multimillions) in sophisticated software, only to find it does not match

---

[3]See for instance, *Compensating New Sales Roles: How to Design Rewards That Work in Today's Selling Environment* by Jerry Colletti and Mary Fiss (New York: AMACOM, 2001); *Compensating the Sales Force: A Practical Guide to Designing Winning Sales Compensation Plans* by David Cichelli (New York: McGraw-Hill, 2003); *The Complete Guide to Sales Force Incentive Compensation: How to Design and Implement Plans That Work* by Andris Zoltners, Prabhakant Sinha, and Sally E. Lorimer (New York: AMACOM, 2006).

their pricing processes, is cumbersome to use, or is expensive to update and maintain.

Why is it so difficult to get systems and tools investments right? Companies tend to make poorly informed assumptions about how much data they need and what types of tools and systems are required to meet their business requirements. After watching many companies wrestle with getting the most out of their systems and tools investments, two lessons from best-in-class companies emerged:

1. *Understand what information you need and when.* Having the right information at the right time in the hands of the right decision makers is critical to creating and sustaining *the price advantage*; best-in-class companies carefully study which roles need what type of information and how they will use it.

2. *Go slow.* Real business needs for systems and tools are best understood over time; this approach avoids costly mistakes and tends to raise the return on investment (ROI) of IT investments.

As companies put together their own systems and tools, they need to remember that there is no one-size-fits-all answer. The data needs, reporting capabilities, and frontline decision tools required for price excellence vary enormously by business. System and tool requirements reflect the scale and fragmentation of the customer base, the number of product/service offerings, the mix of standard versus customized offerings, the number of transactions per period, and the degree of pricing latitude among sales and channel partners. Pricing and margin performance always need to be transparent to managers (ideally at the level of transactions, but at least at the customer/product/market level).

Companies should also be careful not to equate complexity with the need for an expensive solution; plenty of examples exist where a well-crafted spreadsheet supported a disciplined pricing process just as well as a multimillion dollar commercial pricing package. One equipment rental company with more than 30,000 SKUs and hundreds of thousands of transactions per month crafted a practical, successful price management tool over the course of a weekend. The company focused on a handful of pricing metrics and the top 100 SKUs that made up more than 80 percent of their revenue.

WHAT KIND OF PRICING INFORMATION IS REQUIRED AND WHO NEEDS IT?

Pricing systems and tools provide four types of support, including support for pricing negotiations and decisions, analyses to identify pricing improvement opportunities, monitoring of ongoing performance, and help standardizing and tracking pricing actions. Below we discuss some of the systems and tools that best-in-class pricing companies use to address these needs.

Decision Support Tools These tools ensure that the pricer has the data she needs to make an informed pricing decision, whether the person is in the company office (e.g., at a "price desk") or sitting in front of a prospective customer negotiating a price for a deal.

Imagine two sales reps each negotiating a price for a deal with a customer. One sales rep is relying solely on his own experience and the customer's price history to judge what price to aim for and at what price point to walk away. The other sales rep is armed with a quotation tool that generates a fact-based target and walk-away prices using specific character-istics of the customer (e.g., total account size, industry, previous purchase history). Both reps have the *latitude* to negotiate price, but the second rep has more *information* upon which to make a good pricing decision. It is not hard to guess which rep, on average, will achieve higher margins and higher commissions.

One food service company built a simple tool that assisted with pricing individual SKUs; it then deployed the tool on each salesperson's laptop. For a given account the tool highlighted the SKUs priced below average com-pared to the same SKUs sold at similar customers. It recommended the price increase required to close the gap to average and calculated the incremental commission that the salesperson would make. A different view identified the top pricing improvement potential accounts for the salesperson, again sorted by incremental commission available. Finally, a third view showed the sales-person where he stacked up relative to his peers. Salespeople found the tool enormously helpful for recommending pricing and highly motivational due to its linkage to compensation.

Analysis and Exploratory Tools These analytic tools help sustain *the price advantage* over time by using diagnostic and "what if" investigations to sur-face new pricing opportunities. For example, one electrical devices company with a large portfolio of products used such a tool to uncover late-life prod-uct pricing and SKU rationalization opportunities. It found that demand for some of its older products was waning while inventory and carrying costs were increasing—all at a substantially faster rate than prices. The company coupled these insights with a hypothesis that most of the remaining demand was for replacement applications where alternatives were inherently lim-ited. It then used this information to increase prices on these low volume products. The net result was some further volume loss, but a substantial increase in total profit dollars generated from these specific SKUs. Pricing managers or analysts can derive pricing insights from historical price data and rapidly test pricing hypotheses. Armed with these tools, pricers can proactively search out new opportunities for the pricing profit center or triage issues that threaten performance.

Monitoring Metrics, Dashboards, and Reports   All of these tools provide managers with a concise snapshot of pricing performance, enabling them to monitor it across their portion of the business and intervene in areas where performance is not measuring up to desired levels.

The first step is to identify a set of metrics (KPIs or key performance indicators) that measure the essential elements of pricing performance. The KPIs vary across businesses and industries, but a few rules of thumb can help you select ones that work:

- *Easy to understand and update.* Complicated, nonintuitive analysis should not be necessary when using metrics and dashboards.
- *Tailored to the situation.* KPIs should focus on the specific nature of the business and pricing opportunities (e.g., tracking own and industry capacity utilization might be important to a basic materials company).
- *Mix of financial and nonfinancial.* Many companies focus on financial metrics like Average Selling Price (ASP) or pocket margin, but nonfinancial, often operational metrics are also important (e.g., number of pricing exceptions per month).
- *Standardized across the business.* Wherever possible use the same metrics to measure pricing performance across the business. This allows roll-up to the company level as well as drill-down to the division or group level.
- *Target values.* These should be established for each metric. Managers need to know what to manage toward, not just direction.
- *Fewer is better.* It is difficult to monitor and manage more than a handful of metrics. Choosing a small number (e.g., 5–7) and focusing on those is usually most effective.

Companies should let managers see business pricing performance in two ways. The first is a "management dashboard" that shows recent results. This dashboard is often IT-enabled. The second is standardized, regularly published reports on pricing performance, tailored to the manager's level in the organization. Many of the same rules-of-thumb apply: keep the dashboards and reports simple; and ensure that managers are focusing on the same or at least a consistent set of measures and sources of data.

Repository of Pricing Data   One of the most common challenges companies face is collecting all relevant pricing data into a centralized system. The sales and cost information required to construct a pocket price waterfall is often scattered across multiple IT systems, which may reside in different functions or departments. But assembling all this data is critical if the other tools we have already discussed are going to function well.

Many companies take a data warehouse approach, where data from multiple IT systems is regularly loaded into a single large database. Competitive pricing intelligence, historical transaction data, win/loss information, customer master tables, and list price history might all be kept in a pricing data warehouse.

Companies should regularly update this data, though how often the updates need to occur will vary by the type of business. The more important point is that the business ensures that the data is reliable enough for decision making. Managers should also note that pricing data kept in the warehouse is usually not audited financial data, so companies should not be overly concerned if this data does not perfectly match the audited financials (e.g., total revenue in a period).

TO BUILD OR TO BUY, THAT IS THE QUESTION

Many companies wrestle with the question of whether they should buy a prepackaged enterprise pricing solution or have one built from scratch as they journey toward pricing excellence. No universal answer exists and in many cases we advise organizations that are thinking about serious investments in new pricing tools to gain some experience first with what simple solutions might offer. This allows them to get going without having to wait for the all-encompassing IT-based solution to be designed, developed, and implemented. A simpler interim solution also helps them better refine their requirements, experience any constraints imposed by their legacy systems, and develop a more precise feel for what they will get from future investments. They may even be able to use their simpler solutions to "bridge" to a more complete one longer-term, if that is still necessary. It is not unusual for a company that initially expected to make a massive investment to change its mind after experiencing an interim bridge solution and realizing the interim option is actually good enough (Exhibit 6-6).

Exhibit 6-6 Pricing Software Selection

Many companies need to start by...	and beware of the following traps
• Targeting the most pressing issues that software and tools can address	• Thinking software will address all of a companies' pricing issues
• Identifying and solving data problems that could slow down software implementation	• Falling into the "we have to buy big" trap when an internal, inexpensive solution will do
• Refining the pricing processes that software will be aligned to support	• Trying to use pricing-related data to fix every underlying problem
• Adopting short-term "bridge" solutions while identifying longer-term options	• Automating all pricing decisions
• Capturing value from pricing to fund a software purchase, if appropriate	• Not coordinating pricing decision makers
• Sustaining momentum from pricing initiatives during vendor selection	• Not spending enough time driving real cultural change in pricing practices and attitudes
• Cultivating a pricing culture	

* * *

Pricing infrastructure is the key to capturing and sustaining the value offered by the three levels of price management (Market Strategy, Customer Value, and Transactions). Its core elements—pricing processes, organization, performance management, and systems and tools—are the foundation for turning pricing into a significant profit center within a business. But companies must be willing to invest continuing time, energy, and resources into the pricing infrastructure for this to occur. If they are, then the potential for *sustained* value creation—and achieving *the price advantage*—is enormous.

Three

Unique Events

P art Three addresses two critical pricing events, that is, pricing after a merger and price wars that any company might find itself facing from time to time—events that demand deliberate and active management beyond the pricing basics.

CHAPTER 7

Postmerger Pricing

Most large- and mid-size companies will eventually become involved in a merger or acquisition. Whatever their goals—moving into other geographies, acquiring technologies, products, or capabilities, or lowering costs—most mergers and acquisitions (M&As) are entered into with the expectation of huge improvements in profitability. Unfortunately, most fail to meet these expectations.[1] Although this happens for many reasons, one persistent problem is a disconcertingly lax approach to pricing. Despite pricing's enormous potential to drive value, many otherwise rigorous postmerger integration efforts do not put it high on the agenda.

Pricing opportunities can contribute as much as 30 percent of postmerger synergies, but the armies of investment bankers, senior managers, and consultants that swarm M&As rarely pay pricing the attention it deserves. Why not? First, these teams focus on more traditional synergies like reorganization and overall cost-cutting. In addition, as we have stressed throughout this book, they may misunderstand pricing and what it offers. The teams may avoid pricing issues because they incorrectly think pricing opportunities are limited to across-the-board price increases that make headline news, raise regulatory concerns, and alienate customers. In the end, many managers may simply expect market forces to level-set prices automatically as an industry becomes more consolidated.

When postmerger pricing is done well, it delves into the details of the pricing policies of the two merged companies. It assures that new policies reflect any changes in the company's value propositions to customer segments, reconciles different discount approaches, and supports the new pricing architecture that may result from changes in operations and distribution. Postmerger pricing's goal, simply put, is to ensure that the synergies

---

[1]A McKinsey study found that 58 percent of mergers in the United States actually shrink shareholders' interests in the acquiring company and 33 percent ultimately destroy value in the combined entity.

targeted by the merger are revealed and realized; it is not to use the merger to obscure price increases. Such pricing benefits not only stockholders and employees but also customers, who receive greater value from the merged company.

While gains after a merger are never guaranteed, managers who make the effort to harvest pricing opportunities proactively are often richly rewarded. But these managers must act quickly before the short window of opportunity closes. Once the two companies have agreed to combine, they can then work to capture the unique merger potential in each of the three levels of pricing: Market Strategy, Customer Value, and Transactions. Opportunities also exist to move Pricing Infrastructure to a whole new level of capability. But as they pursue this course, they must also be careful to avoid the most common traps and antitrust issues.

A TEMPORARY WINDOW OF OPPORTUNITY

Postmerger integration must focus on creating a winning company and not simply on getting the merger done quickly. Even though the work may need to be done rapidly, the period after a merger is a rare moment to review pricing without the usual internal and external resistance. It is a time during which customers, employees, and competitors *expect change* and are likely to accept any move as just one of the many adjustments triggered by a merger. But the window closes quickly, and then the moment is lost.

CUSTOMERS

During normal business, customers are generally skeptical of pricing changes. After a merger, however, customers expect changes in many aspects of the new company: for example, staff, structure, value proposition, product line, and pricing. This situation is an opportunity to devise and implement the most advantageous pricing approach, in other words, the one that moves prices up to the highest appropriate price rather than down to the lowest.

For example, a company's published schedule of terms, conditions, and discounts—which tends to be complex—may represent a rich opportunity, particularly if sales are through intermediaries such as retailers, wholesalers, and distributors. When two industrial equipment companies merged and compared schedules, they discovered great differences in the terms and conditions each offered their distributors. In particular, they charged different interest rates for financing dealer inventories, had different volume discount hurdles, and offered different rebates for cooperative advertising.

In normal circumstances, the two companies would have had difficulties convincing distributors to accept changes in the terms and conditions, but the merger persuaded customers that the companies had to rectify policy discrepancies. In addition, the newly merged company made the changes more palatable by announcing them in a comprehensive communications package that outlined all the benefits distributors would gain from the company's new pricing strategy. The message explained that changes in the distribution structure would more than offset the changes in terms and conditions. For instance, elimination of overlapping territories would benefit the distributors who remained because they would gain greater volume from the merged product lines. Based on the modifications to terms and conditions, ROS rose almost two percentage points while overall volume remained stable.

However, such opportunities are fleeting. Once customers and distributors start to buy the combined product line from the new company, usually 6 to 12 months after the merger closes, they begin to accept whatever terms, conditions, and discounts are offered as the new pricing model. After this, a company faces much greater resistance to change. Companies needing more time to consolidate pricing structures can keep the window open a little longer by delaying a new price list publication, but even then the opportunity will not last indefinitely.

EMPLOYEES

Like most customers, employees whose jobs link directly to pricing policies—for example, product managers, sales reps, and general managers—sometimes resist price changes. Altering the price structure raises a host of sensitive issues. For instance, who has the authority to grant discounts? Who collects and analyzes account information? These decisions can affect a product manager trying to grow a brand, a sales rep trying to make a commission, and/or a general manager trying to secure profit for the shareholders.

Prices not only may have a direct bearing on these employees' success, but these employees are often *the* key to the success of any pricing change. Their cumulative behavior, guided by high-level policies, produces or prevents a company's net realized prices. Employees are generally nervous following a merger, particularly if job cuts are on the table, but there can also be a sense of anticipation that adept companies can use as a catalyst for change. Employees expect some pricing changes. Resolving conflicting price policies can be one of the first tangible examples of the merging companies working together. On the other hand, a period of uncertainty may mean that both companies could lose sales momentum as sales reps may have to wait too long for new marching orders. For a richer discussion of change management issues, see Chapter 15, "Pricing Transformation."

Pricing policies play an important role in the daily activities and motivations of employees (e.g., impacting relationships with customers and personal compensation). Some change in pricing policies is inevitable unless the two companies' operations remain separate. The policies from one of the companies may be adopted, a hybrid model implemented, or a completely new model created.

To generate the highest improvement in pricing, the newly merged company must analyze each company's pricing processes, structure, performance management, and systems/tools. Exhibit 7-1 shows the pocket price waterfalls for two pulp and paper companies. When the merged company compared similar commodity products, it realized one company was netting a pocket price that was almost 5 percent more than the other was getting. This insight gave the new company the impetus to evaluate critically its entire pricing process to ensure that the merged company would achieve the highest possible pocket prices.

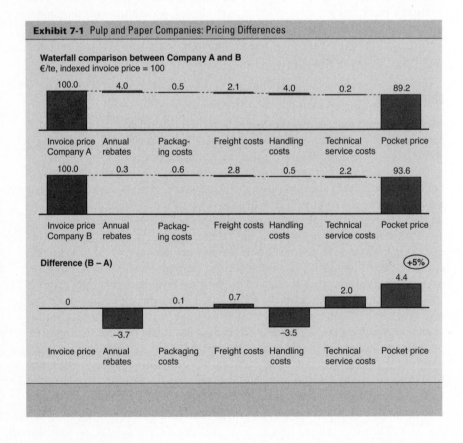

Exhibit 7-1 Pulp and Paper Companies: Pricing Differences

COMPETITORS

Mergers may also provide a promising opportunity to influence pricing conduct. Supply and demand will generally dictate price floors and ceilings within an industry, but individual competitor conduct within the industry plays a significant role in determining where prices fall within that range. For a short time after a merger, competitors are particularly attentive to the merged company's actions. They watch carefully for clues to how the combined company's behavior in the marketplace will change—and changes in marketing strategy and pricing can alter the intensity of price competition for the whole industry. Using our terminology from Chapter 5, "Market Strategy," the postmerger period is almost always a time of enhanced price visibility.

Although the postmerger environment offers an opportune time to reestablish good pricing conduct, both through across-the-board and account-specific actions, this window also closes quickly. Competitors will quickly perceive the new company's actions as the norm for future behavior and will start adjusting their own policies accordingly. Once competitors return to business as usual, it could be harder to establish a firm's fundamental pricing change in its market policy.

Any action that shapes customer, employee, or competitor perceptions and illustrates how the merger may affect pricing policies during the postmerger period can prove invaluable. Some techniques—press releases, internal newsletters, bulletins, and client meetings—can keep the window of opportunity open longer and create a more accepting climate for any moves that prove necessary later on.

TREMENDOUS OPPORTUNITIES AT EACH PRICING LEVEL

Postmerger pricing opportunities exist at each of the three levels of pricing, as shown in Exhibit 7-2 and have important implications for pricing infrastructure. In rare cases, a company's new market and competitive position may justify a price increase for all its customers. There may also be opportunities to consolidate carefully or bundle overlapping products and services. In other cases, a complicated or under-managed discounting approach may indicate Transactions level price opportunities.

MARKET STRATEGY

Mergers can reshape industries. Two midfield players can combine to become an industry leader. The merged company may significantly increase,

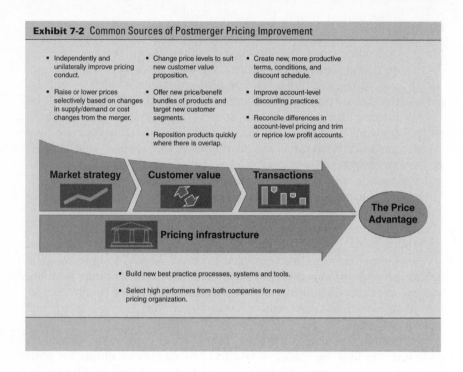

Exhibit 7-2 Common Sources of Postmerger Pricing Improvement

- Independently and unilaterally improve pricing conduct.
- Raise or lower prices selectively based on changes in supply/demand or cost changes from the merger.

- Change price levels to suit new customer value proposition.
- Offer new price/benefit bundles of products and target new customer segments.
- Reposition products quickly where there is overlap.

- Create new, more productive terms, conditions, and discount schedule.
- Improve account-level discounting practices.
- Reconcile differences in account-level pricing and trim or reprice low profit accounts.

Market strategy   **Customer value**   **Transactions**

The Price Advantage

Pricing infrastructure

- Build new best practice processes, systems and tools.
- Select high performers from both companies for new pricing organization.

reduce, or redistribute its product supply to the market. It may force the industry into a destructive price war or choose to focus its competitive efforts on product benefits. A company that understands this potential may be able to independently and unilaterally improve pricing conduct for its own and the industry's benefit.

Newly merged companies can influence pricing conduct through a variety of methods, including making decisions such as whether to focus on market share or profit, and shaping competitors' perceptions of the new entity. An example from the consumer packaged goods (CPG) industry shows how this can work. The two market leaders, Konsprod and Geffrico, traditionally fought furiously for market share, often engaging in destructive price wars. They poached each other's prime accounts and angled, largely in vain, for exclusive arrangements with retailers.

Then Caesar, a company that sold unrelated consumer products, bought Konsprod. Soon after the acquisition it became obvious that the competitive landscape had changed. Caesar fired the Konsprod vice president for sales, who had a reputation for emphasizing volume. Meanwhile, Geffrico's president ordered an analysis of the merger's likely impact on the company's strategy. Managers reported that Caesar focused on profits and rarely competed solely on price. Based on this data, Geffrico announced that it would no longer seek exclusive relationships with retailers and would increase price on a number of its products by 2.5 percent. Breaking from tradition, Konsprod matched the price hike quickly. Both companies also quickly stopped spending all their time targeting accounts held by each other. Instead, they shifted to investments in product and package innovation to drive consumption. Both Geffrico and Konsprod benefited from the new pricing behavior, with profits increasing by 25 and 17 percent, respectively.

Companies can use a host of other ways to influence pricing conduct after a merger. They may shift supply or demand by closing plants or, after extensive market research, decide to increase production on certain product lines while eliminating others. They may pool their marketing budgets and focus them more effectively, which can also promote demand. Any and all of these moves, if done as part of a deliberate postmerger pricing strategy, can raise market prices.

CUSTOMER VALUE

Mergers often change the customer value proposition. The synergies derived from the combined companies can improve product quality, add product attributes and services, or improve the terms and conditions of ownership. The pricing strategy's goal in this situation is to set prices that take into account the additional benefits gained by customers as a result of a merger. That means changes in price should be commensurate with benefit differences, moving the products higher along the Value Equivalency Line (VEL) discussed in Chapter 4, "Customer Value."

A large national bank aggressively expanded its network by acquiring many local and regional banks. After each acquisition, the bank assimilated the acquired branches into its established marketing umbrella. The bank constantly tested its model with customers, both current and future, to ensure that they valued the benefits of the large, established brand.

The integration gave customers who stayed with the bank multiple benefits, including access to the company's ATM network, one of the largest in the country; a large suite of leading-edge products and services, for example, a credit card with innovative features; and a broad loyalty points program that rewarded the purchase of multiple banking products. In addition, many customers felt more comfortable banking with the larger, better capitalized organization.

As each merger was completed, a clear opportunity existed to reposition prices to reflect the service improvements. The newly acquired branches adopted the pricing program of the national bank, including some higher fees and restructured fee schedules. The move invariably improved profitability per customer at the acquired banks with very little customer attrition.

Merging companies should seek to understand intimately whether the additional benefits the merger brings are truly valued by target customers. Market research techniques such as conjoint and discrete-choice analysis can help decipher the likely customer reaction when faced with a new combination of price and benefit levels from the new company. The timing and communication of changes must be carefully handled to ensure that customers recognize and appreciate the increased benefits they are offered and do not misperceive the pricing move as an attempt to take advantage of greater market power, which could easily trigger high attrition.

A second way to pursue *the price advantage* following a merger is to use price skillfully when consolidating product lines during the integration. When two North American auto parts suppliers with similar pricing structures merged, they saw a fertile opportunity to increase profits by consolidating their product lines. Together, they had hundreds of stock-keeping units (SKUs), some identical and many quite similar. To find out how many products they could consolidate, the company formed a six-person pricing team with representatives from both companies' marketing and sales, product development, and engineering departments. The team matched products across the two organizations, looking for opportunities to merge lines or phase out products. In particular, they looked at whether each product was making money, was increasing or losing market share, or was a brand leader. They also looked at minimum efficient production levels to determine at what point a low-volume product should be dropped.

The analysis revealed that the potential for savings was greater than expected. Along with clearing overlaps, the newly merged company dropped some undesirable SKUs, such as unpopular or inefficient package sizes. As a first step, the company discontinued about a third of its products immediately. In other cases where, for instance, profit margins were small, the company increased prices by an average of 20 to 25 percent to wean customers from those products and shift them to another product in its line. Through this program, the company cut about 60 percent of its overlapping SKUs, increased prices on some of its remaining products by 5 percent, and increased overall ROS by 1.5 percentage points.

A third way a company can capture pricing opportunities postmerger is to use synergies between product lines to fuel demand. A new pricing structure that links customer incentives to broader use of the merged company's expanded product line is one way to do this. In a recent integration, two large mattress makers took advantage of their combined marketing and merchandising coverage. The companies came from two ends of the market spectrum—one manufactured high-end mattresses and the other catered to the mid-tier and low-price segments. Following the merger, retailers carrying the products gained several advantages. The merged company now offered a one-stop shop for the complete range of mattresses and, because of its larger size, marketing and merchandising support increased. But nothing in the old price structure prevented retailers from taking advantage of these increased benefits without returning anything to the merged company. For example, many of the retailers used the company's high-end mattresses to get customers in the door, then directed consumers to another maker's lower-end mattresses that were more profitable for the retailer. Because the added benefits accrued to the retailer rather than to the end customers, a price increase on the products to complement the improved benefits, as in the banking example, would not have helped.

After carefully analyzing the various options for its discount structure, the merged company adopted a performance-based "Dealer Partnership" program that encouraged dealers to stock the full breadth of the company's expanded product line. The program rewarded dealers that purchased multiple brands from the merged company and did a large percentage of their business with it. Smaller competitors with narrower product lines could not match the breadth of the product line or these incentives. The merged company gained greater exposure at retail stores, while the retailers got a clear assortment of mattresses for their high-, mid-, and low-tier customers, as well as increased efficiency.

A new pricing structure (or architecture) might benefit a merged company if the merger changes how the combined company wants its resellers to act. If the new company wants its resellers to alter how they order, how much they order, what product mix they order, or which customers they target, the merger might represent an ideal time to alter price structure to influence desired behavior. Chapter 11, "Pricing Architecture," provides more details.

TRANSACTIONS

Transaction pricing also usually holds great opportunity for a newly merged company. As we have seen in Chapter 3, "Transactions," a company's price model is more than its list prices. It includes a range of discounts, allowances, and bonuses, each of which takes away from the revenue that the seller eventually receives—the pocket price. When companies with different price models merge, the leaders of the merged company need to understand the historical pocket prices realized at both companies, recognize leakages that could occur if both structures remain in force, and decide how best to capture the value of transaction price excellence.

A coincidence of events in the commercial printing industry clearly illustrates the value of scrutinizing transaction policies after a merger. Two large printers, X-Act Copy and FastPress, each acquired companies of roughly the same size in the same year. By the end of the year, X-Act Copy posted a 1.5 percentage point increase in ROS, while FastPress marked an impressive 12 percentage point increase. At the same time, a top executive at X-Act Copy said its cost-cutting efforts were on track, but it was far behind in resolving pricing questions. FastPress, on the other hand, had tackled these pricing issues immediately.

Soon after FastPress acquired Line-by-Line Printers, its managers examined both companies' pocket price waterfalls. They had believed that Line-by-Line was an aggressive low-pricer and expected the waterfall tiers to be generous. In fact, some of the discounts FastPress offered had been an attempt to match Line-by-Line prices for key customers. Instead, as shown in Exhibit 7-3, they found that Line-by-Line gave up much less between the list price and the pocket price. Despite Line-by-Line's lower list prices, many FastPress customers were getting much lower pocket prices from FastPress because of the waterfall differences.

On average, FastPress's pocket price was about 18 percent below list, while the discounts and other incentives offered by Line-by-Line reduced its list price by just 1 percent. In addition, FastPress discovered that its

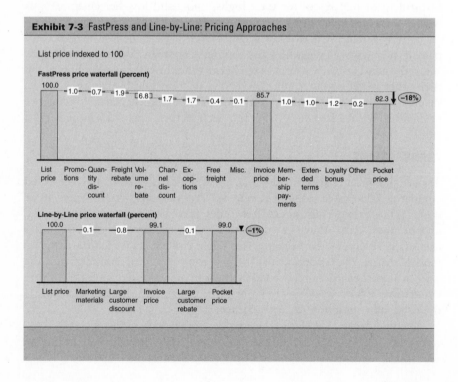

Exhibit 7-3 FastPress and Line-by-Line: Pricing Approaches

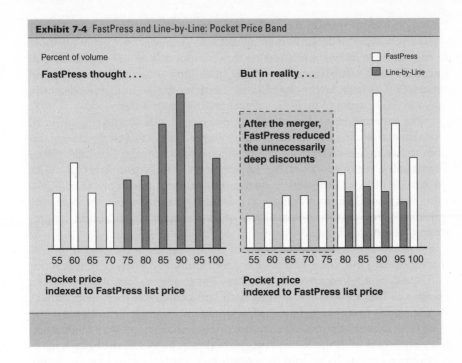

Exhibit 7-4 FastPress and Line-by-Line: Pocket Price Band

pocket price band was much wider than Line-by-Line's band, as shown in Exhibit 7-4.

FastPress worked quickly to correct the situation. Not only did it rationalize the tiers of its waterfall to reflect the knowledge gained from Line-by-Line, but it targeted its own customers that were receiving, particularly deep discounts. In many cases, it trimmed the price waterfall for these accounts, narrowing its pocket price band and increasing profitability.

Reaping benefits at the Transactions level following a merger demands meticulous attention to detail. But as the printing company example shows, careful consideration of all waterfall elements offered by all companies involved and of how each customer or customer segment is treated can be very fruitful.

PRICING INFRASTRUCTURE

Pricing infrastructures are often different in two merging companies. The pricing organization may have dissimilar size and makeup, and may play varied roles within the companies. Pricing tools may differ enough that they provide different recommendations. Reviews may or may not happen, and, if they do, may focus on disparate key performance indicators (KPIs).

Finally, pricing processes may allow various levels of discretion and focus on different types of decision-making. Because employees are generally more open to change during a postmerger integration, it is an opportune time to introduce new infrastructure elements, including organization, tools, and processes. The new, larger organization, with more resources at its disposal, may also have more to invest in critical pricing capabilities.

The experience of a large distribution company illustrates the power of an enhanced pricing infrastructure postmerger. The result of the consolidation of five major companies in the office products area, National Office Distributors became one of the largest players in North America. With 70 branch offices (each with a distribution center), and more than 5,000 sales reps, coordinating pricing was a challenge. Postmerger, the company quickly undertook a thorough review of its pricing practices across the premerged companies.

It found two fundamental types of opportunities in the pricing infrastructure area. First, some of the legacy companies had areas of best practice that could be applied across the regions. For example, one of the previous companies had a policy for dealing with cost changes in its system. Whenever an item's cost changed upward, it would immediately be reflected in the quoting system that reps used to quote prices—so margins were maintained whenever costs went up. When costs went down, however, the branch managers had to manually go into the system and adjust the cost base (knowing the end-customer prices would ultimately go down as well). The idea behind this policy was to make branch managers consciously decide whether the item's end-price really needed to go down to be competitive for the division in the region. On average, the branch managers reduced about half of the prices downward, but used the cost reduction to grow margins with the other half. After instituting this policy, the legacy company had an immediate bump in profitability with no change to its rate of revenue growth. Upon learning this, the newly merged company immediately adopted the policy across all of its divisions—and increased profitability by 8 percent.

Second, the increased scale of the company enabled the new company to redesign some of its processes. Previously, each of the branches sought price improvement by assigning a local "margin manager" to analyze data and prices continually and recommend changes in list prices in each branch. Although there was an effort to share best practices between margin managers, it was ad hoc at best.

After the mergers, the company felt that it would benefit from a central pricing center of excellence that deployed more standardized processes across the 70 divisions. They developed a standardized playbook for each of the margin managers to deploy in their division and created tools for tracking progress. One improvement area was more consistent charging for special orders. The central group developed a manual for margin managers that discussed how to identify special order items and adjust prices. The central group then tracked and compared each division's success rate in obtaining the targeted 20 percent premium on special order items. Lower performing divisions received increased scrutiny and support to ensure achievement of the target.

For the Pricing Infrastructure level, companies should look at all aspects of infrastructure (processes, organization, performance management, and systems/tools), and do a thorough review of each of their practices. They should prioritize areas for improvement based on the opportunities found at the other three levels. For example, if reducing price variation at the Transactions level is a big opportunity, it is probably best to focus on adopting the best practices around managing transaction pricing (e.g., rolling out tools to achieve full visibility on transaction profitability, instituting a transaction review process, and building a pricing organization with sufficient resources to update the data and roll out the new tools). If the opportunities are more at Customer Value level, building tools and expertise to measure elasticity, assessing customer benefits, and equipping the sales force with tools to quantify and sell the economic value of the newly merged company may be more appropriate.

AVOIDING COMMON POSTMERGER TRAPS

Just as astute pricing policy integration can create enormous value, several traps in the postmerger terrain can not only sidetrack but sabotage the unsuspecting manager. Failure to take postmerger pricing actions proactively often results in lost synergies and can destroy much of the value the merger could have created. But even when managers try to take pricing firmly in hand they can make other mistakes that destroy value. Three traps, which we have seen in many companies, are the most common.

THE GENEROSITY TRAP

Sometimes, when one company acquires or merges with another that sells products or services of lesser quality, the higher-quality company decides to be generous. By applying superior practices, managers of the acquiring company improve the acquisition's quality, reliability, or service. But if the new company does not raise prices in tandem with these added benefits, it can inadvertently cause a price war in the low-price segment of the industry or cannibalize its more profitable products.

When Compair International acquired State Compressor, State's products were similar but less expensive, with fewer design features. State also had a weak field service network and a less comprehensive warranty. To reduce the cost of servicing and administering two product lines, Compair International equipped its field service team to support State's products and equalized the warranty terms and coverage of the two lines. But despite the improved benefits, it did not change the prices of State's compressors. Although Compair International's managers thought design limitations and higher maintenance costs limited the customer value of State's compressors, sales of the lower-priced products skyrocketed soon after the service and warranty changes were made. What the managers did not understand was Compair International's superior field service and more extensive warranty had made State's products a great value at the old price.

The new price/benefit position of State's products did not just erode Compair International's market share. It also hurt competitors Micro-Comp and European. Both reacted by cutting prices and Compair International soon felt compelled to follow suit to maintain share. As shown in Exhibit 7-5, industry price levels fell by 7 percent within a year, and the merged company's profits dropped to roughly half what the two companies were recording before the merger. Industry prices eventually recovered after Compair

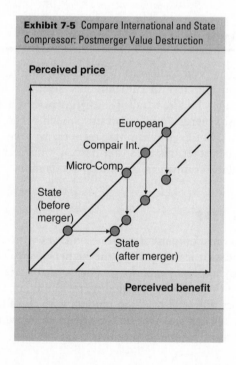

Exhibit 7-5 Compare International and State Compressor: Postmerger Value Destruction

International cut the benefits on State's products, but the generosity trap turned out to be costly for everyone.

THE DISCOUNT ACCUMULATION TRAP

Companies can fall into the discount accumulation trap when they do not properly reevaluate their terms, conditions, and discount schedules after a merger. In the worst-case scenario, a company allows both previous programs to continue, effectively combining the programs and giving customers unintentionally higher discounts. Even if a company chooses one discount structure over the other, a lot of revenue can be lost if trigger points are not adjusted properly.

Take two hypothetical companies, Superior Inc. and Elite Co., which sell to the same retailer. Both offer a 2 percent volume bonus on annual purchases of $250,000 to $1 million, and a 4 percent bonus if yearly purchases exceed $1 million. Before the merger, one retailer bought $950,000 worth of goods from Superior each year and $250,000 worth from Elite, earning a 2 percent discount from each for a total benefit of $24,000. If Superior merges with Elite and keeps the old volume bonus structure, the retailer would be entitled to a 4 percent discount on its $1.2 million purchase from the merged company, or $48,000. Without changing a thing, the retailer reaps a $24,000 windfall.

Multiply this effect across a customer base and it is easy to see that ignoring the accumulated effects of discount schedules could inadvertently destroy significant value for a merged company. Avoiding the discount accumulation trap requires a careful comparison of the customer base of the merging companies. If significant overlap exists, thresholds to qualify for discounts will probably need to be adjusted, but if little overlap occurs there could be less pressure to shift these trigger points.

THE PARENT TRAP

The parent trap can snare any company that arbitrarily believes its approach to the market is superior to that of its acquisition. If incorrect, the acquirer can decrease the value of the merger by imposing its own inferior practices and failing to adopt the acquisition's superior ones. The parent trap can occur around almost any aspect of postmerger integration, but pricing policy is particularly susceptible because it generally receives less attention than other areas.

The consumer durables industry offers a good example, where one company acquired a much smaller company with complementary product lines. The takeover target had superior processes and tools to manage account-level pricing. These included the ability to measure account profitability—right down to pocket margin; strict control processes for discretionary discounts; and feedback mechanisms to identify account-level pricing opportunities continuously. But the acquirer simply assimilated the new company into its more arcane and loosely controlled system.

Without the sophisticated controls previously in place, sales reps of the acquired company began offering customers increased discounts as they tried to maintain or improve volume during the transition period. Not only did the change needlessly destroy a significant portion of the value of the acquired company, but the parent company missed the chance to reap what could have been enormous revenue gains as it failed to adopt the acquired company's excellent transaction management processes throughout the organization.

ANTITRUST LAWS

Many companies are reluctant to use perfectly acceptable and legal opportunities to create value through pricing after a merger. The mere thought of legal repercussions causes them to put pricing considerations on the back burner and accept the status quo, both before and after a deal is completed. As a result, many managers may not feel ready to tackle pricing until it is too late to make a difference.

Antitrust laws rightly protect consumers by barring some activities during M&A processes. However, even with these restrictions, companies can analyze prices safely and legally and be ready, once a deal is closed, to meet pricing challenges aggressively. In Chapter 9, "Legal Degrees of Freedom," and Appendix 2, "Antitrust Issues," we provide a more complete survey of antitrust legislation and other regulations that touch on pricing policies; here we focus on postmerger integration. As always, legal counsel should be called in if there are any questions.

The U.S. Hart-Scott Rodino Act and the EU European Community Merger Regulation police premerger planning in the two markets. In essence, competing companies are prohibited from sharing sensitive information—generally defined as anything not publicly available—on prices, contract details, or customer lists. If the deal falls through, such sharing may constitute illegal collusion. Additionally, it is important to note that any analysis of pricing opportunities before closing, whether it comes from shared proprietary information, may have to be turned over to antitrust regulators either as part of the approval process or later if the merger becomes a subject of litigation. Regulators will closely scrutinize documents that detail potential postmerger changes in prices and discount structures to gauge if the companies involved will wield too much market power after a merger.

Given this understanding, several ways exist to structure early pricing analysis; these do not violate antitrust laws. For example, companies in both markets can use *clean teams*, composed of independent third parties, to work on issues that require competitive information to be shared. Postmerger pricing initiatives have the greatest chance of success if they begin early in the merger process; a clean team can ensure that the work begins as soon as possible and protect the confidentiality of each company's shared data. The merged company can then bring the value of pricing synergies to the bottom line immediately after close, a time when management is typically under high pressure to deliver results.

A clean team would not be able to share competitively sensitive data, such as product-specific price and cost details, with the companies involved until the merger or acquisition is final. But even before the deal closes, both sides could see the conclusions of the analysis and recommendations, as long as the information could not be seen as collusive. If appropriate, these recommendations can be implemented shortly after closure. If the deal falls through, the details gathered by the clean team during analysis cannot be used by either company. Work conducted by such clean teams may be subject to disclosure to regulators as they scrutinize a proposed merger.

Two other options can also help companies get a head start on pricing decisions during a merger or acquisition. Each company can form its own pricing team to begin the often time-intensive process of gathering its own data and analyzing its own internal issues. The companies involved can also create a joint pricing team that, prior to the deal closing, focuses its work on issues that do not require the sharing of sensitive pricing information. This team could become the core of the merged company's pricing team once the deal is completed.

* * *

The immediate period after a merger or acquisition is announced provides a unique opportunity for a company to strengthen its price advantage. Top managers should seize these postmerger pricing opportunities with the same rigor and discipline they apply to operational synergies. This rich potential is available at no other time, and the window can close quickly.

The danger is that CEOs and senior managers are typically swamped with proposals for hundreds of integration projects, and pricing is often on the bottom of the list, pushed down by more operational issues. But they cannot afford to neglect this arena. Companies with *the price advantage* not only think about but implement mergers differently, resolutely pursuing the significant but fleeting pricing opportunity the postmerger environment presents.

CHAPTER 8

Price Wars

A ir travel, microprocessors, diapers, cell phones, medical devices, automobile tires, and fast food—the list of industries racked by price wars in recent years is a long and growing one. Price wars rarely have any winners—and few survivors are as healthy as they were before the wars broke out. Their destruction is often so severe and long-lasting that the only reliable way to come out ahead is to avoid them altogether. All too many price wars start by accident, often through misreads of competitor actions or misjudgments of market conditions. The price war that is initiated as a deliberate competitive tactic is somewhat rare—and rarer still is the one that achieves a positive outcome for either the industry at large or a specific supplier within the warring industry.

No company, however well run, is immune. Even organizations with superior overall strategies and otherwise exceptional execution can destroy themselves by not managing this make-or-break issue effectively.

Navigating a course away from a price war takes effort and genuine helmsmanship. It is important to understand first why prices wars rarely succeed and most often lead to value destruction across an industry, and second what is causing this proliferation of prices wars in recent years. Only then can you find ways to stay out of price wars or, if all else has failed, get out of one with minimal damage. Under rare conditions, a price war might actually be the correct course. In this chapter, we explore all of these areas.

WHY PRICE WARS SHOULD BE AVOIDED

If you have ever imagined that aggressively reducing prices to gain share and increase profits might be a sound strategy for your business, think again. The best-run companies go to almost any lengths to avoid price wars, for a host of compelling reasons. Even if you have a dominant cost advantage—by this we mean costs at least 30 percent below the competition—reducing prices can trigger a suicidal price war. Competitors often quickly follow price cuts because no one wants to lose customers, volume, or share.

PROFIT SENSITIVITY MAKES WINNING ALMOST IMPOSSIBLE

As we say in Chapter 1, "Introduction," profits are extremely sensitive to even slight declines in average price levels. Any decrease in price drops straight off the bottom line. If price for the typical Global 1200 company falls by a single percentage point and costs and volume remain unchanged, then operating profit drops by nearly 9 percent.

What does this mean in a price war? Suppose the war causes a relatively modest 5 percent price decline. As also shown in Chapter 1, "Introduction," volume would have to increase by more than 18 percent for the company to break even in operating profit. Price elasticity would have to be –3.7. That is, volume would have to increase 3.7 percent for every 1 percent reduction in price. Price elasticities in the real world seldom exceed even –2. It is highly unlikely that demand will offset the drops in price that occur in a typical price war. When you do battle on the basis of price alone, your odds of winning from a profit standpoint are very long. Moreover, if your price cut does attract additional customers and volume, your competitors will most likely cut their own prices to meet or beat yours. After all, slashing prices is just about the easiest strategy to emulate. Anyone can do it.

ADVANTAGES FADE QUICKLY

Low price advantages over competitors are usually short-lived. Attempts to boost market share by dropping prices normally lead to retention of traditional shares at lower price levels, rather than increased share. In a skirmish in the PDA market, for example, a 50 percent price cut by Palm was matched in a matter of days by major competitor Handspring. Similarly, it took luxury retailer Saks less than a week to match (and exceed) a 40 percent price cut on designer clothes by rival retailer Neiman Marcus.

PRICE EXPECTATIONS DISTORTED LONG TERM

Amid a price war, customers' price expectations and price reference points are distorted, and these price perceptions remain damaged long after the war ends. A $199 New York–to–Los Angeles round-trip fare was widely available during a summer airfare battle a few years ago. Afterward, tens of thousands of travelers came to believe that $199 was the correct and acceptable price for that trip, and after the war was over many still refused to take that trip again unless fares returned to that level. Weak vacation flight demand during the subsequent summer confirmed that the war had moved travelers' reference points lower.

These developments are consistent with research on price psychology and price recall. Consumer research shows that the lowest price someone pays for a product is remembered longest and remains a reference point for a long time—often for life. Maybe that is why so many remember how little they paid for their first gallon of gasoline. The point, of course, is that the low prices accompanying price wars influence a customer's perception of what is a reasonable price long after the war ends.

CUSTOMERS BECOME LESS BENEFIT SENSITIVE

Customers also become more sensitive to price and less sensitive to benefits during a price war. If you provide a superior product, you probably tend to charge a higher price than competitors. Customers buy your product because they perceive that its benefit advantage more than outweighs the price premium they pay. As long as customers focus on these benefits, superior suppliers can sustain the price premium, as discussed in Chapter 4, "Customer Value."

Price wars often upset the crucial price/benefit balance. As price wars play out, suppliers emphasize price more, bombarding customers with price rather than benefit messages. The inevitable result is that customers become more and more price sensitive—and less and less benefit sensitive. Even when a price war ends, the price/benefit seesaw does not automatically tip back the way it was before. The personal computer industry is an excellent example. Despite a steady stream of quantum performance improvements, evidence shows that an ever-increasing portion of personal computer buying decisions are made strictly on a lowest-price basis. Price wars change customers—usually adversely, often forever.

INDUSTRY SHAKEOUTS ARE RARE

Price war combatants often hope that the battle will bring an industry shakeout, but this rarely happens. Although managers often justify taking part in a price war by claiming it will knock out weak competitors and rationalize the industry, there are at least two problems with this approach:

1. Regulators or the courts may construe such a strategy as illegal predatory pricing—that is, pricing with the intent of forcing a competitor out of business. (Chapter 9, "Legal Degrees of Freedom" and Appendix 2,

"Antitrust Issues" offer a fuller discussion of the legal issues surrounding pricing.)

2. Emotions kick in during price wars, leading companies to stay in a business years after it stops making economic sense for them to remain. In a segment of the electrical controls industry, companies engaged in a price war for five years, each enduring huge annual losses, yet not a single competitor exited. Even when a weak competitor does call it quits, its capacity often stays. Take a key subset of the fractional horsepower electric motor industry: brutally competitive, chronically price-embattled, 20 to 30 percent excess capacity, and most competitors not even earning their cost of capital over the past decade. Not a pretty picture; not an industry that you would expect entrepreneurs to be lining up to enter. But that is exactly what happened. Every time a competitor decided to leave this industry, new players snatched up that player's assets for 25 cents on the dollar. Then the capacity reemerged and operated on a lower cost basis than before.

As these examples suggest, preventing and avoiding price wars should be high on every company's list of strategic priorities. Price wars destroy huge chunks of company and industry profits, and almost never provide a business with an advantage. Price wars often cause irreversible damage to the customer base and seldom alleviate an industry's structural or capacity problems.

WHAT REALLY CAUSES PRICE WARS

Given all of these compelling reasons for avoiding price wars, why do so many companies find themselves fighting them so often? On rare occasions, a company will intentionally embark on a price war as part of a sound overall strategy. It might invest in a new technology that slashes costs and then lower its prices to gain share and block competitors from acquiring that technology. But few price wars are started so deliberately or thoughtfully. Far more often, companies accidentally stumble into price wars—victims of misreads of competitor actions and market changes, or misjudgments of how competitors will react to their own pricing maneuvers.

COMPETITIVE AND MARKET MISREADS

Managers usually hear about competitors' prices when someone in the field tells them, "Enemy Co. is selling at a lower price. We need to match it to survive in this market." But essential collateral information about the price—for

Exhibit 8-1 Price Comparisons

	Old price	Competitor's price	New price
Invoice price	$35.00	$32.00	$32.00
Volume bonus	−2.00	0	−2.00
Marketing allowance	−1.50	0	−1.50
Pocket price	$31.50	$32.00	$28.50

instance, that the lower price applies for no more than two days, exclusively to qualified distributors, and then only to truckload quantities—may never be picked up or communicated back to decision makers. As a result, the company matches the lower price across the board, without qualification or limitation. Enemy Co. then sees the lower price offered by its rival to a wide market, compelling it, in turn, to offer the low price to more customers for longer than was ever intended.

This is one common way for price wars to begin and escalate. A company misreading the market will swear that Enemy Co. started the war, while Enemy Co. will see things in exactly the opposite fashion. One tire company sold a product to retailers at an invoice price of $35. An end-of-year volume bonus of $2 and a marketing allowance of $1.50 brought the pocket price down to $31.50. The company then heard from the field that a competitor was selling a similar tire to retailers at an invoice price of $32. So, fearing loss of business, it lowered its own invoice price from $35 to $32. Only later did it learn that its competitor was not paying a volume bonus or marketing allowance on its $32 invoice price, as shown in Exhibit 8-1. Unable to judge true price comparability, the tire company had lowered its price by $3 to meet a competitor's price that was actually 50 cents higher on a pocket price basis. Unfortunately, this realization came too late to prevent a costly and protracted price war.

Accidents happen. Some years back, an industry association journal erred when it reported total market volume for industrial equipment at 15 percent more than it actually was. Reading the inflated number, the four major competitors in that market all feared they had suffered a serious loss of market share, and immediately dropped their prices in an attempt to recover it, although, of course, it had never really been lost. A correction of the error was published three months later, much too late to prevent a destructive price war that eventually ravaged the industry for more than a year.

Consider still another example: A consumer packaged goods supplier observed a competitor making an unexpected 10 percent price cut. The supplier assumed that the competitor was strategically repositioning its product line and so matched the price cut. In reality, however, the supplier had misread not the fact that prices were cut, but the reason behind the move. Earlier that year, the serving size stipulated by the U.S. Food and Drug Administration (FDA) for reporting nutritional information about packaged foods had been reset to 6 ounces. The competitor had decided to replace all its $6^1/_2$-ounce packages with a 6-ounce size to align with the new regulations.

Rather than repositioning its product line, the competitor was discounting prices only to get its obsolete $6^1/_2$-ounce packages out of the supply pipeline before introducing the new, smaller size. If the first supplier had not reacted with its own deep cuts, prices would have returned to normal in a month or so, once the competitor's obsolete inventory had sold out. Instead, a severe price war erupted that destroyed all industry profits for the year.

VALUE MISJUDGMENTS

Managers often assume that only the lowest-priced supplier in a market can ignite a price war. They are mistaken. The culprit can just as easily be the highest-priced supplier. As discussed in Chapter 4, "Customer Value," customers do not buy simply on price. They buy on value, which is the difference between the perceived benefits that a product provides and the perceived price.

We have shown the value map to be an excellent tool for exploring the way that this price/benefit tradeoff works in markets. In the case that follows, the value map clearly demonstrates how the high-priced player in an industry can inadvertently ignite a price war. The industry here is high-volume blood diagnostic machines used in blood banks and large hospital labs to type and test blood samples. As shown in Exhibit 8-2, Gild-tech was the leading supplier in this industry. Its diagnostic machines were perceived as the highest performing (that is, with the highest test accuracy and fastest test cycle times, among other attributes), and it commanded a justified price premium in this market. Competitors included Jakson Diagnostics, Hemmtech, and MMLabco, whose machines did not perform as well and thus sold at a discount to Gild-tech. As Exhibit 8-2 shows, the competitors traditionally aligned along the value equivalence line (VEL), with Gild-tech occupying the premium high-benefit, high-price position and MMLabco occupying the economy low-benefit, low-price position. Jakson Diagnostics and Hemmtech sat in between. As would be predicted, this market's positioning was traditionally stable with little change in market share.

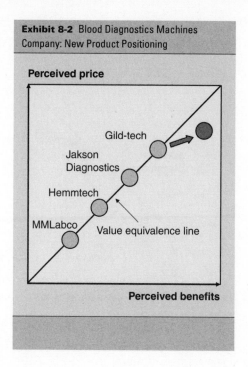

Exhibit 8-2 Blood Diagnostics Machines Company: New Product Positioning

This stability changed when Gild-tech introduced an innovative new blood diagnostic machine with even higher test accuracy, lower false positive indications, and faster test cycle times. In field test trials, Gild-tech quickly realized that its new innovative design would deliver even higher perceived benefits than its old design, and Gild-tech faced the decision of how to price its great new product. Market analysis determined that Gild-tech had the option to raise prices by 10 percent and still stay on the existing market value equivalence line (VEL). Given that the manufacturing cost of their new product was no greater than the one it was replacing, some managers at Gild-tech argued that Gild-tech should price the new product at the same level as the old one and pick up market share from a hugely value-advantaged position. Gild-tech ultimately compromised. It raised the price of the new product about 4 percent above the product it was replacing, but not the 10 percent that the new product's benefits justified. So, even with the 4 percent price increase, Gild-tech clearly occupied a value-advantaged position and expected to gain market share.

When Gild-tech's new blood diagnostic machine was launched, the market recognized its value and Gild-tech's market share rose significantly within three months. Marketers, sellers, and product developers soon began

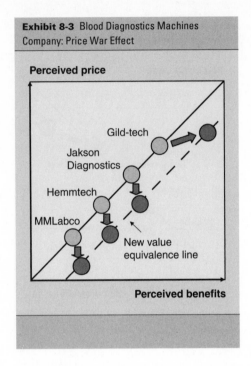

Exhibit 8-3 Blood Diagnostics Machines Company: Price War Effect

celebrating the success of the great new product. The celebration, however, turned out to be premature.

Gild-tech had grown market share at the expense of traditional rivals Jakson Diagnostics, Hemmtech, and MMLabco. These competitors did not have the resources or expertise to match Gild-tech's product innovations, so they defended their market shares the only way they knew: aggressively lowering their list prices. Within six months, each of these competitors had simply cut their price levels to become value equivalent with Gild-tech. As Exhibit 8-3 illustrates, the VEL shifted downward more than 5 percent and Gild-tech's market share slipped back to its earlier level. This turned out to be only the first of several rounds of price skirmishes in this market.

Gild-tech managers were perplexed by the price war that followed their new product launch. They said, "Gild-tech is not to blame for this price war. We *raised* our price 4 percent. Our irrational competitors are to blame." In fact, if Gild-tech had raised its price by 10 percent, as justified by the new benefits, it would likely have held its traditional market share but at a price that would have been 6 percent higher. Because Gild-tech failed to seek a fair premium for its innovative new diagnostic machine, it triggered a destructive price war.

Any player along the VEL—high-, medium-, or low-priced—can make similar mistakes by misjudging competitor response to a shift in the price/benefit position. Ultimately, anyone can instigate a damaging price war.

STAYING OUT OF PRICE WARS

We have shown that price wars usually do huge and often irreparable damage to entire industries and the perceptions of customers they serve, and that they should be avoided at all cost. We have also shown that price wars are all too often stumbled into by combatants—victims of market and competitor misreads and misjudgments. So how can you best avoid them?

It is worth remembering that some industries run an inherently higher risk of price wars than others. As Exhibit 8-4 shows, if a product is an undifferentiated commodity, price is likely to be a more important buying factor, which increases the likelihood of competition on price and of price wars. Shorter product life cycles also tend to spawn more price wars as competitors fight for market position with each cycle of innovation (see Chapter 10, "Lifecycle Pricing"). So do industries with low capacity utilization and declining market size, which ratchet up competitors' hunger for volume. So does customer concentration—when an industry has only a few large customers, each one becomes extremely valuable—and each one tends to exert strong price pressure on all competitors. As the number of competitors grows, the likelihood that one competitor will choose to price aggressively increases and so does the risk of a price war. When it is easy to switch suppliers, when customers are extremely price sensitive, and costs are stable or declining, price wars find fertile ground. Finally, in industries where the ratio of fixed to variable costs is high, companies can be lured into a price war by their high contribution margins (price minus variable costs) and the wish to fully utilize their high fixed-cost base.

Given these different levels of risk, and the kinds of misreads and misjudgments that, as we have seen, usually start price wars, how can managers build an effective firewall to keep their companies safe? Below, we suggest seven steps that managers can take to build such a wall. Many of these steps target the unintentional misperceptions that regularly put tinder to flame.

AVOID STRATEGIES THAT FORCE COMPETITORS TO RESPOND WITH LOWER PRICES

Encourage constructive competition by keeping customer communications centered on benefits and steering clear of actions that overemphasize price. Focus customers on differences in benefits, do not overemphasize price in

Exhibit 8-4 Inherent Price War Risks

Industry characteristics	Lower risk	Higher risk
Product type	Differentiated	Undifferentiated commodity
Industry capacity utilization	High	Low
Market trend	Growing	Stable/declining
Number of competitors	Few	Many
Price visibility to competition	Low	High
Customer concentration	Widely dispersed	Highly concentrated (small number of large customers)
Barriers to switching suppliers	High	Low
Overall customer price sensitivity	Low	High
Cost trend	Stable	Volatile/declining
Fixed/variable cost ratio	Low	High

your advertising, and pass up initiatives designed to steal market share rapidly from one or two main competitors. If you want to gain share, do so gradually, as rapid market share changes almost always set the stage for a price war. The more quickly you grab share, the higher the likelihood that they will respond with an aggressive price move.

AVOID ALL POSSIBLE MISREADS OF COMPETITIVE AND MARKET DEVELOPMENTS

Misreads will kill you. Delay your response until you are confident of the facts. Invest in understanding the qualifiers—and comparability—of competitors' prices. In particular, strive for a balanced reading of the full range of prices offered by your competitor. Never base a reactive price cut on just one or two competitive quotes. These quotes might not be representative; they might be plain wrong. Find out. Do not react until you understand the reason behind your competitor's price cut. If what your competitor is doing seems senseless, you probably do not understand it well enough to react wisely. If you are not sure, do not react with a lower price. The cost of a delayed reaction is always lower than that of a misread that triggers a price war.

AVOID OVERREACTION

Once you get the "what and why" of your competitor's price cut in focus, avoid the knee-jerk response of lowering your price. Though it may sound counterintuitive, the best thing to do is often nothing. Not every competitive price initiative deserves or demands a reaction. Competitors sometimes make unintentional low price mistakes—do not let one of these turn into a vicious price war, especially given the long-term repercussions.

If a response is required, use something other than price if possible. One successful medical supplier reacts to every competitor price cut by increasing benefit delivery—accelerating product improvements, boosting service levels, and shaving lead times—to make its price premium increasingly justifiable to customers. If a price response is required, make it as limited and surgical as possible. If you are feeling pressure in southeast Florida, do not lower your prices across the entire country; close just a portion of the price gap and do it only in southeast Florida.

PLAY YOUR VALUE MAP RIGHT

For important market segments, invest in research to understand your value position and the amount and value of the benefit advantages you hold. Recent breakthroughs in market research make testing your current value positioning less time-consuming and less expensive than ever. Once you understand the magnitude of your advantage, make sure you set your price as high as this advantage will support. Moreover, do similar research to determine the value customers will assign to the incremental benefits for a new or improved product so you can price it accordingly. Goodyear some years ago wisely charged a fair premium for a superior new rain tire, establishing a market position for it without placing undue downward pressure on industry price levels that were already volatile.

COMMUNICATE YOUR PRICE EFFECTIVELY

Price communications to customers should minimize the likelihood that the market will misread your price levels or the reasons behind your actions. Having your own prices misread by the market can be just as damaging as you misreading theirs; either can start a price war. While price signaling is illegal in the United States and other markets, as noted in Chapter 9, "Legal

Degrees of Freedom," communications with a justifiable commercial purpose are generally appropriate, for example, letting customers know about an impending price change and the rationale behind it. If you take actions that might be construed as price slashing, it is proper to include a clear description of all qualifiers and limitations and, in some circumstances, an explanation for the action in your normal price communications to the market.

CONVEY A BENEFITS-ORIENTED APPROACH TO VALUE

Companies that successfully avoid price wars consistently write and speak publicly about the virtues of competing based on delivering superior benefits to customers. Companies emphasize the benefits orientation in articles, in their own publications and media, in analyst conference calls, and in every available public forum.

EXPLOIT MARKET NICHES

If you are a minor player in an industry prone to price wars, the smartest thing to do may be to find a place to hide from the crossfire. Look for a product, segment, or even distribution channel niche that is too specialized, small, or obscure for the big players. Several small computer companies have escaped severe harm in the recent personal computer price wars by placing themselves in specialized, high-performance application niches that were below the radar of the major players.

GETTING OUT OF PRICE WARS

If all preventive measures fail and you find yourself in the middle of a price war, what can you do to extricate your company and limit the damage? First, determine the severity of the price war, which can span a broad range—just like the wars' causes. Simple competitive misreads are quite different from a situation where competitors are hell-bent on putting you out of business. It is vital, therefore, that you align your response with the level of severity. The worst thing you can do is to take a high-severity response in a low-severity circumstance. Such action will quickly escalate an isolated skirmish into all-out price war.

So, before plotting your response, do a careful assessment of just how severe the situation really is. Be cautious: Price wars can become highly emotional, and it is easy for those involved in them to overestimate their severity drastically. More than likely, this will lead in turn to an excessive response, which then throws a company and its industry into a truly severe and devastating price war.

When considering your response, bear in mind you have a number of techniques to draw on. First, continue using the seven methods listed earlier. These are just plain good practices, are easy to do, and just might result in a reduction in price war intensity. If they fail, two more aggressive (and riskier) options exist:

1. *Seek long-term contracts* with key customers. If at all possible, get your major customers out of the crossfire of a price war by signing them up early to extended supply contracts. Such contracts also allow prudent suppliers an extended opportunity to demonstrate benefit superiority to key customers and to create a sustainable barrier to future price incursions by competitors. However, getting customers to sign such contracts is extremely difficult once they realize a price war is raging.

2. Only as a last resort, *actively engage the enemy* with a tit-for-tat strategy. Whenever your competitor makes an aggressive price move, immediately and publicly match it. If your rival steals one of your biggest customers, immediately go after one of its major customers in the same market. You are demonstrating that price aggression is a no-win proposition and that you will match your competitor's every move. Similarly, you should monitor the market closely and return immediately to normal behavior once the price war threat subsides so as not to spark yet another price battle.

We cannot overemphasize the amount of risk that accompanies a tit-for-tat strategy. Your competitor may take an inordinately long time to realize that its actions can do it nothing but harm; rivalry across the entire industry may escalate precipitously; and as the tit-for-tat game plays itself out, all of a price war's detrimental effects on customers will occur. Take this step with extreme care, and only after all else has failed. As a guide, Exhibit 8-5 lays out a broad range of responses and aligns them with the severity of the price war threat.

WHEN A PRICE WAR MIGHT MAKE SENSE

Given the sustained negative profit and market effects of most price wars, situations are *extremely* rare where aggressive price cuts that might ignite a price war make sense. The conditions where a price war *does* make sense fall into two major categories. The first category involves situations where significant latent demand exists at the lower price level. Several years back

Exhibit 8-5 Ending a Price War

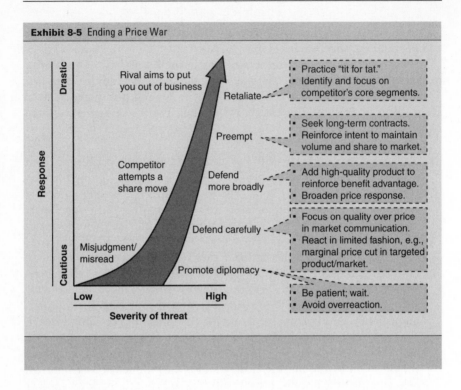

when home PC prices broke below the $1,000 barrier, they unleashed huge latent demand. This rare discontinuity in the demand curve may have allowed combatants in this price action to, at least in the near to medium term, gain both revenue and profits. The second category involves situations where competitors are structurally unable or unwilling to react fully and quickly to your price cut. These situations may include circumstances where a company has a significant cost advantage (costs that are 30 percent or more lower) or an insurmountable technology advantage. Circumstances where a rival has much more to lose by responding also fall into this category—for instance, if a competitor with a dominant share position would have to lower prices across the board to respond to a minor competitor's price cut.

Even these situations are fraught with pitfalls. The surge of latent demand that draws in price combatants is rarely sustained. In the PDA case cited earlier, market demand ultimately flattened. After latent demand is absorbed, the price war leaves industries structurally unable to thrive because prices are too low, costs too high, and demand too flat to sustain long-term viability. If structural barriers make a price war tempting, you should remember that it is often difficult to predict how competitors will react, even when faced with a rival company that has a dominant cost or technology advantage. These wars often become emotional and managers react in illogical ways that may not be in the best interest of their company's financial and market performance.

* * *

What does all this mean for today's management teams, who must deal with the threat of price wars daily? An interesting, albeit bleak, analogy may apply. Price wars are a lot like heart disease. Heart disease is serious, and it can kill you. We all are at risk. Some of us have higher inherited risk than others, just as some industries have an inherently higher risk of price wars than others. Still, however great the risk, you can reduce that risk by the way you behave every day: your diet, whether you smoke, how much you exercise, and so on. In much the same way, your day-to-day pricing behavior will affect your risk of a price war. You increase it with every competitive misread, with every market misread, with every overreaction, with every failure to charge an adequate premium for your superior benefits.

Just as with heart disease, prevention is the best cure for price wars. Each and every pricing action needs to be passed through a price war screen. Managers must constantly ask themselves, "Will this action contribute to the creation or extension of a price war in my industry?" If the answer is yes—or even maybe—do not do it. Ultimately, it will be a string of seemingly insignificant but correct day-to-day pricing actions that provides the firewall to keep your company from suffering the ravages of a price war. Building that wall and keeping it strong is a disciplined and endless struggle—but a struggle well worth confronting and winning.

Four

Expanding the Boundaries

Part Four explores some of the boundaries of *the price advantage*—whether legal boundaries that may limit a company's degrees of pricing freedom or the boundaries that many companies can expand to find opportunities beyond the fundamentals covered earlier.

CHAPTER 9

Legal Degrees of Freedom

More than 60 years ago, the U.S. Supreme Court said restrictions on price competition were threats "to the central nervous system of the economy."[1] Consistent with this view, governments throughout the world have curtailed practices that interfere with market-based price competition; however, governments also continue to pass conflicting legislation such as farm price supports and minimum wage laws that effectively rein in market forces. Although these laws affect many aspects of pricing behavior, they provide relatively little black-and-white guidance, just many shades of gray. Despite the lack of clear direction, in most cases, a company can achieve legitimate business objectives by adjusting the pricing approach to correspond with the degree of risk it wishes to assume. This risk usually manifests itself in trade relations issues or sometimes civil litigation and adverse publicity, rather than full-scale government investigations.

This is a different kind of chapter. Although most of our other chapters are about opportunity, this chapter is about constraints. More precisely, it is about legal constraints—both real and perceived. Too many companies do not know where these constraints start and stop. We do not provide legal advice, but we explore where legal issues commonly arise when implementing pricing programs and highlight some of the legal misconceptions that can get in the way of successful pricing execution.

The pricing strategies of almost all businesses are affected by the law, but many companies respond by either closing their eyes to the implications unless called to task or by adopting an ultraconservative approach that misses many opportunities. Avoiding or exaggerating the legal realities often obscures the potential of price as a powerful lever of performance. Many companies shun pricing programs that are lawful because they believe, sometimes falsely, that there is even a slight chance of legal repercussions. Although it is relatively easy for those affected by a pricing decision to

---

[1] *United States v. Socony-Vacuum Oil Co.*, 310 U.S. 150, 224 n. 59 (1940).

complain and even to take legal action, it is much harder to prevail in court. Companies should view handling these complaints as a cost of doing business. A risk-averse mindset is even more prevalent; companies often adopt this mindset based on a desire to remain well within the most narrow, conservative reading of the law. However, this can foreclose the possibility of considering a valuable price program. Rather than shutting this possibility off prematurely, organizations should consider their true appetite for risk and combine it with the intensity of industry regulation, previous legal problems, the stature of the company, and its general culture when determining whether to embark on an pricing program.

Just about any reasonable strategic pricing objective can be accomplished within a range of legal risk that most companies find acceptable. But businesspeople need to be able to think through the legal issues they will face before they have chosen their specific tactics. Unfortunately, their grasp on the legal issues surrounding pricing parameters tends to be far weaker than on any other pricing issue. This is not surprising, because pricing is a complex, specialized legal area. Recent legal changes that challenged or effectively eliminated some convenient rules of thumb allow more flexibility in pricing but multiply complexity. To accomplish their pricing objectives, executives must overcome these tangles and choose from the many lawful approaches the one that will capture the maximum value from their pricing program.

This chapter does not offer an exhaustive treatment of the legal issues, legislation, and rulings relevant to pricing. We have no intention of offering legal advice. Such a treatment is far beyond the scope of this book, which is strictly descriptive and does not constitute legal counsel. The law is constantly in flux and companies should always consult specialized attorneys if they believe their actions might conflict with applicable law. However, we hope that addressing the subject shows managers that they have more room than many might assume to pursue *the price advantage* within the letter and spirit of applicable laws.

The legal parameters discussed here are broadly applicable to most management decisions involving pricing, particularly in the United States and the European Union. Pricing issues in the United States are generally addressed by the Sherman Antitrust Act of 1890 and the Robinson-Patman Act of 1936, which regulates price discrimination. The European Union is watchful of practices that may inhibit competition, particularly by companies that are viewed as dominant in their markets. The relevant EU statutes are Articles 81 and 82 of the European Community Treaty (formerly Articles 85 and 86). Appendix 2, "Antitrust Issues" has a fuller discussion of U.S. and EU statutes from a business perspective.

Globalization over the last decade has encouraged a trend toward somewhat greater uniformity in antitrust laws of individual nations, as well as a recent, distinct upswing in the active enforcement of those laws. Markets such as Europe, which has strong antitrust laws on the books, have made enforcement easier by eliminating cumbersome reporting requirements and creating competition authorities to coordinate implementation. These revised procedures have resulted in enhanced investigation and enforcement, including more than 1,000 cases based on EC Treaty antitrust law. Other areas of the world such as Brazil have increased enforcement by granting competition agencies additional authority and resources to prosecute cartels. This has resulted in a material increase in cartel cases in industries such as vitamins, security services, and sand extraction. Australia has taken actions against major players in several industries—airlines, telecommunications, paper, and building products. Record penalties have been awarded for price fixing and the Federal Court there recently upheld the enforcement agency's wide power to obtain documents and information as part of their investigations. China's Guidelines on the Definition of Relevant Market were released on July 7, 2009. They are intended to be applied by all of China's agencies that are entrusted with enforcing its Anti-Monopoly law. This increase in enforcement activities reinforces the need for companies competing in these different markets to keep up-to-date with the applicable local laws.

In this chapter we cover three topics: first, the areas in pricing strategy that might trigger particularly close legal scrutiny (and potentially require legal expertise); then, ways to minimize the legal risk while pursuing legitimate objectives like market segmentation, regional pricing, and price war avoidance; and finally, the considerations a company should weigh when working with internal or external experts in pricing law.

PRICING DECISIONS THAT RAISE RED FLAGS

Legal issues can arise at each of the three levels of pricing: Market Strategy, Customer Value, and Transactions. In some jurisdictions, laws can also impact a company's pricing infrastructure (e.g., maintaining an adequate audit trail on discounts and allowances for external financial reporting purposes). At the Market Strategy level, laws generally forbid companies from price fixing either by directly colluding with competitors to affect industry prices or by indirectly reaching an agreement through the inappropriate use of price signaling. Monopoly pricing laws prohibit companies from undertaking pricing practices that establish or exploit power derived from dominance in a given market. At the Customer Value level, vertical price-fixing laws constrain a manufacturer's ability to maintain consistency in prices set by its resellers. At the Transactions level, price discrimination laws limit the ability to charge different prices to different customers based on willingness to pay or perceived benefits.

The likelihood of legal scrutiny increases in certain situations, which could limit pricing flexibility. These situations are not necessarily illegal nor do they automatically prompt legal review, but their presence usually requires more caution. They include:

- *Dominant position.* A company occupies a dominant position in its industry or market. This situation can involve monopoly power, where a company can control prices or exclude competition, such as local telephone companies and utilities, or market power, where a company can maintain prices above competitive levels for a significant time period because of high market share.
- *High visibility.* A company's actions draw attention because of a perceived disproportionate economic effect or its attractiveness as a target for legal scrutiny or action. Examples include major airlines, oil companies, and pharmaceutical companies.
- *New visibility.* A company substantially changes the way it does business, for example, redoing its distribution system or making a significant acquisition. U.S. agricultural and construction equipment manufacturer Case had to defend itself against charges of anticompetitive conduct when it dropped dealers after its 1985 acquisition of International Harvester's agricultural machinery businesses.
- *Previous behavior.* A company or industry has a history of antitrust problems, particularly in the pricing area.

In addition to these issues, which focus on a company's posture within a market, certain customer-specific pricing actions require a clear understanding of the legal boundaries. On their own, these actions are not necessarily illegal and they can all be part of a responsible pricing program. Such actions include:

- *Account-specific pricing.* A company sells at different prices or offers varying incentives to different competing customers. For many companies, this is a way of life as they try to differentiate their offerings or respond to demands from powerful buyers.
- *Performance-based discounts.* A company emphasizes performance-based discounts for resellers to make channels more efficient, which may cause actual or de facto distributor, dealer, or end-user terminations or, at the very least, create "winners" and "losers."
- *Exclusivity and loyalty arrangements.* A company offers exclusivity agreements or loyalty rewards that decrease total cost of ownership for some customers. U.S. beer giant Anheuser Busch was challenged by a group of small brewers in 1997 over its "100% Share of Mind"

program, which gave rebates, attractive payment terms, and reimbursement for some marketing activities to loyal wholesalers. Seven years later, the case remained open, but early court decisions favored Busch.

■ *Product bundling.* A company offers special prices for bundled products or services or does not sell individual products or services separately. This can be an issue when one component of the bundle is not available from competitors, effectively extending monopoly pricing to the entire bundle.

■ *Resale price setting or influencing.* A company formally sets or influences resale prices. Recently, as large resellers have aggressively used their market power to push prices lower, many manufacturers in diverse industries much more actively dictated or influenced the ultimate price of their products.

■ *Global price differences.* A company varies its prices by country or region in order to address differing brand positions, markets, demand, and other factors. This can be particularly difficult within the European Union where, for instance, Nintendo was fined €149 million in 2002 for taking action to prevent the lower prices that it was charging in the United Kingdom from undermining its higher prices on the European continent.

There are also moves that deal more directly with competitors that could increase the legal risks of pricing programs. Two of the more common ones are:

1. *Joint activity.* A company forms a joint venture or engages in joint bidding with one or more actual or potential competitors, or participates with competitors in efforts to exchange data or set standards. Membership in industry cooperatives or trade associations, which may provide forums to discuss pricing issues, could increase the chance of regulatory scrutiny, unless such discussions stay within rather narrow bounds.

2. *Price or price strategy transparency.* A company communicates its prices or pricing intentions to the market. In the 1980s, DuPont and other manufacturers of gasoline additives provided advance public notice of price increases that went beyond the requirements of their contracts with customers. In 1984, a U.S. appellate court overruled a decision of the Federal Trade Commission (FTC) and upheld this practice, among other reasons because such advance notice was useful to customers and permitted them to plan for such increases.

A better understanding of these areas that may raise legal challenges should not prevent a company from embarking on a sensible pricing program. But with this understanding, a company can seek ways that minimize its legal risk while pursuing its pricing objectives.

MINIMIZING RISKS WHILE MEETING PRICING OBJECTIVES

The trend in legal regulation of pricing over the past several decades has been to move away from judging behavior based on economic assumptions and toward doing so based on demonstrable economic effect. For a legal challenge to a company's pricing policies to succeed in court, it must be backed more often by hard data rather than economic theory. This trend has unleashed a great deal more flexibility and opportunity for companies that want to use price to improve performance.

When considering how to use pricing to achieve legitimate business purposes, wise managers acquaint themselves with those approaches that were deemed lawful in the past. By understanding the flexibility that legislatures and courts allow, companies can confidently develop and pursue meaningful pricing objectives based on the degree of risk they wish to assume. In this section, we consider some of the more common pricing objectives and how the law has been applied to these. (For a discussion of legal parameters in postmerger pricing, see Chapter 7, "Postmerger Pricing.")

MARKET SEGMENTATION

As detailed in Chapter 4, "Customer Value," smart companies are justified in considering the perceived benefits customers place on their products and in pricing based on these benefits; in other words, these companies segment the market into groups of customers with different benefit perceptions. Companies may wish to charge different prices based on these customers' or segments' near- or long-term profitability to the company. Chapter 13, "Tailored Value," discusses the strategic implications of this type of value pricing.

But embarking on such a program requires a deep understanding of how value pricing can be implemented without violating the laws against price or promotional discrimination. Although some practices may be well within the law, they may cause tensions with customers, and, as with any business decision, their effects on trade relations should be carefully considered when deciding whether to adopt them.

Several methods are generally acceptable in the United States that could be illegal for dominant companies in the European Union. One is to make price tiers universally available. An example is the use of share-of-wallet discounts instead of those based on volume. Activity-based discounts available to all customers, such as incentives for prompt payment, typically meet with little opposition. Because the Robinson-Patman Act in the United States does not cover services, it has been generally safe in the U.S. to price services differently for various customers based on benefits delivered. Some laws in individual states, however, purport to cover service pricing so companies should check this avenue. This interpretation may also extend to bundled product and service offerings where the benefits of the services predominate, such as the sale of a server along with a maintenance contract. Chapter 13, "Tailored Value," contains more detail on this topic.

Another acceptable segmentation approach creates real differences in products that appeal to the different needs of various customer segments. One element in determining unlawful price discrimination in the United States is whether products within the same grade or quality were sold at different prices. When products have true functional or physical differences that affect styling or actual product performance (different branding is not enough), then price discrimination is not considered unlawful. This approach has also been ruled acceptable in the European Union.

Companies can also charge competing customers different prices based on cost-to-serve differences. These higher or lower prices need to be close to the actual cost differences between these customers. Companies using this approach must be able to quantify clearly the cost-to-serve differences among customers. U.S. companies have also argued successfully that discriminatory prices were necessary to meet a competitor's price and that doing otherwise would have risked losing a customer or breaking from traditional price parity. It was important to have a reasonable basis for believing the discounted price was necessary at the time the decision was made and to establish firmly what the competitive price was. While this approach may work in the United States, it may not be legal for dominant companies in the European Union.

DIFFERENT PROMOTIONAL INCENTIVES

Companies often wish to provide incentives to resellers that market their products in certain ways or that put sufficient resources behind promoting the sale of their products. But when doing this, they must consider the law regarding promotional discrimination in the United States or the law governing price discrimination in the European Union. A dominant supplier has less flexibility under EU law, and the same may be true in the United States.

Because the Robinson-Patman Act does not apply to service providers, companies can lawfully provide different promotional benefits to intermediaries that sell a supplier's services. Purchasers that use the supplier's product to make their own product are also outside the law's scope because they are generally seen as an end user rather than a reseller. The Robinson-Patman Act may become relevant, however, if the end user actively promotes the fact that its product was made using the supplier's product and is then compensated for its marketing efforts. As usual, dominant companies in the European Union have less leeway.

Companies are on firmer ground when they make incentives available to everyone. This way, if a reseller does not receive a certain promotional benefit, it is because the reseller chose not to take advantage of the available incentive. Segmentation is accomplished by designing programs that all competing customers could use, but that have requirements that may mean certain customers are less likely to participate.

Promotional incentives can be linked directly to the value received by the supplier. For example, the size of the incentive payments can be based on the number of units purchased (e.g., an additional $10 in promotional funds for every case purchased), the actual cost of the marketing media (e.g., more money for television ads than local newspaper ads), or the relative value of the promotion (e.g., more money for advertising on shopping carts, which is more effective than window advertising).

REGIONAL AND INTERNATIONAL PRICING

When a company sells its products in different markets, it often does not make sense to charge the same price in each. The markets could be different regions of the same country, different countries, or different global regions. Apart from tariff, tax, and currency considerations, costs in one market may be higher or lower than in other areas (e.g., more investment in brand building). Corporate objectives may also be different. For instance, a company may focus on building market share in Greater China, while its goal in Southeast Asia is to increase profit. Such variances in pricing strategy across markets can call attention to a company's practices, which must be based on a clear understanding of the legal parameters.

In the United States, regional (or even account-specific) pricing is lawful as long as competing customers are treated alike or there are lawful reasons to differentiate. In the European Union, this strategy has historically been troublesome if the different prices are enforced by mechanisms that inhibit the movement of goods or services between countries or into the European Union.

Companies in the European Union can keep lower prices outside the Union from threatening a higher-price position within the Union. In addition, if they own a product's trademark a company can prevent a product's resale within the EU if it was originally sold outside the EU. To do this, the company refuses to give the non-EU buyer permission to bring the product into the EU; they also set up their distribution and pricing so that prices are different inside and outside the EU. If all this works out, the company will be able to bring trademark infringement proceedings if a buyer tries to resell goods within the EU.

PRICING CONDUCT IMPROVEMENT AND PRICE WARS

Pricing conduct improvement can unlock tremendous value in a company, while price wars generally hurt everyone involved. These issues are covered in Chapters 5, "Market Strategy," and 8, "Price Wars," respectively. But preventing price wars can be difficult; companies might want to engage in strategies to improve conduct or avoid a war, but they are often held back by prohibitions against price agreements with competitors. Most companies are appropriately cautious about even the appearance of such an agreement. However, the truth is that companies can independently pursue and support good pricing conduct in ways that do not create legal issues.

Simply imitating a competitor's pricing behavior, a tactic known as *conscious parallelism*, is lawful in the United States and the European Union as long as no agreement exists among the companies involved. For example, airlines frequently announce price increases and, in some cases, competitors match those changes within hours. To casual observers, this may look like collusion. But the move is economic, rather than collusive. Armed with new information (e.g., one carrier raised its prices), the followers recognize that profits will increase more with a higher price than with the additional volume that continued lower prices might bring. As a result, they, too, raise prices.

Communicating prices or pricing intentions publicly to stakeholders is lawful, even if a competitor sees and reacts to it, although there is an extremely important caveat. The communication must serve a legitimate and justifiable commercial purpose for stakeholders. It could, for instance, give customers needed information for their own budgeting or inform shareholders of a likely impact on earnings. An important limitation is that the communication should not be speculative; it cannot be a trial balloon that says a company is "thinking about" raising prices. A company must announce what it *is* doing, rather than what it *might* do.

Using public announcements to explain the reasoning behind a pricing change can help companies manage their own pricing strategies. Such clarity, for example, would have helped a packaged food manufacturer when it lowered its prices in the early 1990s to clear its inventory in response to a regulatory change. Chapter 8, "Price Wars," also covers this case. To avoid a price war, the company could have communicated the reason behind the new prices. Such messages help employees, particularly the sales force, understand the rationale for the pricing decisions and what they need to do to support them. These messages are also heard by the market—whether customers, consumers, analysts, or competitors. The content of the messages can combat the type of destructive market behavior that often leads to price wars—whether it may be consumers thinking that they can always get lower prices, competitors misinterpreting the meaning of a pricing move, or analysts and the press sending a message that the rest of the market picks up and misinterprets. Ensuring that messages are clear, with strong business purposes and explanations, and supported by credible mechanisms that convey the futility of a price war, can help companies try to avoid these situations. Such efforts can change a competitor's calculation of its actions and the market's perception of the company.

Two common methods for avoiding price wars are "meet-the-competition" and "most-favored-customer" clauses. Meet-the-competition clauses commit a company to match any lower price offered by competitors. This can discourage rogue competitors from undercutting prices in key accounts or key markets. Although price-matching practices have been challenged as anticompetitive, the practice has generally prevailed in the United States and the European Union because it is similar to the lawful practice of following a competitor's prices. In addition, price matching that lowers prices is less likely to trigger an antitrust challenge, since lower prices are generally seen as a sign of healthy competition.

Under a most-favored-customer clause, a supplier guarantees a key customer that it will be charged the lowest price offered to anyone by the supplier. Such a commitment helps assure the customer that they will get the lowest price; at the same time, it usually means that the supplier is unlikely to use price as a lever against rivals since any price reduction would have to be passed along to the supplier's core customers. In the United States, such clauses (also sometimes called most-favored-nation clauses) have generally been allowed, although in the health care industry the government has challenged them, saying they foster coordinated pricing or discourage price-cutting. These provisions may be unlawful in the European Union for dominant companies, but are permitted for nondominant companies.

GUARDING AGAINST EXCESSIVE RESELLER DISCOUNTING

As the power of resellers in many industries grows, suppliers increasingly want to protect against heavy reseller discounting of their brands, which could result in brand dilution and channel conflict. For example, a company wanting to maintain a premium brand image would not want a large retailer to heavily discount its products. As a result, suppliers often seek to set price floors or otherwise encourage resellers to price at certain levels. At the same time, they need to ensure that they do not violate the laws governing vertical price fixing.

In the European Union, suppliers have little room to try to influence or control the prices charged by resellers. In the United States, however, a company can use several approaches to influence resale prices and protect its market position, including:

- *Direct dealing programs.* A company can negotiate directly with a distributor or dealer's customer and dictate the price, even if an intermediary facilitates the transaction. As long as the intermediary does not take title of the product, no vertical price fixing is involved. (This is one of the few methods that can also be used in the European Union.) In a variation of this practice, a U.S. supplier can agree with the distributor's customer on a purchase price, then find a willing intermediary that would take title to the product and fill the order at that price. This approach is common when it is necessary to have inventory in the field, but direct negotiations with the distributor's customer are needed because of the size or complexity of the project.
- *Minimum, maximum, or exact price policies.* A company can generally establish a resale pricing policy that is a stated policy by the supplier requiring resellers to price the supplier's products to end customers at a minimum, maximum, or exact level. Historically, the only way to implement this policy was for the seller to do it unilaterally—because any conversation or negotiation on the terms of the policy would constitute an agreement and be *per se* illegal (meaning illegal on its face). A recent Supreme Court ruling, Leegin *Creative Leather Products Inc. v. PSKS Inc.*, liberalized the federal law of resale price setting to permit a supplier to set a minimum, maximum, or exact resale-selling price by agreement with its wholesalers, distributors, dealers, or retailers. In doing so, the Court overturned its own 1911 ruling that such conduct was *per se* illegal and replaced it with a standard called the *rule of reason* that required customers to prove real economic damage as a result of the policy. The practical implication of this change is that suppliers can much more easily implement these policies as plaintiffs' suits are more difficult and expensive to win. Resale price policies are often enforced by dropping the reseller if it charges prices that are outside the range allowed by the policy.
- *Minimum advertised price (MAP) programs.* A supplier may encourage a certain resale price by offering a promotional allowance if the reseller agrees that the advertised price will not be less than the price set by

the supplier. Such programs were challenged in the United States until 1987, when the FTC began permitting them on the basis that they were voluntary and only the promotional allowance was threatened if a reseller did not join.

- *Retail price support policies.* The reseller can receive an allowance, usually in cash-back, based on the closeness of its selling price to the supplier's suggested or target prices. Like MAP programs, resale support allowances in the United States are allowed as long as they are voluntary.
- *Shared price advertising.* For a specific promotion, a supplier can advertise in a particular market and offer to mention the reseller in the ad if it sells at the advertised price during the promotional period. This is a variant of MAP programs and is allowed because it is voluntary.
- *Price waterfall engineering.* One of the most efficient ways of influencing the price that a reseller charges is to change the price that the reseller is charged. Price waterfall engineering, which is sometimes called buy-price engineering, refers to adjusting the price or price model offered a reseller to drive a desired resale price behavior. This could be simply raising the price or it could be something more complicated, such as shifting on-invoice discounts to off-invoice. Chapter 11, "Pricing Architecture," provides more information. Since price waterfall engineering can result in price differences between competing channels and customers, companies must take care that their practices are consistent with the legal requirements of the local and national price discrimination laws.

Companies in the United States, the European Union, and elsewhere can also turn to a more fundamental approach to influencing resell prices: fact-based persuasion. Using market research and an economic analysis of the reseller, a supplier can demonstrate the advantages to the reseller of increasing (or even decreasing) the resale prices of the supplier's product. Then the reseller makes an independent decision. Although the conversation raises few legal risks, care must be taken that there are no illicit agreements with the reseller, such as a promise to extend preferential treatment if a reseller prices in a certain way.

CALLING IN THE ATTORNEYS

Since little in the law is black and white, most business decisions carry at least some legal risk. A company that decides to take this risk, whether in pricing or any other area, is not purposely ignoring, much less violating, the law. More likely, it believes that its interpretation of the law is reasonable and would prevail if challenged. When there is the possibility that a pricing program or decision will trigger enhanced legal scrutiny or will venture into an area where customers, competitors, or the government may question the legality of the move, it is crucial to bring attorneys in early to assess the legal risks. Legal counsel with experience in pricing can provide important guidance regarding both the legality of the actions and the process the company should follow to chart the safest course.

At many companies, attorneys collaborate with business managers to outline the limits of pricing policies or to structure approaches to business objectives in a manner that is consistent with the risks the company wishes to take. In some cases, however, the internal (or external) attorneys may be quite conservative in evaluating strategic decisions or may try to eliminate risks completely, even when company executives, armed with accurate information, would choose to assume some risk to pursue a valuable pricing program.

Where the advice of counsel historically tends toward eliminating risk (i.e., not attempting to balance potential risk with potential reward), it is especially important for executives to think carefully about how they want to use and involve both internal and outside attorneys. Executives pushing toward *the price advantage* must be confident of the legal advice they receive. The following questions can help assess attorneys' experience and qualifications:

- Do the attorneys discuss both sides of an issue, balancing the risks and the potential rewards, or do they focus only on risk and how to minimize it?
- Is engaging the attorneys in the early stages of strategic planning constructive? Do they bring useful insight that helps shape the outcome, or do they take a "can't do" stance?
- Do the attorneys have significant experience in the laws governing pricing? Does their advice reflect an understanding not only of the elements of illegal behavior, but also the myriad defenses and how to make a strong case in favor of pricing action?
- Do the lawyers have incentives to improve shareholder returns and make real risk/return tradeoffs, or is the department measured solely on avoiding all legal and public relations risks and never being wrong?
- Does your internal legal department or law firm have a healthy turnover, with attorneys coming from or leaving for private practices or antitrust authorities, or is it insular, without a great deal of experience in antitrust matters outside your company or industry? Are there lawyers on staff with significant antitrust experience?

In addition, it is important to consider the concept of legal privilege. Under this protection, companies cannot be forced to disclose in court and/or to antitrust authorities the content of communications seeking legal advice and communications providing legal advice. In the United States, communications with both external and internal counsel are privileged, while in the European Union only communications with external, EU-admitted counsel benefit from such privilege.

* * *

It goes without saying that managers need to ensure that their company's pricing practices are consistent with the current relevant laws. Unfortunately, in trying to do this, all too many companies avoid sound pricing efforts because of a misguided assessment of the legal risks they may face. There are ways to achieve just about any reasonable pricing objective while still being in compliance. Ensuring that overly conservative—or worse, incorrect—interpretations of pricing laws do not inappropriately restrict management decisions on pricing requires managers to think creatively through different pricing options. Managers must also ensure that internal or external attorneys have the right background and expertise to help develop and evaluate such options properly. Companies with *the price advantage* maintain a superior understanding of the relevant pricing laws and assure that pricing strategy and execution always meet the letter and intent of those laws—without being unnecessarily constrained by them.

CHAPTER 10

Lifecycle Pricing

Adjusting and managing prices over the course of a product or service's lifetime has never been a simple discipline for most businesses. But rapid new product introductions and accelerated price compression are making this discipline more difficult and more critical for an ever-growing number of industries—including IT hardware and software, consumer electronics and durables, pharmaceuticals and medical devices.

But what is lifecycle pricing? Simply put, it is the strategy and discipline companies use to maximize returns from their products' pricing across the products' lifetimes. Businesses have to think longitudinally about their product pricing—that is, they need to consider the critical pricing decisions and opportunities that arise at each stage of a product's life—during launch, mid-life, and late-life. Lifecycle pricing capabilities are important enablers of success for many businesses in innovation-intensive industries. When we surveyed executives of high-tech companies, we found that lifecycle pricing was the *single* biggest differentiator between top and bottom quartile scores across numerous pricing capabilities.[1]

Failure to pay enough attention to lifecycle pricing can erode returns for an entire industry, in addition to preventing companies from recovering their R&D costs. Hard-disk drive producers provide a classic example of this in the late 1990s. In four years, the three major independent hard-drive makers invested about $6.5 billion in R&D, regularly delivering new products to the market—only to see nearly $800 million in net losses as prices continued to fall. Roger Johnson, the former CEO of Western Digital, called the sector "the longest-running industrial philanthropy" in history.[2] What is especially remarkable is that a *70 percent* price decline ($ per unit of surface area of

---

[1]Survey of 120 high-tech senior executives in *High Tech Marketing & Sales: Aiming for Excellence*, McKinsey & Company, 2003.
[2]Scott Thurn, "Costly Memories—Behind TiVo, iPod and Xbox: An Industry Struggles for Profits—Disk-Drive Makers Provide Backbones of New Gadgets But Miss

disk) occurred during a decade where data density (bytes stored per unit of surface area) increased a *thousand-fold*. Although improved operational efficiency no doubt accounted for some of the lower prices, it is still amazing that such an innovative industry could create so much value for customers and capture so little for itself.

This example is only one of many across diverse industries. Continuous innovation in contrast media (fluids injected into patients during radiology procedures) has allowed existing x-ray machines and scanners to produce increasingly precise medical images. However, rather than capturing the rewards of this innovation through increased pricing; the contrast media industry has seen the average price per dose drop 60 percent over eight years, costing the industry nearly $1 billion in lost earnings during this same period.

This chapter deals specifically with issues around the pricing of *product or services* over the course of their lifecycle. Two other forms of lifecycle management are not addressed: *customer* lifecycle management (e.g., improving account profitability by altering product mix) and *market* lifecycle management (e.g., maximizing profit and managing risk across the ups and downs of economic cycles).

WHAT MAKES LIFECYCLE PRICING TOUGH

Many factors make it challenging to fully capture *the price advantage* over a product's lifecycle, especially for innovation-intensive technology companies operating under relentless pressure to "bloom often and quickly." If they yield once on price, it is hard to claw their way back. Yet technology buyers (consumers and businesses) have deeply engrained expectations that product prices will decline. Exhibit 10-1 illustrates this scenario for the implantable pacemaker market. Despite rapid innovation (Products A, B, C, and D in Exhibit 10-1) and steadily increasing product performance that justified much higher prices, weighted average pacemaker prices actually *dropped* more than 2 percent per year over five years—driven largely by poor management of mid- and late-life pricing of product lines. This lifecycle pricing mismanagement and the resultant drop in average prices cost the industry hundreds of millions of dollars annually.

In our experience, we have seen four factors complicate many companies' attempts to succeed at lifecycle pricing:

Out on Rewards—A Promising Year Turns Sour," *Wall Street Journal*, October 14, 2004, A1.

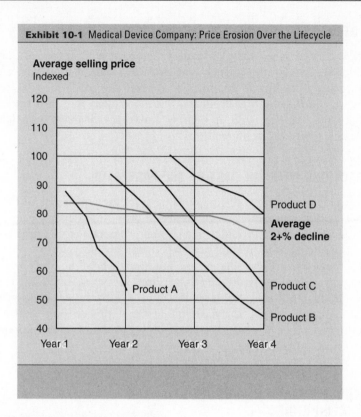

Exhibit 10-1 Medical Device Company: Price Erosion Over the Lifecycle

EVER-SHORTER PRODUCT CYCLES

Many product cycles now number in months instead of years. Companies must adjust pricing models constantly with little room for error—a difficult task with high stakes. As businesses push for rapid new product launches, they are often so focused on product development and commercialization that they seldom devote adequate time to the initial pricing model and longer-term pricing strategy. All of this tends to create and reinforce incentives that emphasize volume/share over pricing/profit.

INTERNAL AND EXTERNAL PRESSURE TO SELL AT LOWER PRICE

Customers increasingly want more for less and expect prices to fall rapidly (e.g., in consumer electronics prices can drop 50 percent in a few months). Manufacturing operations can compound this problem by ramping up new product production; while this may help lower unit costs, it also can create internal incentives to sell product at depressed prices if it is not moving.

HIGH-STAKES LAUNCHES

Pricing is treated as a "make or break" factor for many product launches. Rapid market penetration, which may provide a critical footprint or allow the company's product to become the market standard (see Chapter 14, "Software and Information Products"), is more likely with low prices. But the company may also wind up owning a market that may never deliver a satisfactory return on its innovation.

INTERACTIONS WITH THE REST OF THE PORTFOLIO

It is not uncommon for a company to have multiple products in the marketplace at the same time. As we discuss shortly, interdependencies in the perceived value among products in a company's portfolio can further complicate the pricing of individual products over their lifecycle.

We focus most of this chapter on situations where the lifecycle pricing challenge is indeed most difficult (i.e., short lifecycles, rapid-fire product introductions, steep price compression, and a portfolio of adjacent products). Despite this focus, the basic guidance of this chapter applies to a much broader range of situations where only a subset of these complicating characteristics might exist.

THE THREE PHASES OF PRODUCT LIFECYCLE PRICING

Each stage of a product's lifecycle presents managers with a unique set of pricing issues—so unique that one needs to bring a whole different mindset into the process depending on the phase (i.e., launch, mid-life, or late-life). In this chapter, we discuss in detail the unique requirements for pricing success at each phase.

Despite the distinctiveness of each stage, two critical themes are essential to all stages of lifecycle pricing:

1. *Active management of the price/volume/profit tradeoff.* In innovation-rich industries with short product lifecycles and steep price compression curves, the price/volume tradeoff is seldom fixed; rather, it often changes dramatically from phase to phase and even within a phase. Most companies, however, fail to test customer perceptions and price sensitivity after product launch; as a result, they have no idea how the critical price/volume/profit tradeoff is shifting over time. Price-advantaged companies, on the other hand, routinely test price elasticity, at regular time

intervals and in response to specific trigger events (e.g., the introduction of a competitive offering). Ultimately, they can create pricing strategies in terms of price/volume "trajectories" (in which they actively shape price/volume trend curves) that help companies clarify profit expectations over time.

2. *Making pricing decisions in the context of the broader product portfolio.* When a company has multiple generations of its products in a market, a price move for one product can have important implications for others (e.g., make adjacent products more or less attractive to customers, exert up or downward pressure on other products). These interactions can be dramatic and diverse, and the best companies deliberately consider and manage them. For example, as they ready the next generation product for market they rethink their current product portfolio positions to see what might lead to the success or failure of the new product (or the portfolio as a whole).

With these themes as backdrops, let us now explore the imperatives for success at each lifecycle stage. (Exhibit 10-2 summarizes these imperatives across the phases.)

LAUNCH PHASE

Getting the price right at launch is one of the most important lifecycle pricing levers. Value-based pricing can properly position a new offering, establish an appropriately high-market launch point, and potentially reset market price expectations. (See Chapter 4, "Customer Value" and Section Three, "New Products," in Chapter 13, "Tailored Value.") Doing this right can also boost the product's price trajectory across all three phases. In this phase, several imperatives stand out.

Launch to Maximize Long-Term Value Capture Conducting scenario-based analyses of different launch price points and price/volume evolution curves can help companies avoid crucial mistakes by looking at a range of alternative pricing models and potential competitive responses to them. During this process, companies must try to resist two common temptations: the first is setting a lower launch price than analysis suggests. A chip manufacturer avoided this mistake by launching a fourth-generation processor chip at a price almost double that of the chip's predecessors. Previous generations were all launched at roughly the same initial price—in spite of increasing performance—and all saw rapid price declines. With the new launch, the company boldly sought a higher price point (more in line with the true incremental value of the chip) and kicked off a significant marketing campaign

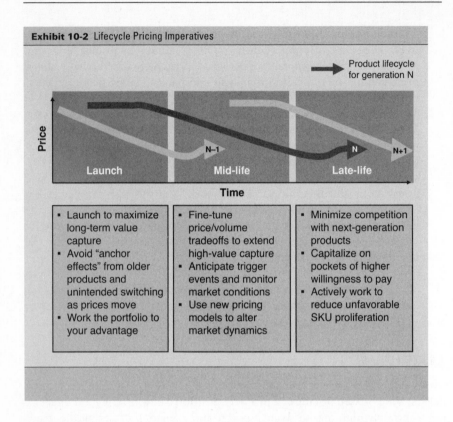

Exhibit 10-2 Lifecycle Pricing Imperatives

Launch	Mid-life	Late-life
• Launch to maximize long-term value capture • Avoid "anchor effects" from older products and unintended switching as prices move • Work the portfolio to your advantage	• Fine-tune price/volume tradeoffs to extend high-value capture • Anticipate trigger events and monitor market conditions • Use new pricing models to alter market dynamics	• Minimize competition with next-generation products • Capitalize on pockets of higher willingness to pay • Actively work to reduce unfavorable SKU proliferation

at the launch. The company reaped early sales at a much higher margin than before. Over time the chip's price trajectory declined the same way the earlier ones had, but the net effect was to reset market expectations of value and to secure much greater profit for the company (Exhibit 10-3).

The second mistake is reducing the product price soon after launch out of fear the company will not achieve enough market penetration. This can be particularly deadly when an initially high price (targeted at a subset of customers) is set for launch, but high levels of production produce an abundance of inventory and inadvertent pressure to reduce price to clear it.

A networking equipment manufacturer that provided both network hardware and related application software astutely observed the gradual commoditization of the hardware and the shift to software as the source of differential value to customers. Industry practice had for decades been to concentrate virtually all of the price in the hardware, and provide software for free or at very low prices. As hardware became more of a commodity with regular price declines of 15 to 20 percent, it became

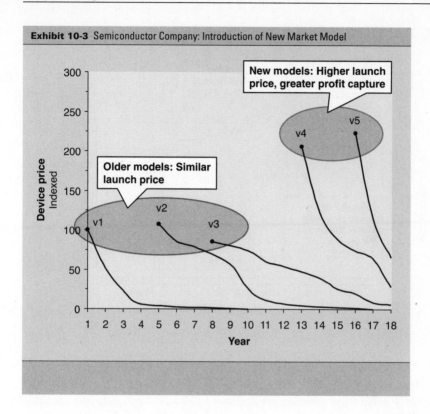

Exhibit 10-3 Semiconductor Company: Introduction of New Market Model

clear that software was where value pricing and returns were possible. So the company decided to change the game. It priced hardware and software separately and significantly increased and differentiated the software pricing. These changes achieved a 24 percent premium on its original system pricing, reinforced the value of the company's intellectual property and innovation, and helped hedge against the price erosion for networking hardware. It also enabled the company to differentiate pricing for the various software packages and scale it based on companies' needs.

Avoid "Anchor Effects" from Older Products and Unintended Switching as Prices Move Careful initial pricing can minimize the degree to which existing products drag down new product prices. In one example, a medical device manufacturer launched a new version of each major product every 6 to 18 months. Each version—whether a significant innovation or minor improvement—was priced only slightly above (2 to 6 percent) the existing one, to encourage migration and mitigate customer backlash. As the new

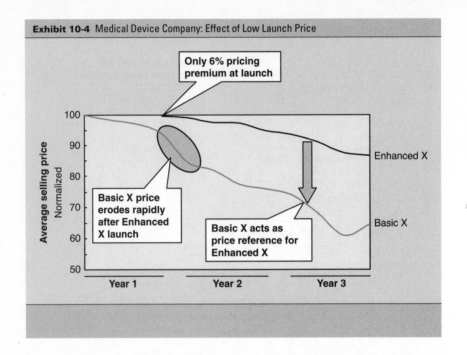

Exhibit 10-4 Medical Device Company: Effect of Low Launch Price

product version gained traction, the company would drop the price on the previous generation product precipitously (20 to 40 percent) but continue to sell it for an extended period (because of continued demand from some customers and the desire to provide other customers with a lower cost alternative). Unfortunately, the old product's price cuts effectively dragged down the new product's price (as the incremental value of the new product versus the old remained more or less constant).

Despite annual R&D investments of hundreds of millions of dollars, the average price for every product line the company offered declined each year. Mix shifts to higher margin product lines masked this trend for a while, but eventually the company faced declining margins in its overall business (Exhibit 10-4). In other words, the company was rapidly innovating itself from a market leader into an average performer! Once the company saw what was going on, it took immediate action. It eliminated "fire sales" on older products and changed sales force incentives to support its new lifecycle pricing strategy. It also carefully launched subsequent products at greater premiums (up to levels justified by their incremental value).

Work the Portfolio to Your Advantage Businesses should assess new product pricing in the context of the existing portfolio and—as importantly—examine the impact that moves in the existing portfolio might have on the success or failure of the new product and the portfolio as a whole. As it prepares the next generation of products, a company should rethink product portfolio positions. Should any of the current offerings be retired? How should their prices change to support the price position of the new product and/or speed its adoption? These questions are fundamental and should be addressed well in advance of the product launch. The "anchor effects" example we discussed illustrates some of the product linkages that can wreak havoc if not properly managed.

More sophisticated portfolio moves ("chess moves") are also possible as illustrated by the following case (Exhibit 10-5). This company was planning to refresh its product line. It had two older products in the market, A and B, with a relatively wide price band; it was introducing two new products, A+ (superior to A) and C, (superior to B). It wanted to replace A with A+ and reposition B. In preparing for A+'s launch, the company *raised* A's price (Step 1 on exhibit), creating a better value reference for A+. After A+'s launch (Step 2), the company then *raised A's price again* (Step 3), this time to a point *above* A+. This accelerated A's end-of-life and migrated users to A+. The company then targeted a niche high-end customer segment by launching C at a price point *above* B (Step 4). Once the dust had settled,

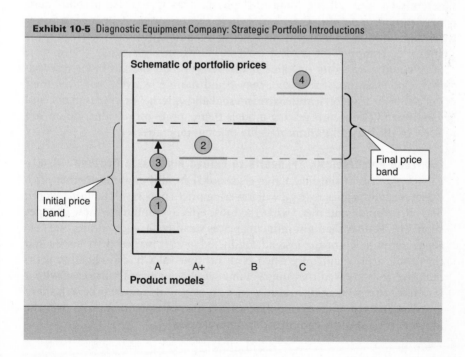

Exhibit 10-5 Diagnostic Equipment Company: Strategic Portfolio Introductions

the company had moved to a higher, tighter, and more differentiated band consisting of A+, B, and C.

In another example, a consumer electronics company followed the successful launch of a new product with additional models targeted at higher-willingness-to-pay customer segments. In this way, the company "raised the bar" by introducing additional high-end offerings. Over the next couple of years new competitors began to enter the market with lower priced models. In an effort to combat these new entrants—while still preserving the value of its existing offerings—the company then introduced new lower benefit models, effectively "reaching down market" to penetrate previously untapped customer segments and create price-competitive options for customers without resorting to heavy discounting. Despite the fact that introducing lower benefit/lower price products can be a risky strategy because it can depress the value of new products, the strategy worked here because there was a huge amount of latent demand for lower priced products, and distinct customer segments who would continue to buy the higher benefit products at higher prices.

MID-LIFE PHASE

Once a product is fully launched and gains stable market acceptance, it enters what we call the "mid-life" phase. This is a phase of both huge opportunity and risk—the phase where the majority of operating profit for a product is earned but also where "me-too" products often appear and price compression is most extreme. Organizations rarely revisit their price/volume tradeoffs or value maps here—or do the customer research that is so essential. If they did, they could more effectively fine-tune their price/volume tradeoffs, anticipate internal and external pricing triggers, and identify and adopt new pricing models that capture more value. Below are a few of the most important mid-life pricing imperatives:

Fine-Tune Price/Volume Tradeoffs to Extend High-Value Capture   Before changing prices in mid-life, managers should carefully analyze whether price changes are appropriate (e.g., will lowering prices now result in more overall lifecycle profits), and if so, what the most effective timing of these changes should be. Rather than just reducing prices steadily during mid-life, one personal computer company instead conducted *weekly* market price tests—and then took a price cut *only* when both (a) unit sales had declined *and* (b) the price tests showed that unit volume would significantly increase with a lowered price. Managing mid-life price erosion in this more precise fashion generated tens of millions of dollars of incremental operating profit over the lifetime of most of this company's computer models.

In a second example, a server manufacturer typically introduced each generation of a particular product family at a relatively high price point, aiming for early adopters with a high willingness to pay. Several months after introduction, it would cut the price significantly, producing a substantial uptick in volume. After several months of strong sales, volume typically declined rapidly because of new competing products. At this point a second substantial price cut revived unit sales for several more months until the product finally became obsolete. Careful analysis revealed that almost *all* of the cumulative profit occurred between the first and second price cuts. Early sales at launch (with lower volumes and higher initial costs) contributed relatively little profit, and most volume sold after the second price cut actually generated a loss! Equipped with this information, the vendor changed its basic lifecycle pricing approach by delaying the timing of the first price cut and eliminating the second price cut altogether. This resulted in a 2 to 3 percentage point increase in profit margin. (Exhibit 10-6.)

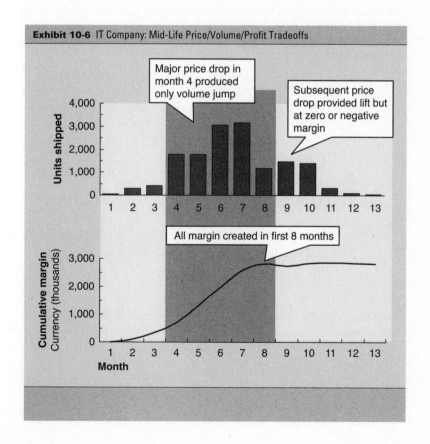

Exhibit 10-6 IT Company: Mid-Life Price/Volume/Profit Tradeoffs

Anticipate Trigger Events and Monitor Market Conditions There are many mid-life trigger events for pricing, both internal (e.g., launch of a new model or change in cost position) or external (e.g., competitive price moves and product introductions, or shifts in customer demand). Companies need to monitor the market so they can anticipate such events. Changes in competitors' behavior can provide valuable opportunities. One medical devices company missed this chance. It had enjoyed a period of product exclusivity but decided to drive prices downward anyway based on its standard practice of discounting after product launch. No other reason existed. The company also failed to respond when its two main competitors introduced products similar to its own at much higher prices. Instead of raising its own prices to capture greater margin—or at least maintaining them—the company continued to discount, hurting prices and margins for everyone.

ROUNDUP AVOIDS A MID-LIFE CRISIS BY ANTICIPATING A MAJOR TRIGGER EVENT

In 1973 Monsanto launched Roundup—a glyphosate herbicide that kills just about anything green. Roundup is still the number one herbicide and the best-selling agricultural chemical product ever. Over time Monsanto souped up Roundup's status through what analysts say was a brilliant strategy of dropping its price years ahead of its mid-life patent expiration and positioning it for use with genetically modified crops that were just being introduced—crops made to work in tandem with the herbicide.

The company lowered the retail price of Roundup several years before its patent expired in 2000—dropping it from about $44 a gallon in 1997 to $34 in 1999 to about $28 in 2001 (although prices remained above costs). This drove up demand and may have also deterred competitors. At the same time, these moves provided an acceptable long-term profit stream for Roundup over the remainder of its lifecycle.

Monsanto also decided that once its United States patent expired, it would supply its glyphosate molecule to competitors. The 35-plus percent drop in the price of Roundup and the substantial size of Monsanto's production volume seemed to deter competitors from building production plants because the economics made it difficult to compete. According to Jeffrey Peck, an analyst at Bear Stearns, "[Monsanto] said, 'We'll license you the molecule, and you can buy it, repackage it, do whatever you want. Or you can build your own plant.' Just about every company they offered it to took the deal."

In 1996 Monsanto also began marketing genetically modified crops that were immune to Roundup. The crops, called "Roundup Ready," allowed farmers to spray the herbicide on the fields, killing weeds but not the crops. Few competitors were willing to produce a generic version of Roundup because Monsanto protected its market share by cutting the price while finding new uses. This built loyalty with customers while reducing the profit potential competitors could reap by trying to lure away customers.

Source: David Barboza, "A Weed Killer Is a Block for Monsanto to Build On," *New York Times*, August 2, 2001, section C, page 1, column 2.

Use New Pricing Models to Alter Market Dynamics   Strong performers are always searching for ways to capture value. Just as they can do at launch, they sometimes introduce a new pricing model at mid-life. Done here, it can reinvigorate a product. Maintenance services for jet engines provides a well-known example. Historically, such services were often performed by the engine OEM using a standard pricing model of "time and materials" associated with each service shop visit. Over time, however, third-party service providers entered the market at lower prices and began to gain in prominence. In response to this, one OEM company introduced an alternative service pricing model built around a long-term service agreement based on hours of flight operation (which roughly correlates with engine wear and tear). The new model appealed to airlines because it made their service costs highly predictable, eliminating uncertainty about the frequency and magnitude of service costs. Moreover, the OEM company's scale, extensive experience, and proprietary technical knowledge enabled it to take on the risk in the new pricing model better than its competitors. As a result, the company saw its volume and margin grow substantially, and the long-term compression of pricing in this service industry slowed.

LATE-LIFE PHASE

Savvy companies often tap opportunities that other organizations miss in the late-life phase. Late-life may be the time to raise prices, rather than lower them. The costs of the product may have increased over time or the inherent value for some customers may not have decreased in the same way as for others (or may have even increased)—which may translate into willingness to pay a higher price. But whatever the choice, the company must have deep insights into the true costs to serve the market and into the customer segments still buying the product. Whatever is done, organizations should be guided by the three late-life pricing imperatives below.

Minimize Competition with Next Generation Product   Even if a company's first instinct may be to discount older products in advance or just following a new product launch, excessive markdowns may hinder the newer offerings by making the older products seem like a better value. Businesses should instead consider raising prices to hasten the older products' exit and to achieve higher margins on their remaining sales. Winnowing out these products can also reduce needless complexity in supply chains, service operations, and customer service. At the same time, companies must guard against creating obsolete or expired inventory.

Capitalize on Pockets of High Willingness to Pay   Certain customers may be fairly price-insensitive on an older product, either because they are more comfortable with it or because switching costs are prohibitive. Many major banks still have their transaction systems on mainframes because they believe the business risk of switching to more modern computers is too high. The maintenance of these aging systems is now a significant source of revenue for some technology vendors.

A semiconductor manufacturer who profitably managed the transition from a legacy product to a new product offers a different example. Traditionally this company launched products at a relatively high price point, then radically reduced price during the remainder of the product's life. On this occasion, the company realized its legacy product still had a strong value proposition for some customers. Wanting to migrate customers to its new offering, the company actually *raised* price on the late-life legacy product after the new product launched. By continuing to sell the older legacy product at significantly higher margins for several more quarters, the company captured at least $250 million in additional profit that it would have otherwise given up had it followed its usual practices (Exhibit 10-7).

Actively Work to Reduce Unfavorable SKU Proliferation   Many companies, especially those selling to other businesses, do not manage SKU proliferation well. Quotes like "we never kill a product" are not uncommon. Equally true, few companies carefully evaluate their products' economics over time—and especially during late life. Although this is troublesome for all, it is especially problematic for those organizations using a cost-plus

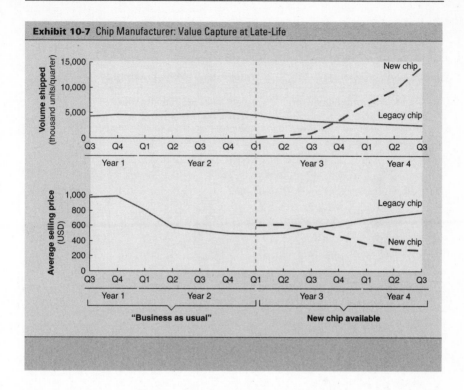

Exhibit 10-7 Chip Manufacturer: Value Capture at Late-Life

methodology. (See Section One, "Custom-Configured Products," in Chapter 12, "Complexity Management.") One industrial equipment manufacturer selling spare parts did not fully account for lifecycle differences in its part costs, instead spreading costs across all products. This flawed approach made it appear that the company was still making a reasonable margin on older products. However, a closer examination of their costs in each phase showed that the costs of older products were substantially higher than expected and many were really unprofitable (Exhibit 10-8). Once this came to light, the company either eliminated the older, unprofitable parts or changed its prices so it was paid appropriately for producing and stocking them.

SUSTAINING RETURNS ACROSS THE LIFECYCLE

Companies that capture *the price advantage* across the lifecycle possess several distinct characteristics. Their perspective on pricing is not myopic—their pricers continuously strive to think across the lifecycle stages, building all their questions and analyses into that framework. Managers constantly scan

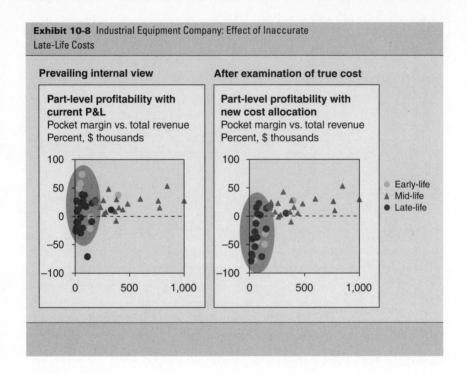

Exhibit 10-8 Industrial Equipment Company: Effect of Inaccurate Late-Life Costs

internally and externally in search of potential "trigger events." Their level of energy and activity—whether the ability to do fast, deep customer research or insightful analysis on a multitude of variables—is at a point above that usually seen elsewhere. In short, their capabilities reflect the more dynamic and interdependent pricing environment that exists when managing over product lifecycles.

The list below is far from complete but provides a flavor for some of the most important steps that businesses take as they manage and price their products over the lifecycle.

PUT SUFFICIENT EMPHASIS ON LIFECYCLE PRICING UPFRONT

Savvy companies develop an initial pricing strategy early in the product commercialization process—early enough so that any desired or required price moves in the existing portfolio can be determined and implemented. New product pricing is not a reactive, ad hoc process, but instead a core pricing competency that is done at the earliest stages of product design. These companies consider alternative price/volume tradeoffs and strategies over time and envision how each scenario might play out across different customer segments. Such considerations lead to a rich spectrum of pricing strategies that go well beyond the basic skim or penetration pricing options. The process explicitly incorporates price moves during the lifecycle and anticipates internal or external triggers that might prompt the company to shift its prices up or down (as much as possible given market uncertainty).

ENSURE THERE ARE CLEARLY DEFINED ROLES AND RESPONSIBILITIES FOR MANAGING ONGOING LIFECYCLE PRICING DECISIONS WELL AFTER THE PRODUCT LAUNCH

In essence, the idea is to ensure that nothing "falls between the cracks" in managing price over time and across products in a portfolio. By emphasizing this element, these companies prevent situations in which there is a "launch and forget" attitude regarding pricing once the new product hits the market. Review processes explicitly monitor lifecycle pricing performance and properly aligned incentives keep the organization focused on the opportunity. Much of lifecycle pricing inherently involves setting expectations about the way in which price and volume may play out—these companies track these assumptions and regularly check performance against them.

CONSTANTLY SEARCH FOR WAYS TO INCREASE PROFIT DURING THE PRODUCT'S LIFETIME

Good lifecycle pricing companies are dynamic and adaptive (e.g., they identify potential responses ahead of time, which enables them to take more thoughtful actions). Often this requires cross-functional coordination that transcends the pricing function (e.g., product development, marketing, competitive intelligence, sales, and operations may all be involved). Beginning with a high-level plan for managing the product to the end of its lifecycle, they constantly monitor market conditions, competitor actions, internal operational changes, and customer perceptions to refine their approach.

* * *

Pricing wisely over the lifecycle of a product or service presents a daunting challenge for many companies—a challenge that is intensified further by the rapid product innovation, offer proliferation, and shrinking product life spans in so many industries today. But making the investments of time and effort required to overcome this challenge are worthwhile. Price-advantaged companies that are masters at lifecycle pricing consistently enjoy competitive advantage and exceptional bottom-line returns.

Mastering pricing across the three lifecycle phases—launch, mid-life, and late-life—requires a dynamic approach and often a shift in perspective. Each phase demands a unique method tailored to the specific issues of that stage. Across all phases, you need to routinely revisit the price/volume/profit tradeoff—and adjust it to maximize your returns. Furthermore, all individual offer pricing decisions need to be made in the context of the adjacent portfolio products. Companies that are distinctive innovators assure they reap the full rewards of their innovation by doing the things above and creating *the price advantage* for themselves.

CHAPTER 11

Pricing Architecture

An architect, when designing a building, usually pursues objectives in two areas—some around form and others around function. The form objectives relate to the desired visual impression and *perception* of the building, while the functional objectives address the *performance* of the building and how well it works—for example, adequacy of room sizes and shapes, effectiveness of the heating and air-conditioning system. In much the same way, there is an architecture to pricing that, when executed well, can actively shape customers' *perception* of price and even drive customers' *performance*—that is, the desired behavior of end-customers and intermediaries, like retailers and wholesalers.

The thoughtful pricing architect has many design elements and tools with which to work. They include the list price and how it might vary by segment, the discount components to include in the pocket price waterfall, and the specific policies and guidelines to apply to each of these components. Additional design elements include the unit of sale (for instance, whether a telephone service is priced per minute used or with a fixed monthly fee) and the approach for communicating price.

In this chapter, we explore how companies that have achieved *the price advantage* use these and other design elements to create price architectures that influence customers' perceptions of price most positively and most effectively persuade customers to behave in ways that maximize benefits to the companies. We not only address price architecture for a single product or service, but devote a separate discussion to the special challenges and added degrees of design freedom that arise when creating the price architecture for an offering that is a package of products, services, or both.

MANAGING PRICE PERCEPTION

Skillful pricers appreciate that price perception can be influenced in the same way that benefit perceptions can, as the following examples illustrate.

To research the impact of price communication, a term life insurance company that markets primarily by mail sent three sets of solicitations that were identical except for how price was communicated in the brochure headline. In the first set, the price was conveyed as $360 per year; in the second, $30 per month; and in the third, $1 per day. The annual price was, of course, identical in all three cases. And in each case, the same payment of $180 was due twice a year. Amazingly, respondents were three times more likely to buy the policy when given the monthly quote compared with the annual quote, and almost 10 times more likely to buy when the price was quoted on a daily basis rather than an annual basis.

In a second case, a retail bank wanted to increase the price of an interest-bearing checking account it offered, while minimizing customer defections. The bank test-marketed two price increase alternatives that, while different in form, resulted in the same monthly price increase for customers in a specific segment. In the first alternative tested, the monthly account service fee paid by the customer was increased by $3 and the interest rate paid on account balances was held constant. In the second, the monthly service fee was only raised $1 but the interest paid on account balances was decreased by 0.2 percentage point. Although these two options generated an equivalent price increase for most customers, nearly four times as many customers defected when presented with the first price increase alternative versus the second.

These two cases illustrate how pricing architecture can influence consumer price perceptions. It can affect those of intermediaries as well. Exhibit 11-1 shows the pocket price waterfall for a microwave oven manufacturer selling to appliance retailers. The price structure was complicated, with 10 on- and off-invoice discounts in play. Thinking that its price structure had grown too complex, the microwave oven company commissioned a market study to determine retailers' satisfaction with its price structure.

In interviews, retailers said they found the company's price structure somewhat complex, but no more complex than that of most other appliance manufacturers. Retailers indicated that competitors' waterfalls were quite similar to the company's *on the invoice*. It was off the invoice where competitive price structures varied widely, with highly diverse designs around volume rebates, promotional programs, and payment terms. Furthermore, retailers stated that this off-invoice diversity made price comparison across microwave manufacturers difficult. As a result, most retailers compared manufacturers' prices on an *invoice price* basis when choosing which microwave brands to carry; they assumed that the totals of each competitor's off-invoice discounts were about the same.

Knowing now that retailers paid much more attention to on-invoice discounts, the microwave company made a simple change to its price structure. It moved its largest off-invoice discount, the annual volume rebate, onto the

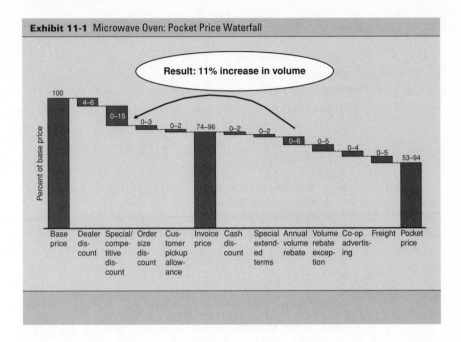

Exhibit 11-1 Microwave Oven: Pocket Price Waterfall

Result: 11% increase in volume

Percent of base price

| Base price | Dealer discount | Special/competitive discount | Order size discount | Customer pickup allowance | Invoice price | Cash discount | Special extended terms | Annual volume rebate | Volume rebate exception | Co-op advertising | Freight | Pocket price |

invoice. In other words, the company estimated each account's annual sales volume, projected the account's year-end rebate, and then included this as a discount on each invoice. If account volume at the end of the year differed significantly from the estimate, the rebate was adjusted at year-end. This reduced invoice price by up to 6 percent and left pocket price unchanged, but it increased sales volume to this category of retailers by 11 percent. This volume increase was *not* the result of lowering price. Rather, it came from changing pricing architecture to make the company's price look better against the yardstick that retailers used to compare competitive supplier prices.

The design of pricing architecture can significantly sway perception of price among both consumers and trade intermediaries. As the examples above show, market research helps companies explore pricing architecture alternatives—just like customer benefit perceptions. Companies that excel at pricing regularly bundle price perception research with their general customer value research.

INFLUENCING CUSTOMER BEHAVIOR

Well-designed price architecture can drive a host of customer behaviors that may be crucial to a company's success. The first principle of price

Exhibit 11-2 Influenced Customer Behaviors

- Total volume purchased
- Product mix
- Resale price
- Order size
- Order timing and frequency
- Freight mode choice
- Payment behavior
- Stocking behavior
  - Which products stocked?
  - At what inventory levels?
- Competitor lines carried
- Promotional behavior
- End-customer application support/service
- End-customer development/focus
- Dealer development (when 2 steps or more)
- Quality of warranty/claims service to end-customers
- Returns behavior
- Distribution structure
  - Distributor/dealer size and concentration
  - Existence of buying groups or co-ops

architecture is that your pocket price waterfall should *work* for you. In other words, every element of your waterfall should be viewed as an investment that drives a specific customer behavior. For instance, a company would pay a cash discount to encourage customers to pay their invoices in a timely fashion and minimize receivables carrying costs. Or a supplier would provide an order-size discount to encourage customers to order in quantities that are logistically and economically attractive for that supplier.

Exhibit 11-2 shows a partial list of the numerous and diverse customer behaviors that price architecture can influence; some of these are relevant only for resellers rather than direct customers.

Let us explore four of the most important customer behaviors that can be affected by thoughtfully designed and well-executed price architecture.

Exhibit 11-3 Auto Parts Company: Annual Volume Bonus Structure

Account volume ($ thousands)	Volume bonus discount (percent)
<100	0
100–200	1
200–500	2
500–1,000	3
1,000–2,000	4
2,000–3,000	5
>3,000	6

TOTAL VOLUME PURCHASED

Some of the largest discounts along the pocket price waterfall can be the least effective at influencing desired customer behavior. Annual volume bonuses—discounts paid at the end of the year, tied to total annual volume purchased—are often large waterfall elements that just do not work for companies. They seldom stimulate as much sales volume and growth as expected, and seldom enough to justify the magnitude of the investment. An auto parts supplier's annual volume bonus program illustrates what so frequently goes wrong.

This company sold its line of products to auto parts wholesalers and retailers. Exhibit 11-3 shows the structure of its annual volume bonus program. Accounts with annual purchases of between $100,000 and $200,000 would receive a bonus equal to one percent of their volume at the end of the year. Those with annual purchases of between $200,000 and $500,000 would receive a two percent bonus, and so on.

A look at how this company's accounts were distributed based on annual volume, illustrated in Exhibit 11-4, shows why this volume bonus structure was not working. Since the business was stable and mature, account growth greater than 20 percent was almost impossible. As a result, any account that had to increase its purchases by roughly 20 percent or more to reach the next bonus level was entirely unmotivated by the volume bonus structure. For example, if an account's volume was in the $300,000 to $400,000 range, as was the case for 17 percent of the accounts, it would have to grow by 25 percent or more to reach the next volume bonus hurdle at $500,000.

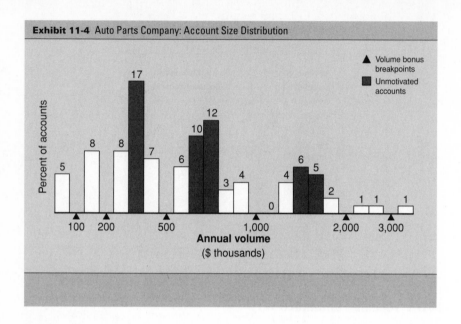

Exhibit 11-4 Auto Parts Company: Account Size Distribution

That was too large a volume jump for those accounts, which are shaded as "unmotivated accounts" in the exhibit. More than half of this company's accounts, representing nearly 75 percent of the company's sales volume, fell into the unmotivated category. Each account gladly accepted its annual volume bonus check at the end of the year, even though the bonus often had no impact on actual volume purchased.

It is no wonder that the auto parts company's expensive annual volume bonus program, which paid accounts up to six percent of sales, was not providing an adequate return on the sizeable investment. Following this analysis, the company refined its annual volume bonus program by realigning its volume bonus break points to better match the distribution of its accounts' sales volumes and provide achievable stretch volume targets for more accounts.

PRODUCT MIX

Companies that sell multiple product lines often experience large variations in profitability across those product lines. One firm that manufactured hydraulic equipment had six major product lines that it sold through industrial distributors. As Exhibit 11-5 shows, its most profitable lines (Gold, Silver, and Bronze) regularly generated pocket margins that were two to four times higher than its low-margin lines (Tier 3, Tier 2, and Tier 1). The company

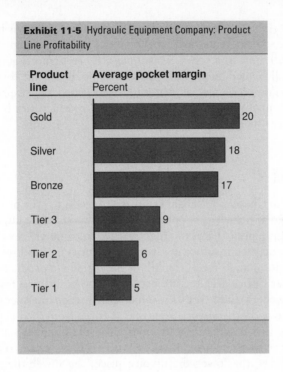

Exhibit 11-5 Hydraulic Equipment Company: Product Line Profitability

Product line	Average pocket margin Percent
Gold	20
Silver	18
Bronze	17
Tier 3	9
Tier 2	6
Tier 1	5

was not aware of this extreme profit variability across lines until it created its first pocket margin transaction database. A host of factors, including which plant made the product, design efficiency, and the level of market competition, contributed to this wide average pocket margin variation by product line.

In this situation, a mere five percent shift in product mix to high-margin products would increase total pocket margin dollars for this company by more than eight percent. However, the company's price structure was blind to these differences, providing no incremental award to distributors who chose to purchase a richer mix of product lines. All discounts, allowances, rebates, terms, and conditions applied equally to all lines.

With such a high payoff for improving product mix, the company decided to refocus its price structure to stimulate sales of the higher-margin product lines. It rebalanced its annual volume bonus program to pay a higher reward for Gold, Silver, and Bronze sales, and a lower reward for Tier 3, Tier 2, and Tier 1 purchases. It concentrated all of its cooperative advertising and promotional discount programs on the high margin lines. Furthermore, it allowed slightly longer payment terms on the three high-margin product lines, allowing 45 days to pay while still qualifying for a 1.5 percent cash discount, rather than the usual 30 days. These more generous terms caused distributors to stock greater inventory levels of the high-margin lines and ultimately to sell more as a result. This thoughtful reengineering of the pocket price waterfall yielded huge returns for the company. While total dollars invested up and down the pocket waterfall remained virtually unchanged, the hydraulics company increased its high-margin product mix by 14 percent within one year while operating profits rose by 23 percent.

RESALE PRICE

As discussed in Chapter 9, "Legal Degrees of Freedom," the price at which a trade intermediary resells a supplier's product has strategic importance. If a retailer charges a price that is too high relative to competitive offerings, then sales volume may be insufficient. If the retail price is too low, the desired premium position and brand strength of the supplier's product may erode.

A supplier's price architecture provides a powerful tool for influencing prices that resellers charge for its product. Most trade intermediaries trigger their resale price off the *invoice* price that they see from their suppliers—not the pocket price. In other words, they take the supplier's invoice price and add a specific margin to it to come up with the price to charge their customers. Thus, the lower the invoice price, the lower the resale price. By shifting discounting between on- and off-invoice, a supplier can change invoice price without affecting its pocket price.

With that in mind, if you want to influence your resellers to sell your products at a higher price, you should shift discounting from on-invoice to off-invoice. This will increase the invoice price that the reseller sees and, in most cases, engender higher resale prices. If, on the other hand, you want resellers to sell your products at a lower price, you should do the opposite—shift discounting from off-invoice to on-invoice. This will lower the invoice price and usually result in lower resale prices as well. Care should be taken, however, to clearly communicate such changes and prevent misreads in the market from other stakeholders, for example, industry analyst, investors, suppliers. A variety of other ways exist to use pricing architecture to influence resale prices, including giving resellers bonuses based on their achieving target margins, changing the price that a distributor pays based on the level of the distributor's resale prices, and so forth.

Consistently managing list prices can also help influence resale prices. Discounting that occurs between starting point list price and invoice price can often be large and vary widely. Too many companies assert that "my list prices don't mean anything, since none of my direct customers buy at list price anyway." This attitude can result in inconsistent management or no management of list prices and the loss of a potential opportunity to influence resale prices constructively.

Price-advantaged companies actively manage list price and use it to communicate price to the market. While *list price* may take on different meanings for different companies—"suggested retail price," "the day-to-day price that a certain class of resellers pays," or "the price, when 20 percent is subtracted, at which the best retailers buy"—the point is that list price is not just a random starting point for negotiation, but rather a price level that has tangible meaning in the market. When list prices are managed with consistency and diligence, then changing list price can deliver important and credible messages to the marketplace, messages about market price direction and even about the desired value repositioning of specific products.

MARKETING ACTIVITIES

There is often a wide variation in the support that resellers give to a supplier's product line. Some resellers may provide full service and support while others provide only the bare minimum. A supplier's pricing architecture should reflect these differences. Companies often want to encourage their resellers to invest in resources, which will enhance the attractiveness of their products. For example, one company that provided advanced technology used in mining operations greatly benefited when their resellers provided on-site technical consultation to the mining companies. When the resellers did this, the customer was much more easily convinced about the economic benefits of using the advanced and more expensive technology, versus when the customer merely purchased product over the phone. The technology company developed a pricing structure that offered prequalified resellers (based on an assessment of their technical rep capabilities), as much as an 8 percent better price versus distributors that operated strictly "off-site."

Total volume, product mix, resale price, and marketing activities are just a few examples of the wide range of customer behaviors that can be influenced through price architecture. In our experience, we have seen companies successfully influence customer conduct in all the areas we have mentioned and more, using thoughtful design and careful execution of price architecture.

PRICE ARCHITECTURE BASED ON SUPPLIER ROLE

Crafting a pricing architecture becomes an even more intricate challenge when a buying decision encompasses more than one product or service from an individual supplier. A supplier can play any of four fundamental roles for

Exhibit 11-6   The Four Supplier Roles

Supplier types	Supplier role	Typical pricing mechanisms
Component provider	▪ Provides discrete products or services to customers.	▪ Unit list prices less standard and/or negotiated discounts ▪ Standard service fees ▪ License fees
Bundler	▪ Provides a collection of products and/or services to customers.	▪ Unit list prices for each product/service ▪ Performance-driven discounts/rebates, e.g., for total volume, share of spend, desired product mix ▪ Service surcharges, e.g., minimum order size, rush delivery
Integrator	▪ Glues together components provided by others and helps them work well together.	▪ Fee for service (plus unit pricing for pass-through components) ▪ Project-based fees ▪ Pay per use
Solutions provider	▪ Meets a unique customer need by providing (and assuming ongoing implementation responsibility for) a customized package of components anchored on a proprietary component.	▪ Pay for solution's performance/output ▪ Risk/gain sharing

a customer—each of which entails a different approach to price architecture. Exhibit 11-6 lays out these distinct roles. Let us explore each role—and its pricing implications—in some detail.

COMPONENT PROVIDER

A component provider is the most basic type of relationship between buyer and seller. It offers stand-alone products or services, sells these to the customer directly or through a channel partner, and does not integrate various parts together. A customer ordering widgets gets widgets. They may be off-the-shelf or customized to match a specific need, but the customer still pays for and gets widgets. A customer wanting standard maintenance service gets that service. The benefits delivered by these components, whether products or services, rest on the discrete functional features and other attributes of the component. Although extras such as shipping or financing may be part of individual transactions, these additions are tangential to the core business of the component specialist.

The price model and price architecture implications for component providers are generally straightforward. Some form of standard or list price or base price is often used to indicate the desired value position relative to competitors. Beyond list price, the pocket price waterfall should be structured to (a) provide a positive customer perception of price, and (b) drive desired customer behaviors—as discussed earlier in this chapter.

BUNDLER

A bundler also offers components but, unlike a component provider, it may have a more comprehensive package. It may be a single-source provider across a wide range of components and offer lower prices through its own volume discounts and other cost advantages to the customer. This offering is standard and available for all customers whether the bundle comprises products and services, such as a pizza shop that offers home delivery within 30 minutes, or a package of products, such as a distributor offering a range of garden supplies. Components offered by bundlers may be produced by the bundlers themselves or by other companies. Wholesalers, distributors, and multiproduct manufacturers are common examples of bundlers.

The price architecture approach for the bundler is a logical extension from that of the component specialist. In most cases, each component of the bundle has a list price that individually reinforces the value position of that component. And just like the component specialist, the bundler should deliberately architect a price waterfall that gives the customer a positive perception of price level and encourages desired customer buying behavior. A key desired behavior is for the customer to add more and more products and services to the bundle being purchased.

Designing a price architecture to achieve this is often a delicate balancing act, in other words, providing enough of a discount to cause customers to purchase more volume and purchase more broadly across components but, at the same time, not discounting so much that overall customer profitability declines. Doing this well requires an accurate *pocket margin level* understanding of customer profitability along with an understanding of bundle elasticity and the bundled price levels that cause positive customer bundle choice. Once you understand the level of discounting you can profitably provide, the principles from earlier in this chapter should be applied to engineer a "bundle discount" that really works and positively changes customer behavior.

INTEGRATOR

Integrators provide the knowledge to make a group of components work together but do not produce or supply the components themselves. The components are often collected by their customers or purchased by the integrator from third parties on behalf of their customers. The key value they add is the ability to put the pieces together and make them work for specific customers.

An example of an integrator would be a wedding planner, who brings all the pieces together—the caterers, the florists, the photographers, and others—and coordinates and manages the whole event. A B2B example is a software integrator, who puts together various components to create a functional system that matches a customer's needs.

For an integrator, the challenge is to price the glue that makes a series of components at the core of a distinctive benefit delivery work together. These components often come from a range of suppliers or even from the customer itself. An integrator maintains the flexibility to choose from a host of qualified component providers and the costs of these components are typically passed through directly to the customer, occasionally with a markup. Ultimate responsibility for component performance remains with the component vendors and ongoing responsibility for the complete package remains with the customer. Therefore, an integrator cannot lay claim to a portion of the ongoing benefits created—a characteristic that makes "front-loaded pricing" (i.e., capturing all or most of price up-front) the preferred pricing architecture in many of these situations.

A global automotive supplier that makes engine and power train components demonstrated excellent integrator pricing. Over time, the company developed such distinctive expertise in the design and fine-tuning of engine and power train systems that it created a separate division to provide those services to car manufacturers. With no credible competition, even from the carmakers' own product development groups, the supplier was able to charge a substantial fee for this service. From the outset, the automotive supplier chose not to link this service business to its component businesses, for instance by offering a "total engine solution," because it feared its high-volume customers would pressure it into giving away the value-added service in order to maintain their large component orders.

An integrator's pricing model should link pricing to the benefits delivered by the service, rather than to the time and expense people who are delivering the service. Instead of the time-based rates charged by general service providers, an integrator should typically quote prices on a per-project or per-usage basis.

SOLUTIONS PROVIDER

Solutions providers work collaboratively with their customers to solve a specific business need. They provide comprehensive, integrated offerings to their customers. Three characteristics are present in most true solutions:

1. A proprietary component that is a core driver of the value creation.
2. The ability to engineer the components to work together seamlessly.
3. The assumption of ongoing implementation responsibility.

When a solutions provider brings these three characteristics to the table, he or she can offer truly differentiated benefits compared with the next-best alternative. Simply put, if a business turns to a solutions provider to meet a specific need, the accountability for making the solution work is clear. If all goes well, the benefits added by the solutions provider can be discretely quantified and apportioned between the two parties as agreed. If the solution does not work, the solutions provider is accountable. Because of this, a solutions provider is held to a higher standard. The benefits offered by a solution must be clearly identifiable and measurable, and the price should reflect how that value is shared between customer and supplier.

The unique role of a solutions provider allows that provider to discuss pricing in a way fundamentally different from other supplier roles. Component specialists, bundlers, and integrators price relative to alternatives. The benefits delivered in solutions are much *greater* than the sum of the component parts and will vary greatly from one customer to the next. So, a solutions provider should have an intimate understanding of its customers' economics and the benefits delivered—often a new and unfamiliar skill for traditional suppliers. If this is accomplished, a true solutions provider can set price to capture the company's due share of customer-specific economic value created. This topic, as well as how successful solutions providers set and manage prices, is discussed in more detail in the Solutions section of Chapter 13, "Tailored Value."

* * *

As we have shown, there is an architecture to pricing that can be more important than absolute price level itself in driving customer behaviors and perception. Too many businesses fail to recognize price architecture for the powerful marketing tool that it can be. They leave price structure, policy, and communication unchanged year after year, feeling bound by tradition and industry convention.

Businesses that have achieved *the price advantage* take a different and dynamic view of price architecture. Whether selling components, bundles, or solutions, these companies set specific market and customer objectives that can be reached through price architecture. The companies regularly reassess those objectives and always make sure that their price structure is working for them—that their waterfall elements are not just entitlements to customers, but rather are efficiently driving desired customer behaviors.

Advanced Topics

P art Five introduces and illuminates a variety of special and advanced topics. These are topics that do not apply to each and every business; but when they do apply, they are particularly challenging and usually vital to a company's realization of *the price advantage*.

Complexity Management

Due to their ever-changing business environments, some organizations have unique needs to consider, which have not been discussed in earlier chapters. Chapter 12 is broken into three sections showing that there are special ways to capture the unique opportunities presented by custom-configured products, high-count product lines, and distributed sales models.

SECTION ONE: CUSTOM-CONFIGURED PRODUCTS

Custom-configured products or services—those designed, built, or tailored for specific one-off applications—create special challenges for businesses pursuing *the price advantage*. Examples abound and include construction projects, design-to-specification capital equipment, managed services, engineering design and installation, and so forth. Even businesses that predominantly sell standard products often create custom-configured offerings for special situations, for example, an electrical controls company that sells a large catalog of standard switches and breakers but also produces custom, made-to-order breaker boxes for key customers.

For a host of reasons, these custom-configured offerings are inherently difficult to price right. Their one-off nature makes useful market reference points virtually nonexistent. They are generally purchased on a request-for-proposal basis that involves multiple vendors and are invariably "winner-take-all"—making competitive dynamics intense. Furthermore, these are often significant, high-priced deals that receive extreme customer scrutiny. Finally, the custom nature of these offerings complicates the cost estimation and calculation of the profit margins certain price levels might achieve. This chapter discusses shortfalls in the way prices are typically set for custom-configured offerings and then suggests a refined pricing approach that builds on and enhances the basic pricing processes that most sellers of this type already have in place.

TYPICAL SHORTFALLS

Against this backdrop of inherent pricing challenges, companies selling custom-configured offerings often resort to a basic cost-plus pricing approach where price is set by adding a standard, or modestly differentiated, profit margin on top of projected standard costs. And although some form of cost-plus pricing may be appropriate for most custom-configured situations, we have observed frequent shortfalls in the common cost-plus approach that many take.

Cost Estimates Are Inaccurate It is difficult to estimate cost accurately for products and services that are highly customized applications. Such inaccurate cost projections—both underestimates and overestimates—can have severe unintended consequences. Underestimate your costs (and add on your standard margin) and you win deals, but your company either loses money or makes much less than the expected margin. Overestimate costs (and again add on a standard margin) and you overprice deals and lose business that you could have profitably won. This erratic costing can also make a company appear erratic in the marketplace, that is, randomly high-priced on some deals/low-priced on others, generating uncertainty that can put unintended downward pressure on market prices. (See Chapter 8, "Price Wars.")

Some common practices can lead to such destructive inaccuracy in custom-configured cost estimating. In the material cost build-up, standard average costs that are either out-of-date or do not reflect expected costs at the time the product will be produced are often used. Fixed average costs are often applied in situations where differences can be large and predictable. For example, a custom steel fabricator applied a standard 2.5 percent freight cost to its estimates despite the fact actual freight varied between 1 percent and 8 percent, depending on product type and customer location. Customer-specific behaviors that create extra costs—for example, customers who routinely pay late, who regularly insist on costly change orders late in the fabrication process—are also too often ignored in the cost estimate. (See Chapter 3, "Transactions.")

Beyond predictable cost differences, there are project or product characteristics that make cost forecasting fundamentally more difficult, or, in other terms, increase cost risk. For an elevator company, the cost of excavating the posthole for a hydraulic elevator was difficult to predict (and potentially extremely high) whenever there was shale or other rock formations in the ground at the building site. The elevator company failed to account for the cost risk associated with the unpredictability of such situations and lost money on a subset of these projects as a result.

Finally, companies remain mired in inadequate cost estimating because they fail to routinely monitor the performance of this critical function. Too many businesses estimate the cost of one job and then go on to the next job, and never close the loop and compare actual costs of a won deal to the costs that were estimated when the deal was bid.

Margins Are Not Systematically Differentiated   Using a standard "plus" in the cost-plus process is the second major shortfall we often see in custom-configured pricing. Common practice is to estimate the cost for a project or product, add the standard margin to that cost to come up with a starting point price, and then adjust up or down based on "feel" for what price will win the business. This common approach fails to incorporate justifiably different target margins for different deal characteristics, for example, deal size, geography, competitive intensity, even customer satisfaction with past products and services. This deliberate, analysis-based margin differentiation, which helps business capture justifiable price premiums when appropriate, is nonexistent at many companies that sell custom-configured offerings. (See Exhibit 12-1.)

Exhibit 12-1 An Enhanced "Cost-Plus" Approach

From typical approach...	...to enhanced approach
Standard costs + fixed margins	**More precise, differentiated costs + situation-specific, value-based margins**
• All costs averaged	• Customer- and deal-specific cost variability explicitly accounted for
• Cost increases/decreases automatically passed through to customer	• Individual decisions made on how cost increases/decrease are passed through
• Project and/or customer risk ignored	• Cost risk explicitly reflected in cost build-up or target margin
• Margin adder same for all	• Margin adder adjusted based on value to customer and other key deal characteristics

REFINE THE APPROACH WITHOUT DISMANTLING IT

The realities of custom-configured offerings discussed earlier (e.g., their one-off nature, the lack of market reference prices, the often complicated cost build-ups) make some flavor of cost-plus pricing unavoidable for most companies in this space. (Notable exceptions might be custom-configured offerings that are integrated solutions, covered in Section Five, "Solutions," of Chapter 13, "Tailored Value.") That said a more refined version of cost-plus pricing that builds on rather than replaces existing cost-plus approaches can enhance custom-configured pricing effectiveness and move the pricing process in a value-based direction.

Exhibit 12-1 summarizes the characteristics we see in typical cost-plus approaches (on the left) and contrasts them on the right to an enhanced approach that many high-performing custom-configured businesses use today. At the highest level, we are proposing refining the "standard costs plus fix margin" approach to one where costs are more precise and differentiated and where margins are situation-specific and more value-based. This refined approach recognizes that accurate, up-to-date, deal-specific costs form the requisite foundation, and that thoughtfully differentiated margins can help link custom-configured pricing to customer value. A more detailed discussion of individual elements of this enhanced approach follows below.

Customer- and Deal-Specific Cost Variability Explicitly Accounted For

In all cost-plus pricing approaches, cost-estimating accuracy becomes critical—because a cost estimate that is 1 percent too low ultimately results in a price that is 1 percent lower (and we all know the value of that 1 percent from Chapter 1, "Introduction"). Businesses that excel at custom-configured pricing are obsessive about estimated cost accuracy. Estimating accuracy is often improved by doing a rigorous analysis of past won bids and comparing estimated costs to the costs actually incurred. The analyses need to be done not just for estimated versus actual *total* cost but, more importantly, for estimated versus actual cost on a *component by component* basis. These analyses typically produce several findings:

- Wider variability in actual versus estimated costs than expected, for example, for a building security systems company, actual costs incurred varied +/– 25 percent from estimates.
- Sources of cost-estimating error concentrated in what is usually a small subset of cost components, for example, for the same building security company, 80 percent of cost-estimating error could be traced to just 8 of the 76 individual cost components that go into a total cost estimate.

So shrinking down overall estimating inaccuracy need not require a total re-creation of your cost-estimating system. Much can be accomplished
by focusing on fixing the small handful of cost components that are creating most of the error. In six of the eight most error-prone cost components for the building security company, the company abandoned its
approach of using average costs and created new costing approaches tied
more to the underlying drivers of those costs, for example, installation labor was always higher in concrete block versus steel-framed buildings. For
the other two components, they broke each into several smaller subcom-
ponents with costs that were individually easier to estimate. This focus on
fixing the most important sources of estimating inaccuracy allowed them
to reduce their estimating error range from +/– 25 percent to less than
+/– 6 percent.

Individual Decisions Made on How Cost Increases/Decreases Are Passed
Through   Companies typically update the cost databases they use for estimating total project costs on a periodic basis (e.g., monthly or quarterly)
with a combination of averages from the prior period as well as expected
trends. So as soon as the cost in that database goes down, it results in project
cost estimates (and thus project bid prices) that are lower.

In custom-configured situations, the best companies do not let these cost
pass-throughs occur automatically. Instead, they make a deliberate strategic
decision about when/which/how much of cost changes should impact the
estimating cost database.

So, *if a cost goes down,* then a business can either:

- *Maintain prices* by essentially leaving that cost component unchanged
  in the estimating cost database. For example, a manufacturing company
  recently reduced its labor costs by 20 percent through an operations improvement transformation program. These savings affected the cost to
  produce everything in the company's product line, including its custom-
  configured products. Because the savings were significant and unmatch-
  able by competitors in the near-term, the company left the labor rates in
  the estimating cost database unchanged—which allowed the company
  to keep millions of dollars in additional profit instead of distributing
  this money to its customers through lower prices.
- *Elect to pass-through some or all of the cost savings* to the market by
  lowering those cost components in the estimating cost database. Some
  input cost changes, for instance, will affect the entire market and justify
  a price adjustment. In those instances, allowing street prices to reset
  may be necessary to remain competitive.

If a cost goes up, the business can either:

- *Absorb small, one-off cost increases and maintain prices* by leaving that cost component unchanged in the estimating cost database. This means margins will decrease—which might be justified in situations where the cost increase is due to a short-term inefficiency (e.g., relocation of a production line) that only affects the company but not its direct competitors. Attempting to pass on a cost increase in this case might undermine the company's competitiveness while the cost increase is in effect and also create a longer-term image problem.
- *Pass the higher costs through to the market* by increasing that component in the cost-estimating database. This could be appropriate where input cost increases were affecting all suppliers in a market in the same way.

Cost Risk Explicitly Reflected in Cost Build-Up or Target Margin   In an effective, custom-configured pricing approach, how does one account for costs that are somewhat "unknowable" where there is high risk that a cost component might escalate way beyond the average, like the elevator company's unpredictable excavating cost where shale and other rock formations are present? Such risks are often too large to ignore in the cost build-up that ultimately results in the bid price.

One solution is to add one or more additional cost buckets (e.g., for complexity or risk), which allows the person pricing the job to account for the risk of higher than anticipated costs. Such buckets can be called risk "adders."

Tactically, companies can alternatively incorporate overall cost risk as a percentage add-on to total calculated cost. Predetermined risk tiers based on a comprehensive assessment of project risk can be created. For example, a "moderate risk" job might add 3 percent to the total cost. A "high-risk" job might add 8 percent to cost. Risk factors to consider in this risk assessment might include familiarity with the products and specifics of the job, extreme quality standards, and the presence of specific job characteristics that have resulted in cost risk in the past, for example, the shale and rock formations for the elevator company. Where possible, cost risk should be conditionally shared with customers, for example, a contract term stating that if posthole excavation hours exceed eight hours because of shale and rock formations, then the customer shares excavating costs beyond eight hours with the elevator supplier.

One could debate whether risk adders should be considered as margin rather than cost elements. In our experience, businesses typically attach more weight and discipline to cost elements. As a result, it is usually more effective to treat these adders as costs.

Margin Adder Adjusted Based on Value to the Customer and Other Deal Characteristics Many companies that sell custom-configured offerings establish a standard margin expectation and apply that target margin to each and every bid situation. But as we mentioned earlier, it is in differentiating this "plus" in the cost-plus approach that a company can capture customer value differences. For instance, a company may have a competitive advantage with respect to a particular customer industry, deal size, project complexity, and so forth, that justifies—all else being equal—a higher, customer value-based price. Deliberately differentiated margin targets can reflect such opportunities.

For the building security systems company mentioned earlier, Exhibit 12-2 shows how they thoughtfully targeted different margin levels for different basic bid situations. The company sold and installed their systems in four basic building types: heavy industrial, light industrial, commercial, and hotels/high-rise residential. The company was particularly well positioned in the heavy industrial part of the market where its highly resilient

---

Exhibit 12-2 Building Security Systems Company: Initial Target Margin Matrix

Target margin (percent of project revenues)

Building type	Less than $100,000	$100,000–$400,000	Greater than $400,000
Heavy industrial	31	27	23
Light industrial	27	23	20
Commercial	24	21	19
Hotel/high-rise residential	21	17	14

Small ◁———————————————▷ Large
Project revenues

systems were well-suited and where fewer major competitors participated. That advantage was reflected in the fact that its highest target margins were in heavy industrial. Conversely, the company's offering was less distinctive in the hotel/high-rise residential sector where a much greater number of competitors played and where the ruggedness of their systems was not so highly valued. This lower relative customer value was reflected in their target margins being lowest there. In all building types, larger projects tended to yield lower percent margin levels, which showed decreasing targets as total project revenues grew.

In their refined pricing approach, the building security company started by creating an accurate, customer-tailored, risk-adjusted cost estimate and then added the appropriate initial target margin from the matrix—based on building type and deal size. But they did not stop there. They then developed a margin "fine-tuning worksheet" that allowed the sales representative to indicate specifics about the customer and bid situation that would justify bidding a price slightly higher or lower than the initial target. Fine-tuning variables were quite granular and included items like the customer's satisfaction with the current vendor, strength of sales rep's relationship with key buying influencers, price level paid by customer for similar systems in the past, and so forth. Having a fixed list of fine-tuning variables to guide the discussion of whether to adjust up or down from the initial target price made those deliberations more consistent, systematic, and effective.

It should be noted that the target margin matrix used by this security systems company was not static, but rather was adjusted on a routine basis. The company tracked win rates for quotes within each cell of the matrix. When a win rate dropped too low, target margins might be slightly reduced. Conversely, if a win rate became too high within a cell, that target margin might be increased to gain margin and assure that no unnecessary downward pressure be placed on market price levels.

This enhanced custom-configured pricing approach—with its more accurate and risk-adjusted costs and systematically differentiated margins—allowed this building security systems company to increase price levels by an average of 3.5 percent while holding market share and virtually eliminating unprofitable projects.

* * *

Basic cost-plus pricing, the approach most commonly used for pricing custom-configured products, is a deeply entrenched practice in many companies and markets. Indeed, a complete departure from the cost-plus framework would be difficult for most companies selling custom-configured offerings. However, incorporating a few of the crucial elements of the enhanced cost-plus approach described above can provide custom-configured product suppliers and other businesses using the cost-plus approach with a practical and rewarding path toward *the price advantage.*

SECTION TWO: HIGH-COUNT PRODUCT LINES

Chapter 4, "Customer Value," discussed the details of pricing based on an understanding of how your product or service is perceived relative to competitive alternatives. The fundamental tenet at this level of pricing is to understand the details of how customers perceive both price and benefits and the implications of your position relative to competitors on the value map. But what happens if you have hundreds of products or hundreds of thousands of products? It is clearly impractical to do the research and analysis to understand the optimal price on all of these different products.

There are many reasons why reaching the optimal price is hard when you have lots of products. First, it is often difficult to get access to complete competitive pricing benchmarks. Second, each stock-keeping unit (SKU) often has insufficient historical transaction data to evaluate the volume impact of past price increases or decreases. Also, the sheer volume of products and transactions requires analytical resources that are quite skilled at scrubbing data and looking for patterns—and that are able to handle the immense amount of information involved. Lastly, companies with a large catalog of products often rely on many third parties to supply raw materials, components, or finished goods and are at the mercy of frequent product cost changes. So maintaining their own price books often requires a tremendous amount of activity merely to keep margins constant, let alone search for additional margin opportunities.

Many companies face this challenge—including distributors or manufacturers of consumer products, spare parts, and industrial products. For example, a construction equipment company that sells spare parts for its line of equipment manages a catalog of more than 300,000 unique SKUs.

How do most of these companies approach the challenge of adjusting pricing? We have found three common approaches to changing pricing in this environment.

- *Use rules to react to cost changes.* Often, companies will have rules that automatically pass along cost increases to their price book.
- *Take across-the-board increases.* Whenever management needs to increase margins, they send the edict over to the pricing group to implement an across-the-board price increase.
- *Make differential increases by category.* As a slight modification to an across-the-board approach, companies may try to "weight" an overall

price increase by taking larger increases in product categories, which they believe are under less price pressure (e.g., because they are more proprietary).

The main shortfall of these approaches is that they miss the unique "DNA" of individual products. Take the construction equipment company mentioned earlier. Historically, they would adjust their prices at a category level (e.g., they would take their hydraulic parts up by 3.5 percent across the board, and their oil filters up by less). The problem is that even in the hydraulics category, there are huge differences in the company's competitive positions for individual parts. They have proprietary and obsolete pumps where there are no competitive alternatives. If the original part breaks, the customer has no alternative but to go with the company—and if the customer does not replace the part fast, they could lose tens of thousands of dollars in lost uptime. For other hydraulic parts, for example, hoses, many different alternatives exist, some of which can be picked up at a local automotive parts store.

The other underlying shortfall of these approaches is that they are reactive, often driven by raw material cost changes or the need for extra profit to meet earnings targets—not by an ongoing program in search of additional profit opportunities. As a result, many products become significantly over- or underpriced over time.

The good news is that there are huge amounts of valuable data that companies can mine when dealing with a large catalog of products. The approach that we have seen work in many large product line pricing environments uses all this available information to develop *multiple indicators* of the *relative risk* of raising prices. We know from past experience that individual indicators *alone* (e.g., historical volume change after a price increase, list price relative to competitors) do not establish a high level of confidence that one SKU can be increased in price. However, when you use a combination of four or five factors, it gives a high degree of confidence that it is less risky to raise price in one SKU than in another SKU (i.e., where the indicators point in the opposite direction).

To illustrate this approach, we will use a recent example from an office products company. This distributor had a catalog of more than 100,000 unique SKUs. It sold products mainly to small and medium-sized companies.

STEP 1: ANALYTICALLY ESTIMATE YOUR PRICE POSITION VERSUS THE MARKET

The first, obvious line of analysis was to compare published list prices relative to the two major competitors in the market. The company initially received pushback from the sales force on this approach, because they knew that competitors (and they) rarely sold at list prices. However, most of the industry gave individual customers a percentage off the published list prices. While on an absolute basis the company did not know where an individual product price fell relative to the competition, on a *relative* basis the company knew where one SKU was relative to another. For example, if one pen was 10 percent below the competitor's list price, and another was 10 percent above, the company might see a stronger *relative* competitor reaction if it raised the price on the latter than if it raised the price on the former.

Because list price alone did not provide an adequate sense of whether one product's price was higher or lower than the market, the company supplemented list price with three other indicators. First, it scored products on whether a SKU was increasing or decreasing in volume relative to other trends in the category. For instance, if a certain type of pen were growing in volume more than the pen category in general, this indicated that the pen's price placed it in a value-advantaged position in the market. Second, the company looked at the margins for an individual SKU relative to other SKUs in the category. If the margin was lower than the average of other similar SKUs, this indicated the SKU was underpriced. Lastly, the company analyzed the volume change after previous price increases. Because there were many outside factors that could influence the volume change in addition to price, it only used this last indicator with large volume bellwether products.

As you can see, each of these individual indicators *alone* is not a sufficient basis for finalizing a SKU's position in the market. However, when combined, these indicators provide a fairly compelling picture of one SKU's position relative to another SKU. So, if a particular pen were priced lower than competitor's list prices (more so than other pens), growing in volume significantly more than the pen category in general, while earning less relative margins, it gives us a high level of confidence that this SKU has less risk of a price increase than if all of the indicators pointed in the exact opposite direction.

The company analyzed all 100,000 SKUs against these three data screens and came up with a high/medium/low total score on *every* SKU's price relative to the market. The process took approximately four weeks.

STEP 2: ANALYTICALLY ESTIMATE RELATIVE PRICE SENSITIVITY

The second step involved a similar approach but focused on the product's relative price sensitivity. Customers who buy from large catalogs face a similar challenge to the company selling the product—how do they ensure they are getting the best value relative to other suppliers? They may not have the time to analyze an individual SKU price versus the competition so they typically use simplifying approaches to make sure that the prices are fair (e.g., looking at high volume products, the products that are the most expensive, or evaluating competitive prices once or twice a year on a given order).

Herein lies the opportunity for the large catalog pricer—identifying those SKU characteristics that give them confidence that one product is *relatively* less price sensitive than another one. So the question pricers should be asking is a bit different in this environment. It is not "What is the optimal price for each individual product?" but rather "Across all the products I carry, what are those that hold the least amount of risk for increasing or decreasing price, so that I am continually moving toward the most optimal price?"

For the office products company, the company analyzed about 15 different indicators of price sensitivity, and landed on four that really mattered (based on statistical analysis of historical price changes).

1. Overall customer share of wallet—A higher percentage SKU will likely get more customer review.
2. Absolute price level for the product—Even if a product did not represent a large portion of a customer's purchases, if it had a high absolute price (e.g., a video projector that costs several thousand dollars), it received more evaluation by customers.
3. Order frequency—Products that were purchased weekly, even if they had a low absolute price level, were likely going to face a higher degree of customer scrutiny.
4. Category advantage—This last one was more qualitative in nature. The sales force was able to command higher margins on some products because of the product advice they provided to customers, and a product line breadth advantage they had relative to competitors.

This step was a little more difficult than the first because there are many indicators one can use for price sensitivity (we have used more than 30 different screens across various situations). It requires managerial and mathematical rigor to screen for the right indicators.

Similar to the competitive pricing analysis in Step 1, the company analyzed and scored all 100,000 SKUs against the price sensitivity indicators and gave a composite high/medium/low score for each one.

STEP 3: DIFFERENTIALLY INCREASE OR DECREASE PRICE BY SKU BASED ON RISK

The last step combined Steps 1 and 2 and resulted in a decision matrix on the price increase. The idea is fairly straightforward—take higher price increases

Exhibit 12-3 Pricing Decision Matrix

Decision matrix: price recommendation for each SKU

Price risk score	Below	Within range	Above
High	0 (No change)	0 (No change)	– (Decrease)
	+ (Small increase)	0 (No change)	0 (No change)
	++ (Medium increase)	0 (No change)	0 (No change)
Low	+++ (Large increase)	+ (Small increase)	+ (Small increase)

Current price relative to benchmark

where indicators of risk are low, and where the distance from market pricing benchmarks suggest current prices are low. And take less risky price increases where the opposite is true. This step also allows for human intervention and judgment. We typically use a matrix like Exhibit 12-3 above to develop an initial recommendation for a price change, and then have product and sales managers review these recommendations and add their expert judgment (e.g., if some products are very closely watched by customers, or if competitors have made some recent changes that are not caught by the algorithm).

This office products company had previously averaged around a 2 percent price increase every year to their catalog, of which about 50 percent would not be negotiated away with additional discounts. Using the approach outlined above, the company was able to implement an average 5.5 percent price increase and had a 75 percent stick rate (i.e., 75 percent of the 5.5 percent increase made it to the bottom line). The company also ran this process continually, where they would monitor and fine-tune the price changes based on competitor and customer reactions. This allowed the company to fine-tune the algorithm over time.

By combining rigorous analysis and the use of multiple indicators, companies can develop pricing for high-count product lines—no matter how many SKUs they have. However, in addition to the process described above, the company should keep a few "lessons learned" in mind:

- The largest opportunities often lie in the "tail" of the product on the Pareto chart. Companies with high-count product lines will often look closely at the top 100 or 200 products, but then use simple rules to manage the rest. As a result, some products that have a beneficial position in the market are averaged out in terms of price increases. Although individually each product might not be a large contributor to profits, collectively this often represents a substantial opportunity.
- By creating an analytical team that is comfortable working on large data sets, the company can ensure that it will obtain and interpret the data it needs to identify and then take advantage of its opportunities. If data is difficult to get on some SKUs, then work on those where it is available while you are obtaining it for the others.
- An ongoing process that updates annually (or more frequently) will enable a company to do an even better job of pricing and capture even more opportunities. One foodservice company reviewed some products weekly (e.g., where costs and supply/demand changed frequently), others quarterly, and still others annually based on product needs and pricing changes.

* * *

Companies with high-count product lines have many opportunities to adjust their prices and capture price improvement. Each SKU has a unique DNA, which must be understood by a company. It is unfeasible to conduct market research on each product, but there are straightforward ways to capture pricing risk "indicators" for each SKU, and translate these into practical guidance for where products should be increased or decreased in price.

SECTION THREE: DISTRIBUTED SALES MODELS

In some companies, senior executives have complete a priori control over the prices they charge in the market. When an airline posts a $199 price from point A to B on its web site, the price is set—right or wrong. Many other businesses do not have this luxury. Pricing, for good reasons, is distributed throughout the field, be it across large numbers of salespeople, branch offices, or distribution centers.

Take a foodservice company selling to small- and medium-sized restaurants. There are many reasons why pricing decisions have to remain local to the branch and salesperson. First, costs frequently change due to local commodity markets, which require quick price changes. Further, many products are locally sourced and/or perishable, which demands a continuous local balancing act between supply and pricing to ensure that inventory is not lost. Finally, every customer uses different products as a benchmark to compare prices between local distributors (e.g., mozzarella cheese for a pizza restaurant, tortillas for a Mexican restaurant); salespeople need to have the knowledge and flexibility to make sure these "key value items" are competitively priced to win the customer's total business.

The hallmarks of distributed sales models include most of the following:

- Sales and branch office dispersion—large number of salespeople and branch offices.
- Geographic dispersion—different competitive intensity (e.g., number and type of competitors and customers).
- Distributed pricing decision making.
- Many customer segments, each with different needs.
- High-count product lines.
- Dynamic supply, demand, and costs.

Many industries have these characteristics, including most distribution companies (e.g., office, high-tech, food, or industrial products), large service companies with local branches (e.g., laser eye surgery, waste hauling, HVAC installation, records management), and rental companies.

As we show, getting pricing right in these environments requires some specialized components at the Pricing Infrastructure level, which, when done right, can create a substantial *price advantage* in the market.

But first, what are some of the typical challenges for pricing in these environments?

Achieving consistent performance across the sales force and branches is one of the biggest challenges in distributed sales models. When there are hundreds or, in some cases, thousands of people making pricing decisions, there are bound to be huge variations in performance. The foodservice company sales force was making 1.2 *billion* discrete pricing decisions per year across their numerous locations and salespeople. However, when an individual salesperson was in front of a customer, it was a lonely undertaking. Apart from a high-level report that showed the margin the salesperson generated each month, there were no tools that brought the collective wisdom of all the previous pricing decisions to bear at the point of making the next pricing decision. That is, there was no *institutional memory* of the company's pricing processes or outcomes on comparable or different products across similar accounts. As a result, comparable products had a wide price band for similar customers.

The challenge in giving good pricing guidance to branches and salespeople lies in the diversity in the product and customer mix in these complex, distributed environments. Many companies with distributed sales models coalesce around simple rules and measurements like gross margins for guidance and score-keeping (e.g., every customer should be at least 40 percent gross margin). This is a huge mistake—and usually the biggest contributor to lost pricing opportunities for many of these companies. The reason is that many salespeople and customers who appear to be generating acceptable margins are significantly underpriced relative to their peers. Product mix differences are what hide this shortcoming. Take a building products company with diverse product lines as an example. Some salespeople were recognized and rewarded for seemingly good margin performance. However, because they were selling to more custom builders of high-end homes, their product mix was rich. And when compared to other accounts of similar mix, they were actually below average. Averages and the use of simple rules of thumb can hide substantial opportunity in these environments.

A related challenge is the sheer magnitude of data in distributed sales models. The pricing organization faces a formidable task. It must have the computing and analytical horsepower to analyze, in some cases, billions of rows of data. If its reports and tools are too complex, managers and salespeople will not use them. If they are too simple, they will fail to uncover opportunities. Another result of the data and process complexity is the increased potential for pricing errors. One office products company identified branches selling up to 7 percent of transactions below costs. Some customers were given a "net" price in the past (i.e., it resided in the billing system as a discrete price versus being a margin over cost); this price had not been revisited and adjusted when actual product costs increased. When transaction volumes are so high, it is easy for even straightforward opportunities to slip through the cracks.

In working with many companies in these types of challenging distributed sales environments, we have found the following have been some of the most critical opportunities and lessons learned.

EMBRACE A PRICING INDEX FOR TRANSACTIONS LEVEL PRICING

Imagine a salesperson is in front of a customer—instead of bringing only their experience to bear in setting a price, they can leverage the collective experience of thousands of other salespeople. Decisions will be better, and the salesperson will be much more confident in defending their prices. Also imagine, when comparing the relative performance of a branch, salesperson, or customer, you can account for important differences in product or customer mix and avoid the pitfalls of using simple gross margin targets and measures as outlined previously. A *price indexing* methodology can help accomplish both of these goals.

A price index is a simple concept—and a fine-tuning of the methodology we describe in Chapter 3, "Transactions." It provides a fair, mix-adjusted comparison of customers and salespeople. So the high-margin building products salesperson described earlier in this chapter is now compared, on an apples-to-apples basis, to other salespeople. Take an office products salesperson selling Bic pens to a mid-sized office. In the past two months, every other salesperson in the region selling to mid-sized offices provides insight into what price is achievable in the market. A pricing index simply groups like products and customers together and provides a grade for each transaction (e.g., showing what is a poor, below average, average, above average, or excellent price for the pen). By starting at the product level, a company can provide a salesperson with insight at multiple levels—for example, what is the grade of my proposed price for this customer for this pen, how does this customer compare to similar customers (by aggregating the score across all products sold to the customer), and, most importantly, how am I doing as a salesperson compared to other salespeople (by aggregating all of my transactions and customers to peers)?

This methodology is a powerful tool to provide guidance and motivation at two levels: (1) transaction target prices and (2) performance measures at the salesperson, customer, and branch levels.

Transaction Target Prices   Companies can use an index to provide specific guidance on target prices for products for an individual customer. Now, a salesperson can bring the *collective wisdom* and *memory* of the organization to each product, transaction, and customer when making pricing decisions—and avoid the shortcomings of simple measures like gross margins. Salespeople will go into negotiations infinitely more confident when they can clearly see what peer salespeople and customers are generating for comparable products and customers.

Salesperson, Customer, and Branch Performance Measures   Another powerful motivational tool is the simple, yet influential transparency that a pricing index brings to the relative performance of salespeople, customers, and branches. Exhibit 12-4 shows a series of cascading reports created for an industrial distribution company from this simple indexing methodology. Salespeople knew exactly how they performed on a relative basis to peers;

Exhibit 12-4 Industrial Distribution Company: Cascading Pricing Reports

Sales group pricing reports

Regional pricing summary

Subregional pricing summary

Subregional sales manager

Sales rep pricing summary

Invoice price as percent of target price

Rep	Current month	Quartile	Previous 3 months	Quartile
Rep A	100.0	Top	97.4	3rd
Rep B	99.8	Top	98.0	2nd
Rep C	98.6	2nd	96.6	Bot
Rep D	98.4	2nd	96.7	Bot
Rep E	97.9	3rd	98.3	2nd

Customer pricing reports

Global customer summary

Top-50 regional customer summary

Top-20 subregional customer summary

Sales rep

Sales rep pricing by customer

Invoice price as percent of target price

Customer	Current month
Customer A	95.7
Customer B	98.2
Customer C	96.5
Customer D	90.9
Customer E	95.0
Customer F	100.0
Customer G	84.8

Product pricing reports

Global pricing summary by product model

Regional pricing by product family

Subregional pricing by product family

Sales rep

Sales rep pricing by product

Invoice price as percent of target price

Product family	Current month	Previous 3 months	Quartile
ML	100.0	99.8	3rd
SPA	97.5	97.6	3rd
AWP	97.2	97.5	Bot
TH	96.1	98.0	3rd
TMZ	92.6	99.0	Bot
LTW	92.1	100.0	2nd

the scores accounted for customer and product mix differences. It also provided the salesperson with clear guidance on which customers and products they were chronically underpricing. Even the best salespeople unearthed opportunities from these reports, finding some products and customers that they did not know were performing poorly (usually hidden because of product mix). Second, these reports allowed sales managers to know which salespeople required more coaching time for improvement (e.g., by riding along with them for a day during the next month). Lastly, regional and branch managers were motivated to spend real time on price improvement because the CEO of the company received a monthly rank-order report on their performance relative to peers (again, based on the same indexing methodology, but aggregated up to the regional level).

RAPIDLY PROTOTYPE NEW PRICING IDEAS

Thus far, we have talked about how to overcome some of the many challenges that face distributed sales models. One key opportunity also exists for companies with distributed sales models that companies with complete a priori control do not have. That is the opportunity to use the distributed nature of the market to test and refine new pricing ideas. Unfortunately, many companies with distributed sales models do not fully take advantage of this opportunity.

A large national company providing local plumbing services to consumers and businesses had a number of hypotheses on areas it could change in its list prices (e.g., standard labor rates for service calls) and terms and conditions (e.g., up-charges for rush service). It knew from competitive analysis that some of the key rates and terms could be raised, but it did not know by how much. It took six local markets (out of 70) and tested two levels of changes (e.g., three markets had a moderately aggressive change, and three had a more aggressive change) and monitored the impact to volumes over a two-month period. It found that it could confidently take the more aggressive actions without impacting the sales growth in these markets.

This prototyping served many valuable purposes. First, it enabled changes to be rolled out more aggressively than they otherwise would have been. Second, it helped fine-tune some of the tools used to help salespeople sell these changes to customers. Third, it created a ton of internal momentum for the new pricing changes by proving their impact in the pilot branches. Since branch managers were compensated on branch profitability, many went from being skeptical and resistant to the new changes to clamoring to be the next set of branches in the rollout process.

CONTINUALLY HUNT FOR PRICING "LEAKAGE"

As mentioned previously, the complexity and transaction volume associated with distributed sales models causes many pricing opportunities to fall through the cracks. These leakages can take many forms. Below are some of the most common types:

- List price adjustments—local adjustments because of cost or market changes.
- Transactional errors—caused by legacy pricing agreements.
- Customer price outliers—low-volume customers receiving high-volume pricing.
- Cost outliers—customers or transactions that are consuming inordinate resources because of special needs or location.
- Terms and conditions—not following best practices or established policies.

It is important for a pricing group to be in continual "search and destroy" mode for these leakages.

A foodservice distribution company created a group of 10 people whose job it was to find these opportunities. It developed a continually evolving "toolkit"—covering 8 to 10 "opportunity scans" that it would complete with all its distributed branches (e.g., below cost transactions, special-order up-charges, delivery cost outliers). For any one branch, usually only two or three of these would provide opportunities, but across all branches, this process was a key contributor to maintaining and increasing profitability. It was a great example of an "activist" pricing organization as outlined in Chapter 6, "Pricing Infrastructure."

FLAWLESSLY EXECUTE THE PRICING CHANGE PROCESS

Chapter 15, "Pricing Transformation," covers the tools and frameworks we recommend for capturing the hearts and changing the mindsets of the frontline when it comes to achieving *the pricing advantage*. A distributed sales environment is quite challenging when it comes to shifting pricing behaviors and attitudes. Many people need to be influenced. By definition, price changes here are more action-oriented, as opposed to policy-based. For the airline example used in the beginning of the chapter, perhaps only one person must be influenced to change the price for thousands of transactions. In a distributed sales environment, hundreds, or thousands of salespeople and pricers might need to be influenced to change the outcome on a similar magnitude of sales and transaction volume.

* * *

Pricing in a distributed sales environment requires specialized pricing infrastructure actions and components. Target prices and performance comparisons between branches and salespeople must account for product and customer mix, and the organization must not only have the skills to manage large data sets but constantly search out pricing leakage. The change management process needs to be managed even more closely, given the sheer number of employees these companies must influence.

CHAPTER 13

Tailored Value

While the overall idea of customer value—perceived benefits minus perceived price—is straightforward in concept, there are a number of situations where the fundamental concepts of customer value need to be applied in a tailored fashion. The sections in this chapter explore a few of the most common situations where customer value must be executed in a differentiated and tailored way. These situations include price segmentation, tiered products and services, new products, "razor/razor blades" offerings, and solutions.

SECTION ONE: PRICE SEGMENTATION

Whether deliberately or randomly, almost all companies differentiate price levels to some extent across customers and transactions. The wide pocket price bands in Chapter 3, "Transactions," demonstrate just how much normal prices can vary. And the value profiling section of Chapter 4, "Customer Value," highlights how variability in the way a company delivers its benefits (or how its customers perceive those benefits) can often lead to wide differences in customer perceived value.

But what if something more fundamental affects the way diverse customer groups perceive the benefits a supplier provides? What if the customer groups assign entirely different importance weightings to individual benefit attributes—so dissimilar that their value maps are dramatically different? By dramatically different, we mean competitors' positions shift significantly, for example, a supplier is value-advantaged for one customer group, value-equivalent for another, and severely value-disadvantaged for yet another. In such situations, these different customer groups (or customer segments) may require some deliberately varied price levels, that is, price segmentation, if the company is going to maximize its price and profits.

THE WINCO PLASTICS CASE

Winco Plastics illustrates such a situation. Winco is a leading producer of engineered plastic resin used in the production of a wide variety of plastic components. It competes with two other major suppliers in this market, Midco and Baseco. Value research across 80 customers showed that, on average, customers perceived Winco as the high-price/high-benefit supplier—with a position firmly on the value equivalence line (Exhibit 13-1). Its superior product consistency, innovation, and delivery reliability earned it a perceived benefits advantage that justified its price premium over Midco and Baseco. This average value map across all customers would on the surface imply that Winco's overall price position was about right and that there might not be much opportunity to adjust base prices.

However, Winco decided to look beyond the average value map in its search for opportunities. It observed surprisingly large variations in the importance ratings customers assigned to the individual benefit attributes that were driving their choice of supplier. Three segments of customers—each with similar attribute weighting patterns—emerged from the research (Exhibit 13-2). A "technology-leader" segment placed particular value on the importance of its relationship with the most innovative supplier in the industry. Customers in this segment were themselves often innovators and

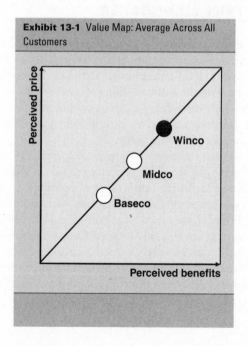

Exhibit 13-1 Value Map: Average Across All Customers

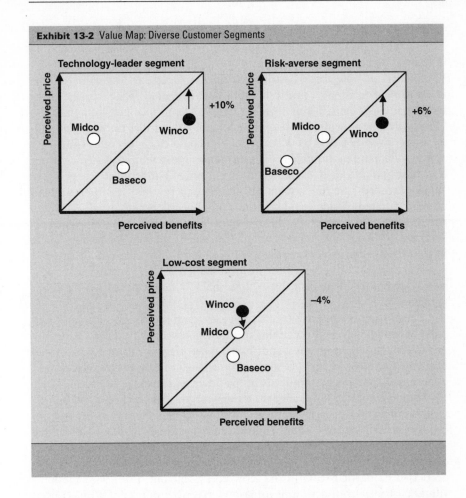

Exhibit 13-2 Value Map: Diverse Customer Segments

saw their partnership with Winco as enabling them to develop and introduce their innovative new products more quickly. This segment penalized Midco for its older technology orientation. It was clear that Winco was value-advantaged in this segment and could raise target prices up to 10 percent with minimal risk of customer loss.

A "risk-averse" segment of customers was less focused on innovation and more focused on supplier reliability. These customers valued suppliers who never put their productivity at risk—who provided products of consistent quality and delivered products dependably. These customers also liked dealing with suppliers who were financially stable and most likely to survive the volatility of business cycles. Winco's reputation and reliable product and delivery performance over the years caused this segment to give Winco an expanded benefit advantage over Midco and Baseco. Winco concluded that a 6 percent increase in target price levels to the risk-averse segment was in order.

Finally, a "low-cost" customer segment placed far less value on the innovation, consistency, and reliability that endeared Winco to the prior segments. Customers in this segment tended to produce more commodity-like plastic components. These customers had low hurdles for product quality and consistency that Midco and Baseco could easily exceed. They were also less demanding on delivery performance and willing to sacrifice order lead-time and fill-rate in exchange for lower price. The attribute areas where Winco excelled just did not matter that much to these customers—who ultimately rated Winco at about the same overall benefit level as Midco and Baseco. So Winco was clearly value-disadvantaged in this segment. With its low price and "good enough" product and delivery performance, Baseco held a value-advantaged position. A target price cut of at least 4 percent would be required to position Winco for any success here, that is, 10 percent to 14 percent lower than the new target prices for the other segments.

These insights caused Winco to place less emphasis on this low-cost segment, where they were not winning much business anyway. They chose only to sell into this segment on a spot basis, when they occasionally produced what they referred to as "off-spec" resin that did not meet the more strict quality and consistency standards of the other segments.

Winco resolutely implemented its new segmented pricing approach. It went through its entire list of nearly 300 customers and, with input from product marketing and sales, assigned each customer to one of the three segments. Winco gradually raised target price levels to "technology-leader" customers by 10 percent and "risk-averse" customers by 6 percent. It also decreased its participation in the "low-cost" segment. Even with the individual customer transaction negotiations that always occur, Winco raised its average price levels by nearly 7 percent over time. It also had a richer understanding of its customers, what they were looking for from suppliers, and which ones would reward Winco most for their product and service superiority.

OTHER CONSIDERATIONS

Although the Winco case is a powerful example of price segmentation done well, it is a specific example that addresses only a subset of considerations around price segmentation. Several key additional considerations are summarized in the following paragraphs:

Segmentation Dimensions The Winco price segmentation was "needs-based"—that is, driven by vastly different needs between customer groups. Customer needs are not the only dimension along which price segmentation can be built. Others include:

- **Geographic segmentation**, where different competitive participation or customer preferences by geography can materially affect the shape of local value maps.
- **Channel segmentation**, where different roles served and values provided vary by channel and justify differences in price.
- **Cost-to-serve segmentation**, where some customers are intrinsically more costly to serve, often driven by characteristics beyond customer needs, for example, costly remote delivery, high-order frequency.

Segmentation Price Architecture With its prices negotiated on a customer-by-customer basis, Winco was able to execute its segmented pricing through differences in target price levels by segment (see Chapter 11, "Pricing Architecture" for more details). A number of alternatives exist for building segment price differentials into your delivery of price to customers:

- Unique price lists for each segment.
- Segment-differentiated standard discounts off of a shared single price list.
- Different terms and conditions by segments, for example, more generous payment terms for resellers who routinely stock and promote your product.

Cross-Segment Cannibalization If Winco's technology-leader and risk-averse customers were able to buy at the low-cost customer price, then Winco's segmented pricing would have destroyed rather than enhanced price levels. Winco prevented that costly cannibalization by only selling "off-spec" material on a spot basis at the lower price levels—a clearly unattractive offer for Winco's higher-price segments. Consumer goods companies often use secondary brands or different package sizes to avoid such cannibalization. Adding conditions of sale, for example, airlines' requiring a weekend stay for their lowest prices to avoid cannibalization of the business traveler segment, can also make the low price offer less attractive to segments targeted for higher price.

Legal Issues All forms of price differentiation—including segmented pricing—carry with them some legal risks. Price segmentation design and implementation should be done with the oversight of legal counsel. Refer to Chapter 9, "Legal Degrees of Freedom," for a more detailed discussion of legal considerations associated with price segmentation.

* * *

Price segmentation sits at the core of tailoring value to customers. As the Winco case illustrates, well-executed price segmentation can help you win volume from a range of customers at price levels significantly higher than a single price approach might allow. While legal and cross-segment cannibalization risks need to be managed with care, effective price segmentation represents for many businesses one of the most powerful—and too often overlooked—sources of pricing opportunity.

SECTION TWO: TIERED PRODUCTS AND SERVICES

As marketers try to appeal to more and more refined customer segments, they have to manage the pricing relationships among groups of related products—in other words, they have to find ways to tier their prices for products and services. Tiering happens for many reasons, whether in response to a competitor's position on the value map, because of increasingly diverse customer needs or uses for a product, or simply because of a change in the company's internal capabilities (e.g., the ability to source or manufacture a lower cost version of a product).

Companies can provide tiered offerings in many ways: by differentiating various levels of the product based on good, better, and best; by offering multiple versions with different features and prices; or by using multiple size packages. This myriad of combinations makes the pricing challenge even more complex. Whether your company is the chemical supplier that offers the same basic chemical with three tiers of performance characteristics or the consumer products company that sells various brands of laundry detergent with different features at different prices, the pricing challenge and opportunity are the same. How do I ensure that my pricing strategy delivers the most profitable share of the market? The only thing that changes is the level of complexity.

Getting the pricing relationships and customer segments right for product tiers is critical. Recall the case study of Compair International and State Compressor in Chapter 7, "Postmerger Pricing." The company lost profits after the merger with State Compressor because it did not create a well-researched, tiered pricing strategy. Specifically, the company assumed that having two products, one high-end and one low-end, would be the right way to appeal to its targeted customer segments. In reality, the customers it targeted for the high-end product were happy with the low-end version—which was backed by the same warranty and technical service as the high-end version.

Companies can optimize price tiers in two ways. First, they can optimize price gaps between different products or different sizes of the same product. Secondly, they can change the mix of products or different sizes offered.

Whatever choice, or combination of choices they make, they need to develop a detailed scientific understanding of how customers make trade-up and trade-down decisions between the different products and then use that knowledge to craft the most profitable pricing strategy. They should also consider how these strategies fit with the product's overall lifecycle and the particular dynamics that emerge from that dimension. Chapter 10, "Lifecycle Pricing," offers more information in this area.

OPTIMIZE PRICE GAPS BETWEEN DIFFERENT PRODUCTS OR DIFFERENT SIZES OF THE SAME PRODUCT

Many companies try to optimize price tiers between different products within the same category or brand (e.g., a good, better, best replacement tire for passenger cars) without scientific testing. We have often encountered this situation with legacy pricing relationships (e.g., 10 percent difference in price between the better and best tire). In our experience, companies can often find great value from building a customer research fact base around these pricing tiers and using it to guide their actions.

One electronics company continually brought new product innovations to its category (the "better") while also offering the older technologies (the "good") at a lower price. They believed that they needed to keep the older technologies (the "good") at a lower price to serve lower income consumers and fight off lower price competitors. Our research found, however, that a significant portion of consumers would not automatically move up to the "better" technology because the old technology was "good enough" for their needs. By pricing the tiers accordingly (both the "good" and the "better" at about the same level), the company captured additional profits.

Another issue that plagues price tiering is the variation in actual prices in the marketplace. The distinctions between good/better/best product line pricing can become blurred when variations caused by differences in the negotiated price, different channel promotions, or channel pricing are included. Detailed price banding analysis, like that described earlier in this book, can help identify channel partners that may be unnecessarily discounting certain products.

Size also plays an important role. Companies will often give price discounts as customers trade up from smaller to larger sizes. This is another area where history and tradition often drive pricing strategy more than rigorous science. The key is to understand the true role that different pack sizes play for customers. Do they need larger or smaller sizes for convenience purposes or do they expect a discount? If a customer buys a larger size, are they likely going to use more of the product, or will they just use the same amount, but make fewer purchases because their initial buy lasts longer?

In one case, a health and beauty product supplier gave a nearly 15 percent discount for buying its product in larger-size containers across its different brands. Based on elasticity research, the company found that there was almost zero cross elasticity between pack sizes. Consumers that bought the larger size packages did so out of convenience, as opposed to the expectation of a steep discount. By closing this price gap, the company captured additional profits.

Analysis of existing package size discounts across retailers and across similar products can also indicate an opportunity. See Exhibit 13-3 for an example. This company plotted the retail prices on its products across retailers. This simple analysis identified several pack size opportunities. First, on product A, one retailer was providing much steeper discounts for larger pack sizes than others. The company analyzed the volume comparison on the large packs and found that they did not get any higher consumer trade up than those retailers with a flatter discount curve.

The company also compared its discount curves across multiple brands in the same category. When comparing product A to product B, it found that both its wholesale and retail prices were more highly discounted for the larger pack sizes in product B. Again, comparing consumer uptake for the larger size packages between the brands, it found no material benefit for the steeper pack size discount.

CHANGE THE MIX OF PRODUCTS OR SIZES OFFERED

Researching customers' trade-up and trade-down behavior often leads to counterintuitive and profitable insights. Companies start to question basic assumptions that may lead to much more profitable and successful solutions—such as how many product tiers to offer, how many segments to target, and whether to even keep an older version of a product around or develop another "better" version.

Pricing psychology is an important consideration here. A high- or low-priced product may serve as an "anchor" to make customers feel better about picking a product in the middle (e.g., a man does not want to buy the

Exhibit 13-3 Pack Size Opportunity Identification

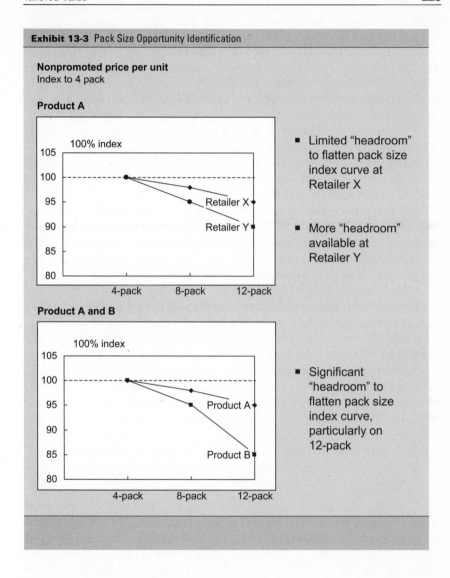

Nonpromoted price per unit
Index to 4 pack

Product A

- Limited "headroom" to flatten pack size index curve at Retailer X

- More "headroom" available at Retailer Y

Product A and B

- Significant "headroom" to flatten pack size index curve, particularly on 12-pack

most expensive or the cheapest wedding ring, but assumes that a mid-priced ring will still be acceptable). This is a common dynamic, observed in many consumer goods categories.

In one telling example, a consumer and business software company historically offered three tiers of software with different price points and features. These tiers addressed several different user profiles, including those that wanted basic levels of functionality on the low end and "super-users" at the extreme high end. As the product tier structure evolved, the company offered entry level, mid-tier, and high-end versions of the same basic software. Hundreds of PowerPoint slides outlined the rationale behind the different features and functionality. The one thing missing was an answer to a fundamental question—Why do we need three products and not one, two, or four?

The company conducted market research to explore this issue. Whenever the company presented potential customers with various software options and prices, it also collected detailed research. However, instead of always presenting the full line of products, the company tested options with fewer or more products.

For years, the company thought that their mid-tier product was what appealed most to the masses—it represented almost 70 percent of their sales volume. They feared that if they did not offer this product, customers would migrate toward the lower-end product, which was about 30 percent cheaper and provided most of the technical features that people needed.

When the company tested consumer response without the mid-tier product, however, they found something different. Even though usage would suggest that customers did not need the higher-end product, almost everyone who currently purchased the mid-tier product was more than willing to pay an extra 12 percent for the higher-end one. Detailed interviews revealed that most customers really did not spend the time to research all of the technical features of the different levels of the software. However, they thought that the extra cost for the more advanced version was added insurance in case they, or a family member, ever needed the most sophisticated features available. By dropping the mid-tier product, the company was able to increase average prices by more than 8 percent with no impact on volume.

* * *

Tiered product and service offerings require an advanced level of complexity at the Customer Value level. Managers need to understand the intricacies of how customers make their decisions when they are faced with a myriad of brands, packages, and sizes. Significant profit opportunities usually exist for fine-tuning the price gaps between products and sizes as well as the number of options provided.

SECTION THREE: NEW PRODUCTS

New product launches are highly visible. Investors, managers, and employees are eager to see signs of success. Consumers may be excited about the possibilities of the new product. However, in the rush for immediate success, companies tend to focus on sales volume and market share figures, which can lead to costly, value-destroying pricing mistakes at launch time. The company takes a conservative approach to pricing a new product, fearing that too high a price could jeopardize the new product's future or lose business that they may not be able to justify the price premium sufficiently, or that share growth or market penetration might take too long.

Not surprisingly, companies often use a cautious incremental approach to price new products within a safe percentage range relative to products already in the market. For B2B products, this percentage is usually based on differences in costs of production or a narrowly defined view of the added benefits the product offers customers. In consumer markets, companies often focus on a price that is a bit above or below their main competitor's price. Even for truly groundbreaking products (e.g., the iPod, the Segway), there is usually some market reference product that the company tries to use to deduce the price. It would be like trying to price laser eye surgery at its debut based on the lifetime replacement costs of eyeglasses or contact lenses.

Such incremental approaches usually underestimate the benefits delivered to customers and set the price too low. For example, one of the first makers of portable bar code readers, the devices used in inventory tracking and management, based its release price on the economic improvement resulting from the faster assembly speeds that its product offered manufacturers. These improvements were based largely on quicker data entry and improved component tracking. Faced by anxious investors, the company also wanted to ensure that it penetrated the market quickly. Using improved assembly times as the yardstick, the company set the price of the portable reader proportionately above that charged for the older, stationary readers.

But the added benefits offered by the portable reader went well beyond the assembly time improvements. It ushered in entirely new business processes by allowing real-time inventory control and improved logistics planning. For many companies, portable bar code readers reduced their need for large inventories and enhanced customer service because of improved inventory accuracy. It also enabled just-in-time delivery. Buyers quickly recognized these substantial benefits and flocked to the low-priced product, outstripping the company's production capacity. Not only did the firm fail to capture the reader's full profit potential, it also set the enduring customer price expectations at a low level. With a single misguided decision, the company not only reduced its own profitability, but also erased more than $1 billion in potential industry profit over the life of the product.

Consumer markets are not immune to these pitfalls, as the classic case of the launch of the Mazda Miata illustrates. Japanese carmaker Mazda introduced its Miata sports car to U.S. markets in 1990. With its retro look,

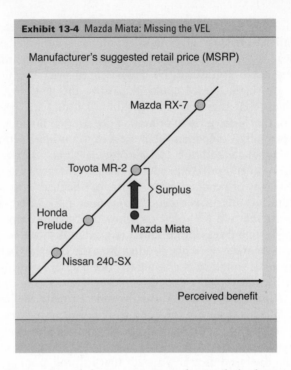

Exhibit 13-4 Mazda Miata: Missing the VEL

Manufacturer's suggested retail price (MSRP)

- Mazda RX-7
- Toyota MR-2
- Surplus
- Honda Prelude
- Mazda Miata
- Nissan 240-SX

Perceived benefit

the little roadster captured the imagination of aging baby boomers nostalgic for the classic British MGs and Triumphs of the 1960s and 1970s. As much fun as its British predecessors but better built and more reliable, the Miata was an instant hit in the United States.

But Mazda grossly underestimated the appeal of the simple, unique Miata. The carmaker set the manufacturer's suggested retail price at $13,800, which was disproportionately low for its perceived benefits, as shown in Exhibit 13-4. Mazda dealers were quick to recognize this imbalance, and added an extra $2,000 to $3,000 to the MSRP in the form of "market price adjustments."

Customers willingly paid the higher price and the dealers eagerly pocketed the surplus for themselves. This type of deep understanding of customer value (e.g., the well-researched value map above) can inform new product pricing and help companies avoid costly launch pricing errors.

THE DIFFERENT TYPES OF NEW PRODUCTS

New products can occupy a range of positions, from groundbreaking to innovative to "me-too" offerings, and each requires a different emphasis and nuanced approach to setting the release price (see box).

LAUNCH POSITION

A critical first step in pricing a new product properly is understanding the true level of its innovation. Every new product hits the market in one of three positions, as described below and shown in Exhibit 13-5.

1. **Revolutionary:** Products so new that they create their own markets pose the challenge of quantifying the benefits delivered to customers in the absence of anything similar. In addition, customers themselves can have trouble envisioning the benefits. The supplier must be creative in explaining the product's benefits to an untested market. Otherwise, the supplier may wind up setting a price that is lower than optimal, leaving little room for maneuvering and severely limiting an industry's potential profitability. Recent revolutionary products include the original Blackberry and the Amazon Kindle.

Exhibit 13-5 New Product Pricing Situations

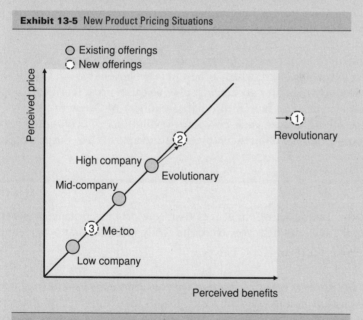

(Continued)

LAUNCH POSITION (*Continued*)

2. **Evolutionary:** These products include next versions, upgrades, and enhancements to existing products. If the new product provides too many new benefits at too low a price, a price war can ensue, so a firm grasp of potential competitor reactions is essential. (See Chapter 8, "Price Wars.") It is also critical to make sure that there is a large enough customer base at this new level of benefits. The Blackberry Curve and Tide Totalcare detergent (formulated to keep clothes looking like new) are examples of evolutionary products.

3. **Me-too:** These are products that bring a company in line with the rest of the market without exceeding customer benefits that are already available from other suppliers. Careful cost and competitor analysis is needed to avoid catastrophe here. Finding a profitable niche in an established market and setting a price that does not push down the existing VEL can be particularly challenging when introducing me-too products. Examples of me-too products abound in almost every product market.

Companies all too often overplay the benefits of a new product, touting it as revolutionary when, at best, it is evolutionary—and rarely acknowledging when they are actually playing catch-up. It is critical for companies to make an honest internal assessment of a new product's launch positioning since each position—revolutionary, evolutionary, or me-too—requires a different emphasis in and approach to the pricing strategy.

Given the unique set of challenges that new product pricing presents, seven general guidelines help you avoid the costly mistakes that occurred in the case studies above:

1. *Invest in customer research to quantify your product's benefit level.* Go out to customers and conduct focus groups and conjoint and discrete choice research to put a number around the perceived superiority (or inferiority) of your new product—and use that quantification to avoid under-pricing that can cause a destructive VEL shift. Also, use this research to understand how customers would trade up or down to your new product from adjacent products.

2. ***Run pilots with cooperative customers.*** Particularly when a product is genuinely revolutionary, give the product to a few friendly, collaborative customers to provide experience-based feedback on the real customer benefits that your new product creates—and what it is worth to them.

3. ***Delay setting/communicating price until the benefit level is clear.*** Most importantly for revolutionary products, reliable customer reference prices often do not exist. So customers will latch onto any early price that you communicate as the "fair and right price" for your great new product. Wait until the customer benefits are clear before creating that important early reference price.

4. ***Target launch price levels to "best fit" segments.*** Early adopters of new products are often less price sensitive and the first to perceive the full benefits of new products. So setting the early launch price based on the higher price receptivity of such best fit segments (as you gear up production) usually makes economic sense. Furthermore, high-benefit perception by early adopters often helps drive up benefit perception of middle and lower segments over time. The Apple iPhone originally sold out at a high launch price ($500) to early adopters. As additional supply became available and Apple wanted to sell beyond the early adopter segment, it lowered the price significantly.

5. ***Help potential customers by articulating/quantifying new benefit levels.*** The genuinely new benefits offered by a revolutionary or even evolutionary product can be difficult for customers to value if they have not yet experienced the benefit. Guide these customers on how to evaluate the difference between the new and current products. For instance, saying that a 15-watt compact fluorescent light bulb gives off the same light as a 60-watt incandescent bulb tells the customer that it uses less energy—but does not translate that increased efficiency into economic impact. Saying that for average daily use and average electric rates, a compact fluorescent saves the user $10 per year in energy costs makes the price/benefit trade-off much clearer to buyers.

6. ***Limit discretionary discounting early, particularly on high-benefit offerings.*** For customers, there is always some uncertainty about whether a higher-priced new product will really deliver on its claimed superior benefits. Excessive early discounting can severely undercut the desired high-price/high-benefit value perception of new products by implying that the manufacturer may not be confident in the claimed superior benefits. (The VEL decline dynamics that we discussed earlier are another serious consideration here.)

7. ***Do not forget to consider lifecycle pricing.*** If the newly launched product will coexist in the marketplace with prior generations of the product, you

should pay special attention to the full range of lifecycle pricing issues and guidance covered in detail in Chapter 10, "Lifecycle Pricing."

* * *

A whole host of forces—internal, customer-based, and competitor-based—conspire to cause business after business to misprice—usually underprice—innovative new products. And the more innovative and revolutionary the product, the greater the risk of severe under-pricing. Mistakes made in new product pricing can condemn even the most groundbreaking new product to a lifetime of mediocre performance and profitability.

During the excitement around new product introductions, a high degree of patience and discipline is required—patience in quantifying the benefits and creating a compelling story for customers and discipline in avoiding the traps of premature surrender to price levels lower than your new product deserves. Taking an informed, customer value–based approach and employing this higher level of pricing patience and discipline will help assure that your new products deliver all of their profit margin potential—both at launch and beyond.

SECTION FOUR: "RAZOR/RAZOR BLADES" OFFERINGS

"We give away the razor, and make it up on the blades" is a common pricing strategy discussed in conference rooms and boardrooms worldwide. It entails getting customers to buy an initial product or service, usually at a relatively low price, and then "locking" them into purchasing replacement components or services for the product at relatively higher prices.

Companies in a wide variety of industries—for example, medical devices, industrial equipment, consumer products—employ this strategy. Examples include glucose monitoring devices with corresponding test strips, cell phones with two-year contracts, even vehicles with after-sales parts and services.

Creating an ongoing revenue annuity from replacement components or services can be lucrative. This model can provide a significant ongoing revenue stream as long as the consumables are reasonably priced and there is no real competition from other providers. However, a razor/razor blades product offering requires a different type of pricing strategy—one that scientifically understands the product's elasticity over its lifetime as well as how much the profit will vary per user per year across segments.

Take an industrial equipment company as an example. It sold equipment and ongoing "consumables" and services to a variety of manufacturing companies in North America. For large customers, contracts were typically three to four years long and covered the initial purchase, the consumables, and service. The equipment usually had low and sometimes negative margins for the company. The main argument for this strategy was that these items were highly visible to the customer and that the company could use these products to "lock in" the customer to the consumables and service. It could then get an ongoing annuity from the other related products and services (the "blades"). This should have meant that customers became more profitable over the life of the contract because the "blades" were much higher margin than the initial equipment sales. But there was a problem (Exhibit 13-6). When analyzing the profitability over the life of large customer contracts, about 50 percent of the customers became more profitable over the life of the contract, while 50 percent stayed the same or became less profitable.

We conducted a detailed analysis of the potential contributing factors to profit performance over time and found some interesting conclusions on what differentiated profitable versus unprofitable accounts.

First, it was clear that some customers were inadvertently or intentionally not purchasing all of their "blades" from the company. Although the

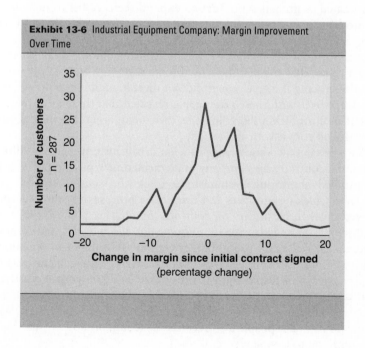

Exhibit 13-6 Industrial Equipment Company: Margin Improvement Over Time

contract pricing was based on the agreement that the customer would purchase all of their needs from the client, some were cherry-picking a few products and not using the company for all their consumables and services needs. They would have months of consistent purchases of some products then zero volume for that category for several months.

Second, product mix differed between customers based on their needs, equipment mix, and where they were in the life of their contract. This variance significantly affected the profitability of the products they purchased. The intensity of manufacturing equipment use strongly influenced whether the customer purchased a high- or low-margin mix of "blades." Customers with high volume use equipment tended to purchase the profitable OEM maintenance parts and services from the company, where the client typically had very high margins. The customer was able to substitute private label and competitive parts, and use third-party services with much lower margins, when they did not use equipment as intensely.

Lastly, small details on the pricing terms and conditions had substantial impact on whether the client had the flexibility to move pricing during the life of the contract. Customers usually negotiated and received net pricing on the 30 to 40 "core" high-volume consumables; they then purchased other products at a percentage discount off the company's standard catalog. These latter were the much more profitable "blades." On occasion, the most sophisticated customers would try to expand the core list to include 70 to 100 products and competitive pressures would force the client to oblige. However, a higher number of products on the core list did not necessarily doom the contract to lower profitability. Some more astute salespeople added a clause that enabled them to automatically restore the core products to catalog pricing if the customer did not meet a minimum volume requirement. Interviews with these salespeople revealed that these terms were easy to insert as customers used volume as their main argument for negotiating the expanded core list.

With this detailed knowledge of what drove customer profitability over the life of a contract, the company implemented new pricing policies. First, they installed monitoring mechanisms to track where customers were potentially cherry-picking products and executed a process to ensure salespeople followed up with customers on contract compliance. Second, they trained the sales force on how to evaluate equipment usage and educated them on its impact on the contract's profitability over time. The question of equipment intensity became one of the key evaluation criteria management used when evaluating very low priced contracts proposed by a salesperson. Lastly, they added standard contract language to ensure, where possible, that minimum volume requirements were added for any consumable product that was part of the core list. Salespeople also received coaching on how to sell this contract condition to customers.

As this case illustrates, several important considerations come into play when crafting a "razor/razor blades" pricing strategy.

MAXIMIZE LIFETIME VERSUS ONE-TIME PROFITABILITY

Most managers conduct pricing analysis where the unit of measurement is the profitability at the sale of a product. In a razor/razor blades environment, it is critical to look at lifetime profitability. In the industrial equipment case, there were good contracts that started out as low profit, and it would have been a mistake to walk away from the deals at the onset.

When there is variation in lifetime profitability, as the case above illustrates, understanding all of the potential drivers of the difference is crucial, as is analyzing which factor is causing the most variation in profit.

UNDERSTAND PRICE ELASTICITY BETWEEN THE RAZOR AND THE BLADES OVER TIME

Developing a pricing strategy that maximizes lifetime profitability depends on a detailed understanding of the price elasticity for the razor and blades over time. The tools and perspectives discussed in Chapters 4, "Customer Value" and 10, "Lifecycle Pricing" apply, but they need to account for both the initial purchase and the ongoing consumables. Issues such as where the most intellectual property is contained (razor or blades), where the greatest barriers to entry from competitors exist, and where customers perceive the greatest benefits will determine the balance between these elements and where the company captures profits.

ACTIVELY MANAGE THE VARIATION IN "BLADES" USAGE THROUGH PRICE STRUCTURE

For some products, like razor blades, if you buy the razor, you are pretty much tied to using the company's razor blades, whose design is protected under patent laws in most countries. For other products, like automobiles, there are many alternatives available for replacement parts.

When there is a wide variation in "blade" usage because of either usage patterns or the nonproprietary nature of the product, the price architecture covered in Chapter 11, "Pricing Architecture" becomes critical. Where possible, companies need to provide incentives to encourage the use of the company's blades and reward the most profitable "super users." It may also structure its warranty to necessitate the use of its "blades."

For example, a medical testing company sold diagnostic equipment (the razor) and testing reagents (the blades). Some of the reagents were proprietary to the company, some commodities. A third group of reagents was somewhere in between. Some customers would not go with another brand because of fear of inconsistency of the diagnostic results. Other customers had sophisticated purchasing departments that were able to convince the lab technicians to switch to alternative reagents across a greater breadth of tests. Unlike the industrial distributor who was able to identify who would be more or less profitable over time due to equipment age, there was no easy way to identify which customers would fit into which category. The only way to protect the profitability over time was to build in contract minimums for the reagents and provide a scaled rebate structure that rewarded higher levels of reagent usage.

KNOW WHEN NOT TO USE A "RAZOR/RAZOR BLADES" STRATEGY

It is tempting to create an ongoing revenue stream from high margin "blades," but this is not always the best strategy. First, customers may value the flexibility of not being tied into proprietary "blades." For example, some consumer electronics products have been successful at gaining market share by having products that run off standard size batteries instead of expensive proprietary batteries. Second, some customers like to have certainty around the ongoing cost of using a product and like to buy an integrated bundle of products, consumables, and service. Aircraft engine manufacturers pricing their engines based on per hour of uptime as opposed to unbundling all of the components (the engine, maintenance parts and service) is a great example.

* * *

Razor/razor blades offerings require some special pricing considerations to ensure that companies extract the full value. Analysis must consider the lifetime profitability of the offering and details of elasticity between the up-front and ongoing products and services. Price structure can also be used to encourage the most profitable customer behavior. Lastly, a razor/razor blades strategy does not make sense in all situations, especially when customers highly value a simple and certain product offering.

SECTION FIVE: SOLUTIONS

In the modern marketplace, you cannot move without bumping into a solution. Increasingly popular, they are touted in almost every business, whether IT, transportation, logistics, energy, or home dining. Even a well-known company in the elevator business described themselves as a "vertical transportation solutions provider." But saying something is a solution does not make it one—nor does it mean the offering has the benefits or potential of a real solution.

What is the allure of solutions? First, of course, is their marketing message. Solutions appeal to a customer's desire to have a problem solved—whether it is about data storage or what to eat tonight—and real ones can be very effective. Second, suppliers believe that delivering a solution forms a closer business relationship with customers and produces increased sales and higher margins.

WHAT IS A SOLUTION?

A company provides a solution when it takes responsibility for a specific need that is unique to a customer. It provides an integrated, customized package of discrete components, such as hardware, software, and services, which have been engineered or tailored to work better together than separately. The solution must also have benefits that can be discreetly quantified and apportioned between the solution provider and the customer. This makes accountability easier, which is a key element of working together with a solutions provider. When a business turns to a solutions provider to meet a specific need, that provider is clearly accountable for making the solution work—and is responsible if it does not. As a result, a solutions provider is held to a higher standard than other suppliers, many of whom do not have to meet such transparent measures.

A leading player in the automotive coatings industry, including paints, laminates, and other spray-on applications, successfully built a solutions business. It developed a process that actually ran the coating operation (providing employees, equipment, and supplies) and optimized the application of different colors at varying thicknesses by vertically integrating into original car manufacturers' plants; this worked even in build-to-order systems. As carmakers began using it to run coatings operations, the coatings company was able to charge by the car, rather than by liters of paint used. Working at a number of plants over several years, the company reduced the coating consumption per car by more than 20 percent. The key to the company's profitability was crafting a pricing strategy that allowed the company to keep a fair share of these savings for itself. As the business model evolved, the company eventually captured more than 60 percent of the global market share for this class of coatings solutions business.

A global lubricants producer took a different tack. Faced with tough competition in its traditional lubricants and additives businesses, the company tried to expand its value proposition by selling solutions. It acquired a series of businesses—primarily service businesses specializing in areas like environmental auditing and technical testing—to complement its robust product line. After spending more than $100 million, the company went to its largest customers with its new solution offer: a full suite of services that covered lubrication needs from application to disposal.

Unfortunately, the offer was not a truly integrated solution and was easily unbundled by customers choosing separate suppliers for each component. Faced with the possibility of losing high-volume customers, the company acquiesced. Rather than pricing to capture the value provided, the company agreed to throw in its newly acquired services for free.

The value destruction was enormous. With a core business with a return on sales (ROS) of about 5 percent, it added acquisitions with ROS's of about 15 percent. In the end the company's ROS fell below the original five percent. The company may have been better off keeping the service businesses separate but part of a bundled offering, rather than trying to include them into a solution. To succeed with a solution, the company may have needed a bolder move—for example, take over an entire process from its customers—and then stand firm under pressure to unbundle the offer. A key question, though, is whether its largest customers wanted such a solution.

It is rare to find a company that delivers a true solution. Rarer still is the solutions provider that makes money off its efforts. The missing link is often an appropriate pricing strategy. The price must accurately reflect the benefits delivered by the package, which requires that a company understand first whether it is offering a solution. As these cases illustrate, a true solution can only succeed if the supplier clearly understands how the new offer creates benefits and how that affects its role in the value chain. Once a company is clear on this role, it must price appropriately and with conviction in order to capture the value of its solution.

SOLUTIONS PRICING

A solutions provider can discuss pricing with customers in a way fundamentally different from other suppliers. Component specialists, bundlers, and integrators, who are discussed in Chapter 11, "Pricing Architecture," price relative to alternatives. However, a true solutions provider is better positioned to set price to capture a high share of the customer-specific economic value it creates.

Price to Economic, Not Perceived Value   Solutions benefits are much greater than the sum of the component parts and vary greatly from one customer to the next. A solutions provider must have an intimate, ongoing understanding of customers' economics and the benefits delivered to them, a skill that may be new and unfamiliar for traditional suppliers. One storage network provider who learned to do this offered customer-specific solutions that combined core and periphery hardware, operating and application software, and professional design services. Leveraging proprietary components, including servers, software, and distinctive engineering capability, the supplier demonstrated that the benefits of the total solution were at least twice as great as the nearest competitor's, allowing the supplier to stand firm on a combined system price that was 30 to 50 percent higher.

Because solutions are tailored to individual customers, the benefits and price often vary widely. For the storage network provider described earlier, much of the core platform of its offering to customers was the same, but the benefits of a fully functional storage network are much greater for one customer than another. For instance, an online retailer or a bank handling real-time automated teller machines (ATMs) or credit card transactions have a critical need for reliable, real-time data storage, while the need is less pressing, for instance, for a hospital or a government agency that must process large volumes of data but can do it during off-peak hours. Pursuing identical pricing strategies in such different worlds of benefit delivery would probably leave significant money on the table.

What portion of the incremental economic value created by a solution can you actually capture in price? Our rule of thumb is that you should communicate 100 percent of the value that you create, target capturing 50 percent of that value, and accept no less than 30 percent. A greater portion can be captured when the benefits are easily quantified, where a history exists and, ideally, third-party validation of the benefits is available, and where the supplier guarantees the delivery of the benefits.

Never Unbundle a Solution   A solution's price cannot be calculated simply by summing the pieces. In the same vein, communications with customers regarding the price cannot be linked to individual components. Since solutions tend to be expensive and attract attention from top management, suppliers must carefully develop a clear message that continuously focuses on total benefits delivered and discourages discussions on component-to-component benefits. Suppliers can accomplish this by simply refusing to offer a price for the individual component parts of a solution and by reminding the customer that service and knowledge tie the components together. Another way is to provide options (e.g., a good/better/best solution), so the customer feels that they have choices, but is still not able to negotiate individual pieces.

Blastomatic, a company that sold explosive detonators through distributors, offered the distributors a comprehensive solution—including highly advanced products, technical training for their salespeople, end-customer product consulting advice, and inventory management. Historically, nothing in its pricing structure tied distributors to selling the company's product, even though they received all these services. This had not been a problem in the past because few competitive alternatives existed with as advanced technology and knowledge.

As the competitive situation changed, however, distributors began to carry their own private label detonator products after receiving the company's training. They would use Blastomatics' brand name and technical support to get the initial sale, then convince their customers to switch to their own private label brand once they earned the customer's trust. Blastomatic responded to this issue by changing their pricing structure to include a share requirement on the part of distributors. The only way they could get the technical service, training, and end-customer support was if they sold the whole package of Blastomatics' products and services to the end-customers. As a result of these changes, their falling market share first stabilized and then increased, and overall price levels went up.

Build Flexibility into Price Structure to Account for Implementation Cost

Risk   A solutions provider needs to configure the price of the solution appropriately. All too often, it errs when configuring price by simply forgetting portions of the offering or miscalculating the business risk it assumes when taking on implementation responsibility. Section One, "Custom-Configured Products," of Chapter 12 goes into more detail. Second, it should carefully handle the increased complexity of the pocket price/margin waterfall. Because of the complexity of a solution, the waterfall must take into account multiple pricing elements that will vary over time—for instance, updated software, replacements, expansions, or maintenance services. When crafting the pocket price/margin waterfall, companies should also take care not to compromise future revenue streams. Similarly, because solutions are commonly delivered and implemented over longer periods of time, it is critical that companies proactively shape the evolution of ongoing revenue following the sale.

And finally, a solutions provider must also manage the profitability of the solution following the sale. As the pocket margin waterfall in Exhibit 13-7 shows, there will be many customer-specific costs that can quickly escalate out of control if not actively managed, resulting in a pocket margin much lower than originally anticipated. For example, a pricing model must allow payments for customer requested moves, adds, or changes (MACs) that would otherwise simply be absorbed by the supplier.

* * *

Exhibit 13-7 Solution Economics After the Sale

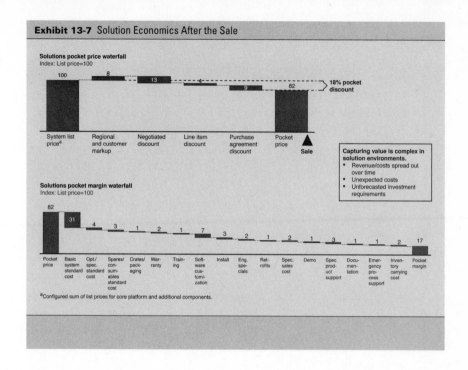

Solutions offer great potential to those few who can truly offer them—and price them successfully. Doing so requires both discipline and flexibility—the discipline to never unbundle the components and the flexibility to consider all the possible cost risks and options. Companies must also ensure that they have a solution that their customers want—and one that delivers the valuable benefits that they can then capture with their pricing strategy.

CHAPTER 14

Software and Information Products

S oftware and information products abound today. Examples of software products include "shrink wrap" consumer-oriented applications (e.g., tax software or video games), computer operating systems, software embedded in physical devices (e.g., automotive engine control software), enterprise resource planning (ERP) platforms, and hosted applications (e.g., sold in the form of SaaS—software as a service). The world of information products is even broader, including digital content like music and video, streaming media on the Internet, electronic publications (e.g., books, magazines, newspapers), and data and research reports (e.g., product usage or financial market analysis).

These products differ from physical ones in ways that create unique pricing issues and opportunities and therefore require special application of the three levels of pricing excellence plus pricing infrastructure. In this chapter, we explore the basic characteristics that make software and information products unique and then show how to translate these into pricing opportunities.

UNIQUE CHARACTERISTICS THAT IMPACT PRICING

Software and information products have five key characteristics that make their pricing issues and opportunities distinctive:

1. *Marginal production costs at or near zero, with no meaningful capacity constraints.* With software and information products, the cost to produce one more unit (the marginal production cost) is so small as to be almost immaterial; moreover, practically no limit exists as to the number of copies that can be made after the software or information

product's creation.[1] Burning one more CD or DVD is cheap (ask any digital content pirate). As a result, gross product margins can be well over 90 percent; at the same time, companies may be prone to discount because the perceived margin "headroom" is so large. It is important to remember, however, that the marginal cost to *sell* one more unit may *not* be negligible due to significant direct per unit selling costs (e.g., sales commissions, packaging, documentation, account registration).

2. *High upfront costs.* Unlike marginal production costs, the upfront costs to develop, market, sell, distribute, and support software and information products are relatively high. This combination of high upfront costs and low marginal costs simultaneously puts companies under extreme pressure to capture high volume and share quickly and produces strong downward price pressure—usually much greater than that seen with physical products.

3. *Greater malleability.* Malleability makes it relatively easy to create different configurations with distinct customer benefits and pricing architectures for software and information products—for example, the "same" digital audio song can be sold at different quality levels—MP3, CD, or Super Audio CD (SACD). It can take multiple forms: altering core product benefits (e.g., quality or features); or bundling/unbundling elements of the offering (e.g., selling a software suite vs. individual applications). More traditional means of differentiating products also apply (e.g., packaging).

4. *Potential for high switching costs.* Users who have invested time and energy installing, configuring, and learning how to use a software or information product are often unwilling to switch to an alternative or newer version of the product because they want to avoid further investment. Software and information products can be even "stickier" when users create other content that relies on the product in a proprietary way (e.g., spreadsheets that only one application can read) or when the product is heavily integrated into a company's business system (e.g., an ERP software platform with many third-party applications that rely on it). Online information-sharing communities that allow dues-paying users to upload content and view other members' content illustrate another form of switching costs (e.g., online dating services where switching costs arise from potentially having to re-create one's profile and losing connectivity with other users in the community). In such cases, convincing a potential customer to switch to a new offering

---

[1]Also, in contrast to most physical goods, there is usually little or no cost associated with scrapping unsold inventory.

can be challenging.[2] High switching costs can create competitive pressure to grab market share at any cost, and strong incentives to develop offerings that increase customer stickiness.

5. *Potential for winner-take-all scenarios.* One of the more intriguing aspects of software and information products is how strong positive network effects derived from market standards[3] can promote winner-take-all scenarios. Strong incentives exist for competing vendors to fight hard to be the winner whose standard prevails; this competition can create strong downward price pressure. The stakes associated with losing the battle to become a market standard can be quite high—in fact, all or nothing (e.g., Betamax lost to VHS in the format battle for videocassettes in the late 1970s, and HD DVD recently lost to the Blu-Ray format for high-definition optical discs in the early 2000s). In contrast, some companies have created tremendous value by establishing a strong standard in their market (e.g., Microsoft with MS DOS and Windows). Others have also created value, but in a more indirect way. For example, Adobe established the .pdf portable document format standard by giving away the software application that enables people to *read* .pdf files (Reader) and selling the Acrobat software that allows people to *author and modify* .pdf files.[4]

Although this chapter focuses on software and information products, other products share some or all of the characteristics outlined above and can benefit from the recommendations herein. In many cases, the concepts outlined below also apply to these products. Hard-copy textbooks are one example—they have high upfront development and distribution costs, low marginal production costs, and limited capacity constraints on production.

---

[2]The corollary to this is that it may easier to capture more surplus from customers over time because they have fewer readily available alternatives.

[3]The classic example of a positive network effect is the fax machine, which has no value if there is only one user, but has increasing value with each additional user as the "network" grows. Negative network effects are also possible, where additional users diminish a product's value (e.g., a financial service firm's proprietary trading model that capitalizes on market inefficiencies—the more users, the fewer market inefficiencies and the less value in the product). Standards can underlie a positive network effect: imagine a world with hundreds of proprietary standards for electronic documents; exchanging content and collaborating would be almost impossible. Then imagine the benefits that a broad user base would receive from having a common standard that allowed them to work together seamlessly.

[4]Laurie J. Flynn: "Adobe Tries to Create Image of a Moneymaker," *New York Times*, July 7, 2003.

Their malleability takes several forms (e.g., publishing full or abridged texts, selling hardbound and paperback formats, releasing revised versions over time). Switching costs and network effects can be quite significant (especially if a text is the standard reference in a field). Cable network programming is another example. It has significant upfront development costs, low marginal costs (easily rebroadcast), high malleability (e.g., shown with or without commercials, during primetime or late night), large network effects (e.g., the community that comes from sharing laughs with others who saw a Seinfeld episode), and some degree of winner-take-all potential (e.g., for a show that dominates a primetime slot).

EXPLORING THE ELEMENTS OF PRICING

Pricing is the single biggest profit lever for software and information products. The 1 percent improvement analysis in Chapter 1, "Introduction," holds for software and information companies (although low variable costs and high fixed costs means that increasing unit volume tends to have a greater impact than for most businesses).[5] Getting the pricing right has substantial upside potential—we have seen many examples of 10-plus percentage points of incremental ROS on the addressable revenue base for software businesses. Unfortunately, many companies do not consider their full range of choices prior to making pricing decisions for such products.

To help make the following discussion concrete, we illustrate the core ideas primarily with software examples, although the underlying principles apply to information products as well. Let us now consider them in the context of the core elements of *the price advantage* as outlined in Chapter 2, "Components of Pricing Excellence."

MARKET STRATEGY—CAPTURING VALUE TODAY VERSUS CREATING VALUE TOMORROW

Software and information products' unique structural characteristics (e.g., low marginal costs, high fixed costs, lack of capacity constraints) make it difficult to apply the classic microeconomic pricing theory of supply and demand. Instead, market and internal forces often make it tempting for companies to accept virtually any price for their products—potentially triggering price wars. We see examples of extreme discounting frequently. Price-advantaged companies, however, deliberately manage the Market Strategy level to avoid price wars by establishing and maintaining good reference price points in the market, emphasizing benefits over price, and carefully managing lifecycle pricing. Chapters 5, "Market Strategy," 8, "Price Wars," and 10, "Lifecycle Pricing," provide more information on these topics.

In most cases, extreme discounting of software and information products is completely unwarranted and value destroying. However, in certain special situations the unique characteristics of these products create the potential for companies to pursue two very different strategies, with a focus on either "capturing value today" or "creating value tomorrow." In the first, they capture more value from their products over the near-term by using the same methods that companies with physical products do: selling each unit at a higher price (while holding volume steady) or selling more units (while holding price steady). In the second strategy—creating value tomorrow—the unique characteristics of software introduce a twist not often seen with physical products. Companies can focus first on creating a standard that will radically change a product's market position, with the hope of subsequently capturing value over the long term. For example, an organization might blanket the market with free or low-priced product to spur demand, make the product the de facto standard, and then subsequently leverage that position by selling products tied to the standard.

It is not easy to determine which of these strategies a business should pursue at a given time. While "creating value tomorrow" may look attractive, companies must consider its risks—it may require significant upfront investment and ultimately leave the business "owning" a dominant market standard, but with no ability to capture value either directly or indirectly. Organizations should ensure that the following conditions are in place; otherwise, "capturing value today" may be the better strategy:

- The product has widespread relevance and the potential for strong positive network effects (otherwise a meaningful standard is unlikely to emerge, either because there are too few users or the standard has no value to users).
- There are no strongly entrenched competitive alternatives with high switching costs already in the market.
- There is a high likelihood that the company can capture substantial value from the standard over time.
- Once the new standard is created, there should be relatively high switching costs that "lock in" customers.

Adobe successfully pursued the "creating value tomorrow" strategy with the .pdf portable document format and its free Reader software (mentioned earlier).[5] Online newspapers are an information product example; online newspapers allow users to view current stories and editorial content for

---

[5]Laurie J. Flynn: "Adobe Tries to Create Image of a Moneymaker," *New York Times*, July 7, 2003.

free, which builds up a loyal reader base, but then charge for access to archived content.

In the rest of this chapter we focus on situations where the explicit goal is "capturing value today"—either because this is the preferred business strategy or because the business has already taken the first step in "creating value tomorrow" by establishing a standard and is now intent on capitalizing on it.

CUSTOMER VALUE—EXPLOITING MALLEABILITY

Software's inherent malleability provides incredible degrees of freedom and flexibility around product architectures, packaging options, and pricing architectures, which companies can exploit as they move toward *the price advantage*. Together, these factors open up unparalleled opportunities at the Customer Value level—opportunities that are rarely leveraged to their full extent.

We will explore malleability across the two dimensions of Customer Value: (1) perceived benefits (i.e., *flexing product architecture*—tailoring product offerings to increase perceived customer benefits in specific segments), and (2) perceived price (i.e., *aligning pricing architecture*—using smart licensing models to win and drive favorable price perceptions).

Because software is so malleable, best practice software pricing efforts frequently involve broader topics like product packaging, product architecture, and pricing strategy topics (e.g., how can the company capture the most value from the product's intellectual property over time). Software also makes it easier to maximize perceived customer benefits and value by considering product and pricing architectures jointly and early. Product and pricing architecture questions should be tackled well before products are launched—ideally during product development. The company can then optimize software design and packaging and align the product architecture with the most appropriate licensing model (e.g., usage-based versus flat fee; bundled or unbundled).

Flexing Product Architecture—Tailoring Product Offerings to Increase Perceived Customer Benefits in Specific Segments Software businesses need to understand the perceived value drivers (benefits and price architectures) of customer segments (see Section One, "Price Segmentation," in Chapter 13, "Tailored Value")—and how malleability can help them enhance their offerings to their current segments or target additional segments. Software's malleability allows companies to easily, quickly, and cost-effectively create product architectures and licensing schemes that match the needs of the various segments. Companies do this in many ways, including:

Exhibit 14-1 Value Capture Through Malleability

	Description	Examples
Versioning	• Create different product/service versions (at small incremental cost) to meet specific customer or segment needs	• Silver/gold/platinum versions of software • Customized content delivery
Bundling/ unbundling	• Aggregate/disaggregate products and services to build value-driven solutions	• Application suites • Subscription software service models
Delivery mechanisms	• Identify differentiated approaches to deliver products/services to customer segments	• Hosted applications • Software embedded in devices
Platforming	• Establish platform as market standard through low pricing and generate value through application sales or customization	• Commercial Linux products • ERP platforms • e-commerce infrastructure service platforms

versioning,[6] where different product versions have different benefit levels (e.g., digital stock photos available at different resolutions); *bundling/ unbundling,* where stand-alone products are aggregated and sold as a single product (bundling), or a single product is disaggregated into components that are sold separately (unbundling); and *platforming,* where a free or low-price product is used to create a basis on which additional modules are sold separately to capture value from specific segments. Exhibit 14-1 summarizes these and a few other options.

As a simplified example, consider a software product that has 10 discrete functions (or modules). The vendor can create a low-cost "base" version with two of the functions, to drive penetration, then upsell the other eight functions as separate, optional modules. Vendors can also release multiple products with different function combinations that appeal to various customer segments; this allows them to use differential pricing to maximize current value. A significant difference between physical products and software in this case is that these differentiated products can be offered with low incremental production costs—as long as the software product architecture is designed to allow this. The cost per product variant for software can thus be significantly lower than that for a physical product.

Businesses selling bundled products (e.g., software suites) should periodically ask themselves if unbundling features and functionality might better

---

[6]C. Shapiro, H. R. Varian: "Versioning: The Smart Way to Sell Information," *Harvard Business Review,* Nov./Dec., 1998, 106–114.

address customer segment needs or be a better way to communicate or capture more value (e.g., sell more units at higher average prices). Businesses should conduct market research to understand the likely price/volume trade-offs of such moves. In other cases, bundling can simplify the buying decision and drive additional volume (e.g., charging $700 for a single query of proprietary data versus $5,000 for the entire database—many users might be compelled to buy the entire database). Finally, in some cases offering *both* bundles and components can be attractive (e.g., selling a business productivity suite at a discount relative to à la carte–priced word processing and spreadsheet applications).

In the following unbundling example, an established ERP company found that adopting new product and pricing architectures around licensing allowed it to not only capture more value from current markets but also penetrate new ones. It did this by better understanding customer perceptions of its current product as well as the needs of the segments it wanted to serve. The business traditionally sold its product on a licensed basis that included all features for a flat fee. The company soon realized that most customers placed low value on much of the base ERP functionality; however, certain customer segments placed relatively high value on some of the newer, more advanced functionality modules.

The business then split its advanced functionality modules out from the core ERP package. It sold the core package at a low price to drive adoption and priced the advanced modules to capture value from those segments that valued them (Exhibit 14-2). These moves enabled the company to compete at lower prices in the base ERP market and capture more value for proprietary functionality in specific industries.

The changes helped the company create value for tomorrow as well as today. It targeted product development to allow continual, independent replacement of modules that could be sold to individual segments, rather than all-or-nothing upgrades. By dropping the absolute price level of the base ERP package, it penetrated the small and medium enterprise market and increased its total market for future products. What began as a pricing exercise for software products became a fundamental redefinition of its business strategy and generated a 20 percent increase in revenue.

Aligning Pricing Architecture—Using Smart Licensing Models to Win   Although many different pricing models are possible for software, most are some form of licensing; the primary exception is "shrink-wrapped" software that companies sell to consumers in a way similar to other packaged goods. The rest of this section explores licensing, which is flexible and offers a rich palette of options for value capture if companies can manage it well.

Exhibit 14-2 ERP Company: Impact of Unbundling Software Suites

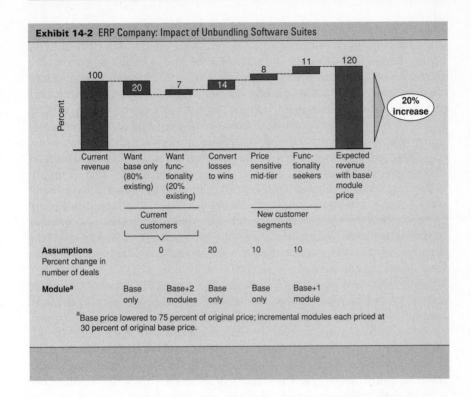

^aBase price lowered to 75 percent of original price; incremental modules each priced at 30 percent of original base price.

Software licenses range from named-user licenses sold to professionals (one per user), to concurrent licenses shared among a group of professionals (giving everyone access, but limiting the maximum number of simultaneous users), to enterprise ERP software sold for an upfront, one-time license fee, with separate ongoing maintenance/support charges (and possible upgrade fees to migrate to newer versions). More recently, alternative licensing schemes have emerged, including subscription models like Software as a Service (SaaS), which bundles product usage rights, maintenance, and upgrades into a monthly service fee; no upfront fee is charged and usage rights extend for as long as one pays for the service.

When choosing a licensing approach, companies need to align it with the drivers of customers' perceived benefits while keeping it relatively simple to communicate and administer. For example, B2B software applications often price based on the number of users (e.g., one license fee is incurred per user); this is appropriate for many applications where benefits scale, or ramp up, based on the number of people using the products (e.g., engineering design software). However, in other situations, the right approach may be different.

The inherent benefits of an enterprise human resource (HR) administration software package might scale more closely with the number of employees versus the number of users, and so should be priced based on the number of employees in the company. Companies make such pricing architecture choices by assessing customer needs, benefits, and existing market precedents at a segment level, estimating the impact on sales and profit, and by striking a balance between high potential but highly tailored and complex ones and others that are more streamlined, but probably are less optimal ones.

Whatever licensing model the company selects, it is as important to choose the right pricing variable (e.g., per user or per server CPU). A simplified example shows how using the wrong one destroys value. Two companies, A and B, sell competing software applications that run on third-party servers but use different pricing variables. Company A uses the *total number* of servers deployed as the basis for its software pricing (e.g., it charges a fixed price for each server on which the software is installed). Company B uses the *total operating capacity* of the servers as its licensing basis (e.g., it charges a fixed-price based on the total number of processors in the servers—many servers are "multicore" and have more than one processor—rather than the number of servers). Customer interviews and analyses showed their perceived and actual value drivers were more aligned with B's capacity-based approach than with A's. Under these conditions, the prices proposed by A and B would scale similarly for single-core servers, though in absolute terms its prices were somewhat higher in these situations. But in other situations with multicore servers, A's pricing will be lower than B's and, all other things being equal, A will win the deal. However, because customers are more aligned with B's model, A will win precisely in those situations where it could capture much more value by pricing in accordance with the way customers (and in this case competitors) perceive benefits.

Being open to alternative types of software licensing structures can help companies address business issues with customers (e.g., ease of doing business, alignment with buyer business model). One supplier of design and engineering software (Exhibit 14-3) changed from a traditional perpetual license to an annual subscription model to encourage customers to upgrade software more frequently and to help them spread their expenses across cost centers. Revenue went up dramatically and was more consistent over time (i.e., driven more by a steady stream of users paying on a monthly basis than a few large up-front license deals).

Yet another company used a radical change in the way it structured license upgrades to smooth and grow its revenue flow. Customers were not upgrading to new software versions regularly, the cost of supporting multiple versions was rising, and upgrade revenues were hard to predict. The business adopted a new approach, launching a software maintenance

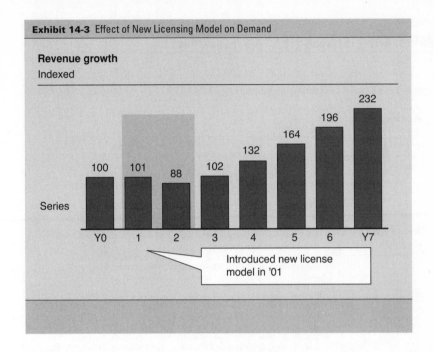

Exhibit 14-3 Effect of New Licensing Model on Demand

offering that replaced all prior upgrade models. Customers who purchased this service paid a percentage of license revenues each quarter to receive upgrades. The software company collected recurring fees on a steadier, more predictable basis; not only that, the overall demand for the software maintenance service was higher than for periodic upgrades as it better fit many customers' needs.

SOFTWARE LICENSING BASICS

Best practice software license models should be developed with a few critical goals in mind (Exhibit 14-4). Specifically, they should align the software product value proposition with customer segment needs; provide great power to price discriminate and capture fair value within and across segments; and establish more mutually beneficial operating relationships with customers.

(Continued)

SOFTWARE LICENSING BASICS (*Continued*)

Exhibit 14-4 Goals for Software Licensing

Software licensing objective	Description
Align offering to customer's business requirements	• Easy to buy software—vendor offerings match customer functionality, service and financing requirements • Alignment with customer business requirements means shorter sales cycles for vendor, less senior management involvement in buying • Software licensing enables customers to buy functionality they require in a manner consistent with their budgeting process
Structure pricing to capture fair value	• Software license fees align with software value • Software licensing enables vendor and customer to realize value from deployment, usage, and scale • Appropriately sharing value gives customers revenue/profit upside for deployment and vendors money to fund continued innovation
Establish mutually beneficial operating relationship	• License is easy to manage—payment terms and administrative requirements structured for win-win scenarios for vendor and customer • Effective operating relationships reduces ongoing cost of software for customer and cost of support and administration for vendor • Licensing addresses customer need for low risk and low overhead, and vendor need for predictable revenue and compliant use of product

To ensure that software licenses achieve these goals, they are usually structured around six basic dimensions:

1. *License scope*—details the product features and services (e.g., technical support) that the license grants to a specified set of users.
2. *License terms*—addresses questions of fair usage, license duration, transferability, and so forth.
3. *Scaling of license fees*—covers situations in which the license fee depends on well-defined parameters that scale with customer value (e.g., telephony software for a small business that scales with the number of phone desk sets operated by the business).
4. *Packaging/segment approach*—defines the levels of functionality and corresponding price points as well as segment-specific pricing that might exist (e.g., discounts for academic institutions).

5. *Financial structure*—specifies payment terms, financing options (which might be important in the case of large upfront perpetual license fees), and risk/reward sharing arrangements (as applicable).
6. *Compliance mechanisms*—clarifies the processes and mechanisms that might be used to ensure agreed-upon usage and accurate determination of license fees (e.g., audit rights to verify proper number of users).

TRANSACTIONS—PRESERVING VALUE

Software products have many of the same transaction pricing issues and opportunities as physical products—and are amenable to many of the same improvement techniques. However, relative to physical products, their low marginal production costs can create much greater pressure (even a willingness to discount significantly) in the heat of a competitive customer negotiation. Over time, customers become accustomed to and, indeed, expect, steep discounting from list price levels. Exhibit 14-5 shows how these levels can play out for a software company where each dot represents a deal (note that the horizontal axis is a logarithmic scale). This wide discounting range (from 0 percent to 80 percent) is indicative of the poor transaction pricing capabilities many software companies have.

The end of quarter "hockey stick" that many software and technology companies face is another large complication—one that is extremely difficult to address. It is not uncommon for companies to book half or more of quarterly sales during the last few weeks of each quarter. Savvy buyers exploit the pressure on salespeople to make their quarterly quotas; they play hardball and close deals only at the 11th hour, and at substantially discounted prices. Exhibit 14-6 shows a typical example. Although the end-of-quarter "hockey stick" can affect many other types of businesses, software companies selling perpetual licenses with a large upfront fee are especially vulnerable to this type of manipulation because of the major impact that the delay of a large deal would have on sales compensation or reported quarterly financial results. To deal with this dilemma, some software companies have migrated from perpetual license models to subscription ones where the impact on the current quarter of closing a deal one or two weeks into the next quarter is significantly lessened. This approach reduces internal perceived risk as well as the incentives to discount significantly.

Exhibit 14-5 Effect of Excessive Discounting Pressure

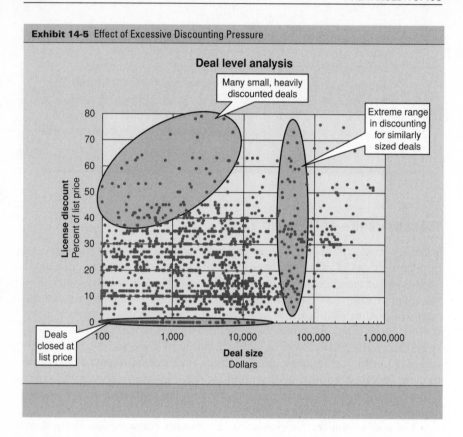

Companies must also be wary of assuming that marginal costs are effectively zero. Although the cost to produce one more unit may be low, the marginal selling and delivery costs may not be (e.g., sales commissions). Pocket price/margin waterfalls for hybrid deals with a mix of hardware, software, maintenance services, and professional services look remarkably similar to those for typical physical products (Exhibit 14-7). In these cases, many of the strategies and tactics discussed in Chapter 3, "Transactions." would apply. In addition, a few types of leakage are unique to software. One is license management compliance (e.g., ensuring that actual users are covered by the license agreement and that no cheating is going on, whether intentionally or not); a second and related source involves entitlement (e.g., ensuring customers who get upgrades and technical support are actually eligible under their license and support agreement).

Discounting software is an area that possesses many pitfalls—and one where companies must therefore be extremely careful. In deals with both

Exhibit 14-6 Value Destruction Based on End-of-Quarter Discounting

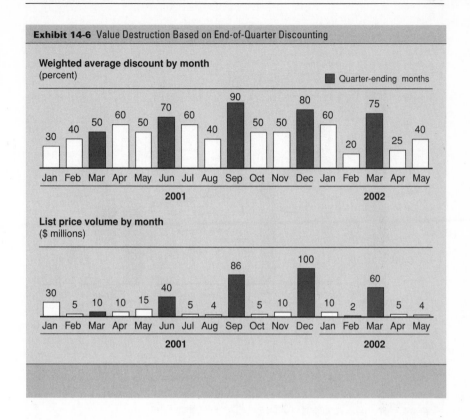

hardware and software, sellers may be more inclined to discount software than hardware—a move companies must carefully monitor. Both buyers and sellers may perceive that the price of software has more room to move than that of hardware. Many reasons exist for this belief (e.g., the more tangible nature of physical products, software's low marginal costs, or the greater familiarity both buyers and sellers may have with physical goods). Companies should be on the alert for disproportionate discounting of the software. By comparing any discounts with the average discount for the same software sold on a stand-alone basis, the business can avoid a situation where it gives too much away. Exhibit 14-8 shows an example where the average software discount sold on a stand-alone basis was discounted 25 percentage points less than the same software sold with hardware. Much of the sales force was familiar with the hardware, but had a much harder time conveying the value of the software and reconciling what seemed to be a high price from a "cost plus margin" perspective. As a result, they often discounted the software in mixed deals. In contrast, software-only sales were mostly driven by more software-savvy sellers with better results.

Exhibit 14-7 Drivers of Above-Zero Marginal Costs

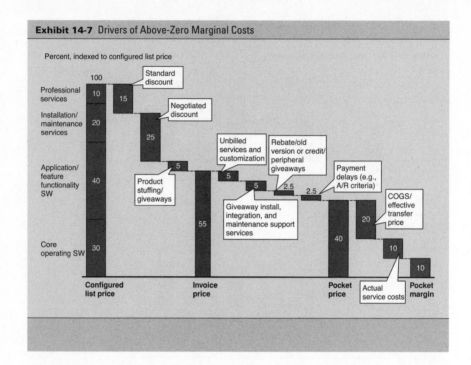

Exhibit 14-8 Over-Discounting of Software in Combined Hardware/Software Sales

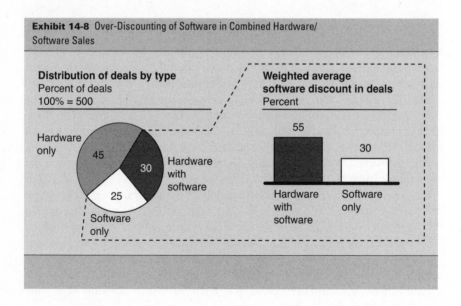

Companies should also avoid discounting software maintenance at the time of license sale (or at license renewal) because maintenance provides a steady, recurring revenue stream long after the initial license sale. Discounting maintenance at the initial license sale is particularly bad as it may set a "low price" expectation for the future. Companies also need to stick to their target price points for maintenance at renewal. One way to do this is to establish tight discount policies and practices for software maintenance, with incentives to discourage heavy discounting of any recurring revenue (e.g., sales commission "carve outs" where a salesperson is penalized for discounting maintenance outside prescribed guidelines).

Finally, large customers will often attempt to negotiate enterprise-wide or "all you can eat" deals that bear little or no resemblance to "list" pricing. For example, instead of paying for and administering named-user licenses for all of its employees for all products they are using, a large company might try to pay a single, heavily discounted fixed fee that is independent of the number of its employees and of the products they are using. Software companies need to limit exceptions and ensure, whenever possible, that any granted ones allow the software company to capture fair value. Software's malleability can work against you in the sense that it makes it easy to offer licensing variations that are not in the best interests of the business. For this reason, it is imperative that a central approval process with rigorous guidelines exists for all Enterprise License Agreements (ELAs) and other nonstandard deals.

PRICING INFRASTRUCTURE—RECOGNIZING SOFTWARE AND INFORMATION PRODUCTS ARE DIFFERENT

The infrastructure needed to support pricing excellence for software and information products is similar to that for other products and services, with a few noteworthy exceptions. First, physical products generally do not have compliance and entitlement issues that require license management tools and capabilities.

Second, and more importantly, software applications, more so than most physical products, are constantly under development. A natural problem is when and how to release an updated version or new software module to the market. Software companies must address some tough strategic and tactical pricing issues. Resolving these issues requires an essential price-related decision process that differs from those in most physical product companies. For example, at what point should the next release occur? If releases are too frequent, customers may be upset and have a hard time paying for what they may perceive as minor improvements. If releases are too infrequent, customers may perceive that the offering is less attractive than those of competitors or that the company is not keeping up with competition. Good software pricing functions are equipped to work with the product management function to tackle these questions.

* * *

Software and information products offer a unique set of issues and opportunities for pricers that requires thinking in new ways about strategies. Companies can create value tomorrow as well as capture it today (by leveraging standards and network effects), exploit the inherent malleability of these products (more effectively differentiating pricing and targeting customer needs), and preserve transactions' value (despite very low marginal unit costs). Only those software and information product companies who combine technical prowess with a deep understanding of how to leverage the elements of pricing excellence with these unique products will be able to achieve *the price advantage*.

Making Change Happen

Creating and sustaining *the price advantage* can present managers with one of the most daunting change management challenges. Part Six examines the practical enablers and constraints to making enduring and positive pricing change happen in an organization.

Pricing Transformation

The decision to seriously pursue *the price advantage* launches a company on a transformational journey that touches virtually every aspect of its business system. This wide-ranging effort is not about mastering a handful of clever pricing tips and tricks, but instead about creating a fundamental step-change in an organization's pricing performance, capabilities, and mindsets. This journey is a true transformation that transcends other initiatives in terms of its bold aspiration, priority within the overall management agenda, executive-level mindshare, breadth of scope, and commitment to organizational capability building.

Evolving from a business that treats pricing as a tactical necessity to a price-advantaged company whose pricing function is a true profit center is not easy. It demands significant senior commitment and engagement as well as the substantial investment of critical resources ranging from subject matter experts and implementation teams to enabling tools and performance management systems.

Whether a company is already on its way to *the price advantage* and searching for ideas on how to continue or correct its course, or looking for ways to jump-start its efforts, the ideas in this chapter can help accelerate its progress. These pages provide a "reality check" on what is truly required to drive change and capture lasting pricing impact. In our experience, companies must pay heed to two crucial areas: *designing a clear change program* for the pricing journey and *accelerating and embedding change* within the organization. The first area clarifies the company's pricing aspirations, sets the scope and pace of the change, and outlines the resources and talent required for the journey. The latter one specifically addresses ways to build enthusiasm, overcome internal resistance, and instill the organizational mindsets and behaviors that must be present in a price-advantaged company. It is only by doing both that companies can motivate employees to transform and capture pricing's full potential.

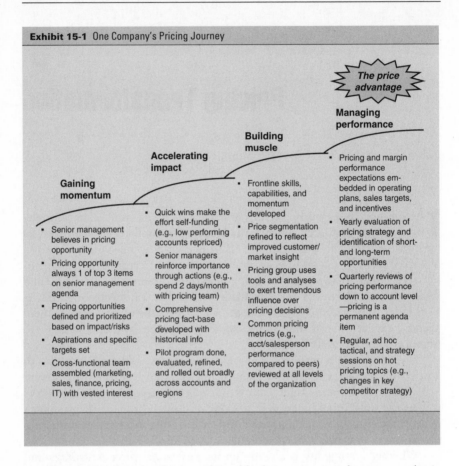

Exhibit 15-1 One Company's Pricing Journey

The price advantage

Managing performance

Building muscle

Accelerating impact

Gaining momentum

- Senior management believes in pricing opportunity
- Pricing opportunity always 1 of top 3 items on senior management agenda
- Pricing opportunities defined and prioritized based on impact/risks
- Aspirations and specific targets set
- Cross-functional team assembled (marketing, sales, finance, pricing, IT) with vested interest

- Quick wins make the effort self-funding (e.g., low performing accounts repriced)
- Senior managers reinforce importance through actions (e.g., spend 2 days/month with pricing team)
- Comprehensive pricing fact-base developed with historical info
- Pilot program done, evaluated, refined, and rolled out broadly across accounts and regions

- Frontline skills, capabilities, and momentum developed
- Price segmentation refined to reflect improved customer/market insight
- Pricing group uses tools and analyses to exert tremendous influence over pricing decisions
- Common pricing metrics (e.g., acct/salesperson performance compared to peers) reviewed at all levels of the organization

- Pricing and margin performance expectations embedded in operating plans, sales targets, and incentives
- Yearly evaluation of pricing strategy and identification of short- and long-term opportunities
- Quarterly reviews of pricing performance down to account level —pricing is a permanent agenda item
- Regular, ad hoc tactical, and strategy sessions on hot pricing topics (e.g., changes in key competitor strategy)

Companies that simultaneously tackle these two crucial areas can obtain dramatic improvements in pricing performance, establish a cultural climate that sustains success, and capture *the price advantage*. Exhibit 15-1 depicts one company's progress through this journey at a high level.

DESIGNING A CLEAR CHANGE PROGRAM

Many of the companies we advise on pricing have asked, "How do we help ensure our pricing change effort will succeed?" Pricing change programs are similar to business transformations in many ways.[1] Successful companies usually set unambiguous stretch targets, develop a clear structure for the project, maintain energy and involvement throughout the organization for

---

[1]See, for example, Josep Isern and Caroline Pung, "Driving Radical Change," mckinseyquarterly.com, November 2007.

the entire project, and ensure strong, visible leadership at all levels. Our experience in working with companies undergoing major pricing change programs has revealed a few areas that require special attention. The seven key lessons described in the following sections can help organizations ensure that their pricing change efforts capture the types of opportunities discussed in prior chapters.

SIZE AND ARTICULATE THE PRIZE EARLY

Fundamentally transforming a company's pricing performance is both daunting and yet extremely rewarding. In many cases, the overall financial "size of the prize" is substantial and well beyond what many would expect. Indeed, the potential profit often compares to that of a sizeable company division or to that gained by acquiring another business that is 25 to 50 percent of the original organization's revenue (with similar profit margins). A successful pricing journey can often deliver the same or better bottom-line profit impact as this acquisition. This point reinforces the "profit center" perspective introduced early on in Chapter 6, "Pricing Infrastructure." When viewed this way, a pricing change program can easily be a top management priority for a company that has yet to achieve *the price advantage*.

Estimating the financial upside of the pricing effort should occur early in the process (even if the initial assessment is crude). This estimate can then be shared with the organization to help them understand the importance of pricing. For example, the financial end-state aspiration for a pricing change effort might be to achieve a 4.5 percentage point increase in return on sales (ROS) in 18 months. A diagnostic may help refine the number over time.

Companies should also set nonfinancial aspirations if they want to achieve *the price advantage* (e.g., a new Revenue Management Office staffed with high-performers, led by a senior vice president reporting directly to the business unit [BU] head; sales incentives aligned with pricing goals; pricing performance reviewed regularly by the executive team). As they strive to achieve these goals, laying out a series of milestones can expedite progress (e.g., Exhibit 15-1).

DON'T UNDERINVEST

The most successful pricing transformations are the ones where organizations dedicate talent and resources commensurate with the opportunity—both upfront and over time. Companies should ask themselves: Given the fact that a pricing change effort often has the same or greater profit potential than a new division does, are we dedicating the same level of talent to our pricing journey as we would to run such a division? Underinvesting not only makes reaping full benefits unlikely but also sends the message to the organization that management may not genuinely believe in the upside of *the price advantage.*

Unfortunately, this underinvestment occurs all too often in pricing change programs. Even when all these factors are understood, underinvestment can sometimes still be driven by a false sense of how easy the journey will be, based on early diagnostic or pilot results.

DEDICATE THE RIGHT LEADER AND TEAM

The leader of the pricing change effort is one of its most important ingredients—one that interacts constantly with both the broader leadership group and many other organizational elements discussed later in *accelerating and embedding change.* Although all the senior leaders of the company need to be visible and committed to the pricing journey to some degree, there must be a single, carefully chosen leader that is dedicated to driving the pricing change effort.

But what does an ideal candidate look like? Although there are no hard and fast rules, individuals with the following characteristics seem to work best in the role of pricing change program leader:

- Credibility in the organization—most people will look up to and listen to this person.
- Good interpersonal and leadership skills—able to inspire and influence others to change.
- Proven track record of success and initiative taking—real "up and comer, go-getter."
- Sales background or experience—can bridge the gap with skeptical/resistant frontline salespeople.
- Analytic capacity, business acumen, and openness to new ideas.

After selecting this leader, the company should assemble a team of high-caliber individuals to work with and support him or her.

In many cases, these roles are only interim ones that last as long as the pricing change effort—which should not make anyone nervous. In the vast majority of cases, being a dedicated, integral part of a successful pricing transformation provides tremendous professional development for the senior leader and core team. Often, these folks advance more quickly to higher positions than their peers. The senior leader does not need to be the existing or future pricing lead; similarly, many of the core team may assume other roles in the organization over time. Dedicating such talent to the pricing journey is not unlike dedicating quality resources to the integration of an acquisition. It is completely wrong to staff these roles with "available" bodies—said differently, if some part of the organization does not scream when an internal person is pulled for the effort, then that person is probably not qualified to play the role.

STRUCTURE TO ACCELERATE PAYOFF

The scope of pricing change programs can often seem overwhelming. However, our work with companies pursuing *the price advantage* shows that those who followed a rigorous, structured approach can make strong headway toward capturing the pricing potential.

The approach contains a few core steps but is flexible enough that companies can tailor it to fit their own needs (e.g., different levels of production or channel complexity). It usually follows a similar sequence within different organizations, taking several years to complete (Exhibit 15-2).

The first—and extremely important—step is often an upfront **diagnostic** that clarifies the sources and magnitude of the pricing opportunity. Companies should resist the temptation to skip this step, as it provides a "from" and "to" for the pricing journey by creating a baseline for measuring future progress, a strawman for the end-state, a first-cut gameplan for getting there, and a refined estimate of the financial payoff.

Exhibit 15-2 Typical Transformational Design and Implementation

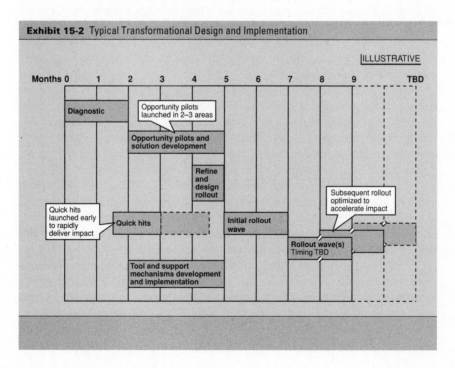

Hungry for action, many companies also identify a set of **quick hits** that they can launch independently, quickly, and with relatively simple effort. As early as possible, they will also start to develop **requirements for future pricing systems and tools** (given potentially long lead-time items to develop, debug, and implement).

The next major piece of work often combines **pilot tests** (e.g., for new service fees) and further **initiative development** (e.g., to finalize new discount authority and escalation criteria). A **rollout design and refinement** step then occurs where the remaining implementation plan is developed and refined using early results from quick hits and pilot tests. Finally, the **rollout** itself proceeds, frequently with an initial wave or two before going either into a sequence of waves that cascade more and more deeply into the organization or one "big bang." The rollout waves should be prioritized to accelerate overall impact (e.g., largest addressable revenue opportunities first).

One of the best ways to achieve early momentum is through the quick hits mentioned earlier, which can take many forms. They are often managed centrally to help drive traction and ensure coordination across markets and businesses. They can be relatively straightforward changes in commercial guidelines, policies, or terms and conditions. The pricing leakage topic covered in Chapter 3, "Transactions," usually represents a significant source of quick hit opportunities that companies pursue. Other common examples include changes that affect net pricing (e.g., modest changes to discount authority levels), new fees or adjustments to existing fees (e.g., moving the threshold for free freight), or modest changes to obsolete or infrequently purchased specialty items.

Quick hits also help fuel one of pricing change programs' most distinctive traits: their ability to become self-funding and accretive early on. From the earliest stages of the journey, companies can identify and launch low-risk/low-difficulty initiatives with significant impact potential. This strategy accelerates overall impact, builds early wins and confidence for the effort, and even fuels the remainder of the pricing journey's investments.

This structured approach helped one Fortune 500 services company capture hundreds of millions in incremental earnings before interest and taxes (EBIT) even before the program had fully rolled out. Prior to embarking on its journey, operating cost growth outpaced revenue growth and compensation programs rewarded volume at the expense of profit. Because the company operated in a distributed sales environment, pricing decisions were made locally across dozens of regions with different competitive environments (see Chapter 12, "Complexity Management"). After launching a pricing transformation that spanned almost two full years, the company achieved tremendous bottom-line impact. They used several themes from the diagnostic (Exhibit 15-3) as the heart of their pricing change program,

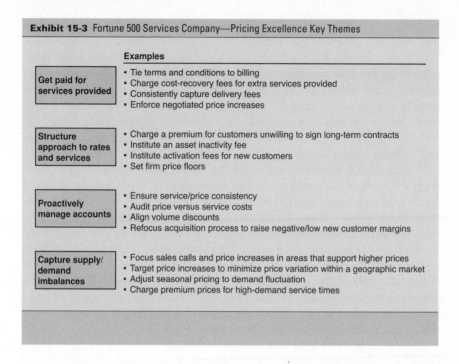

Exhibit 15-3 Fortune 500 Services Company—Pricing Excellence Key Themes

	Examples
Get paid for services provided	• Tie terms and conditions to billing • Charge cost-recovery fees for extra services provided • Consistently capture delivery fees • Enforce negotiated price increases
Structure approach to rates and services	• Charge a premium for customers unwilling to sign long-term contracts • Institute an asset inactivity fee • Institute activation fees for new customers • Set firm price floors
Proactively manage accounts	• Ensure service/price consistency • Audit price versus service costs • Align volume discounts • Refocus acquisition process to raise negative/low new customer margins
Capture supply/demand imbalances	• Focus sales calls and price increases in areas that support higher prices • Target price increases to minimize price variation within a geographic market • Adjust seasonal pricing to demand fluctuation • Charge premium prices for high-demand service times

initiated a set of centrally driven quick hits, and ramped up multiple teams to simultaneously drive rollout in the field in multiple areas.

MANAGE THE RISKS—BOTH INTERNAL AND EXTERNAL

A pricing journey contains many inherent risks that companies must be aware of and the pricing team must properly manage. Companies can do this by creating an oversight body, running pilot tests, overinvesting in early moves, and using a well-developed communication strategy.

Why is it so important to manage risks? Some, perhaps many, customers will notice pricing changes and may feel unnecessarily singled out, under-appreciated, or even gouged. Competitors may try to take advantage of the situation through their sales and marketing messages or even by undercutting prices. In complex pricing environments, or when changes to pricing policies and practices are substantial, there is always the risk that the data, approach, or execution may be flawed. If pricing is improperly applied, it can do real damage—the flip side to the point that it is the biggest profit lever. Any missteps or excessive noise from customers may also cause frontline decision makers to lose faith in the change program.

Best practice companies establish a cross-functional Steering Committee composed of senior executives at the start of the pricing change effort. This group should include leaders with a range of experience from sales, marketing, product management, operations, and finance. The committee's primary roles would be to clarify overall aspirations and direction, test specific change ideas, approve recommendations/quick hits, assign or reallocate resources, monitor progress, and remove any internal obstacles.

A pilot test in a limited market is a safe way to evaluate proposed "high risk" changes (e.g., instituting a new fee for a previously free service). The test manages risk by narrowing scope, by letting customers and other audiences know that the change may not be in its final form, and by utilizing direct feedback from internal and external stakeholders to refine the concept. The company may also be able to gauge competitive responses. One electrical equipment company used a pilot test to launch an eventual across-the-board price increase. It announced a modest price increase to customers in one small market, obtained customer feedback (somewhat negative but largely understanding), and examined competitive responses. Based on this information, the company tweaked its pricing and communications strategy and then launched a national price increase that was highly successful—the first in the industry in more than five years.

Investing in pilot tests and early rollout waves is worthwhile—it helps ensure that the pricing team gets it right and creates a clear, positive proof of concept for the change program. These investments include allocating additional resources to pilots and early waves, engaging senior leaders in significant, visible ways (e.g., active at kickoff, major interim events, and subsequent reviews), extending the length of the first implementation wave, and monitoring progress and impact closely.

Finally, companies need to develop and implement a robust internal and external communication strategy as an important part of their pricing journey. Because pricing change efforts often face a large degree of internal skepticism regarding the ability to realize profit improvements, it is critical that early wins be widely celebrated, that senior managers constantly reinforce basic pricing themes, and that perceived risks or concerns be openly addressed. Externally, organizations often lack a clear supporting rationale to share with customers about pricing changes—a topic on which they need to be well-prepared to address common questions and customer pushback.

DO NOT VIEW SYSTEMS AND TOOLS AS "SILVER BULLETS"

All too frequently organizations are so excited by a pricing tool's capabilities (or potential capabilities) that they are lulled into a false sense of having solved the problem. Although there can be no debate that systems and tools play a critical role in the success of a pricing change program, they are no substitute for the many other elements discussed in this book. A fuller description of the role of systems and tools is included in Chapter 6, "Pricing Infrastructure." We focus here on those elements particularly relevant to the pricing journey.

One of the most valuable things a company can do during a pricing transformation is to take the time to understand its real system and tool requirements properly. Starting with a makeshift interim tool allows you to obtain a sharper picture of what you really need to have (versus initial impressions of system needs, which may turn out to be overly complex and costly). It is common to see systems and tools requirements in a pricing change effort evolve as quick hits and pilots bring a new (sometimes more streamlined) set of requirements to light.

At the same time, the pricing team must start the systems and tools design process early enough to have it ready for rollout—especially given that the time required to fully design, build, test, and implement an IT-based solution is almost always longer than initially thought. The team must balance the desire to build a "100%" solution versus the total investment and length of time required to arrive at a practical, field-ready working solution. It needs to wrestle with a couple of important questions:

1. *Build or buy?* Is there an existing off-the-shelf or readily customizable solution you could buy that might get you further, faster? Would you be better off building an interim (e.g., spreadsheet-based) solution before pursuing a full-blown IT-enabled solution?
2. *Wait or go?* To what degree can we begin rolling out the program (or even elements of it) before the tools and supporting mechanisms are fully ready? Can we sequence the work to minimize the need to wait on tool development for rollout?

DO NOT LET CHANGING MARKETS THROW YOU OFF TRACK

The transformational journey to achieve *the price advantage* is rarely easy. However, changing market conditions can sometimes make the journey seem even tougher. When this happens, it is important to realize that in both up and down markets the journey is still usually worth pursuing. Two principal challenges exist:

Creating Sufficient Focus and Energy for Pricing Change in a Booming Market
When sales are growing and demand is hot, companies may pay much less attention to pricing and the near-term and long-term impact it can create for a company. This is truly a missed opportunity because the

conditions are often ripe for making fundamental pricing changes (e.g., at the Market Strategy and Customer Value levels).

Maintaining Faith in a Down Market   Getting pricing right is always challenging in a down market, where decreasing demand, excess capacity, and greater price sensitivity all exert negative price pressure. Striving for *the price advantage* can be particularly difficult as managers must deal with demands from multiple angles: customers who want lower prices, competitors who seem eager to oblige, and internal instincts to lower price and defend market share. These conditions can result in less discipline (e.g., greater numbers of pricing exceptions). This "looseness" not only allows percentage points of profit to slip away, but can also set a dangerous precedent with customers who will expect the same pricing flexibility in the eventual market upswing. Even worse, abandoning a pricing change program during worsening market conditions sends a strong message to the organization that "when times are tough, our pricing isn't." For all these reasons and more, senior leaders and managers alike must remain vigilant in seeking *the price advantage* throughout all cycles—up or down.

ACCELERATING AND EMBEDDING CHANGE

Let us imagine a company that has followed the pricing change program we just laid out and done everything right—and still is not capturing the complete potential of *the price advantage*. As we stated earlier, making the journey does not just mean designing an effective program; companies must also find a way to accelerate and embed change throughout their organization. Otherwise, they will never capture the pricing potential, much less instill and sustain *the price advantage*.

Managers invariably encounter cultural and even emotional resistance along the journey. The freedom to set price can be seen by individuals in product management, marketing, and sales as central to their personal power and authority within the organization. Pricing authority may even heighten the customer's perception of the importance of an individual in the seller's organization. When that authority is controlled more tightly, which often occurs as an organization moves to create the price advantage, some resistance is unavoidable.

To make it all the way through the journey, organizations must find ways to not only get through this resistance but also build and maintain high levels of energy and commitment. Quick wins may provide early momentum, but the real returns typically occur over several years as the company institutionalizes its pricing knowledge and improves its pricing capability.

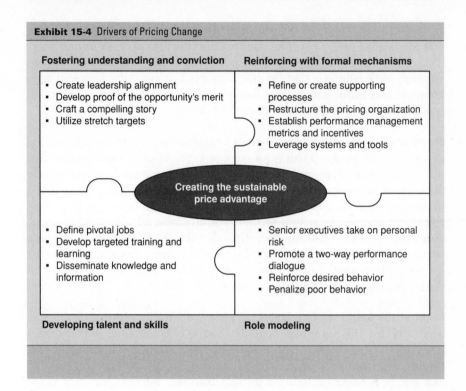

Exhibit 15-4 Drivers of Pricing Change

Fostering understanding and conviction

- Create leadership alignment
- Develop proof of the opportunity's merit
- Craft a compelling story
- Utilize stretch targets

Reinforcing with formal mechanisms

- Refine or create supporting processes
- Restructure the pricing organization
- Establish performance management metrics and incentives
- Leverage systems and tools

Creating the sustainable price advantage

- Define pivotal jobs
- Develop targeted training and learning
- Disseminate knowledge and information

- Senior executives take on personal risk
- Promote a two-way performance dialogue
- Reinforce desired behavior
- Penalize poor behavior

Developing talent and skills

Role modeling

Time and again, we have seen such pricing success breed upon itself. After reaching initial targets, successful teams attain increasingly aggressive ones.

A company that wants to enter this virtuous cycle must first accelerate, then embed change as it carries out its pricing journey. In our work with hundreds of companies over the years, those that most effectively did this employed the four elements in Exhibit 15-4: fostering understanding and conviction; reinforcing the change with formal mechanisms; developing talent and skills; and role modeling. These elements need to be applied simultaneously and constantly reinforced, although a "start up" sequence is often followed: setting the stage (fostering understanding and conviction); creating enablers (reinforcing with formal mechanisms, and developing talent and skills); and closing the loop (role modeling). We explore each of these in some detail and then discuss the issues that can short-circuit them.

FOSTERING UNDERSTANDING AND CONVICTION

Before individuals can step up to their role in creating *the price advantage*, they need to understand what they are being asked to do and why. Senior executives must align the organization around *the price advantage* vision, make a credible case for success, and point to the path they are taking to get there. They cannot delegate this job. Only top managers can clearly, convincingly make the case that the company can achieve *the price advantage*. Frequent and consistent communications across the organization and to all stakeholders are some of the best ways to do so.

Broad Leadership Alignment   For an organization to rally around pricing change, the top management team must be firmly aligned and committed to achieving a price improvement target. Any disagreements will spread quickly throughout the company. This alignment will be particularly important in the face of hard choices: letting go of unprofitable customers, dealing with customers angered by new policies or enforcement of old ones, or abandoning entire markets. If top executives do not act on and talk about these challenges with a single voice, employees will quickly sense it and support for the initiative will wither. Broader management must also align around the pricing change program and champion it.

Proof of the Opportunity's Merit   A clear, believable, and substantial success story for the organization is the best way to show that the impact from pricing excellence is real, meaningful, and attainable. Piloting a well-resourced pricing program in a carefully chosen subset of a business—for example, a product category, a distinct customer segment, or an isolated geographical region—can do even more to build credibility and address skepticism. A successful pilot can become a rallying point for pricing improvement initiatives across the remainder of the organization.

A Compelling Story   Once a credible case has been established, the next challenge for senior management is to craft a compelling and credible story that will start to drive the broader organization to work hard to change. This story is a tangible, fact-based explanation of why the company is upgrading its pricing capability, what needs to be done, and what rewards lie at the end of the journey. It may or may not be easy to create. For example, if a company is in significant financial trouble, that alone may be enough to rally employees to take on pricing excellence to improve profitability. The story needs to be shared across the organization by all leaders and managers in a consistent way to reinforce the pricing change effort.

Stretch Targets   A successful pricing change program must be anchored in credible stretch targets. These targets are often quantified pocket price or pocket margin goals that cascade across all company levels. In other words, the pocket margin goals of all the sales representatives in a region would be the pocket margin goal for the region; the sum of the region goals would equal the pocket margin goal for the division, and so forth. The targets should also provide a healthy tension between competing company goals like pocket margin or share growth.

CREATING ENABLERS: REINFORCING THE CHANGE WITH FORMAL MECHANISMS

A reinforcing pricing infrastructure forms the backbone of a pricing change program. The core elements from Chapter 6, "Pricing Infrastructure," provide our framework, although we focus primarily on those elements specifically geared toward accelerating and embedding the pricing change.

Processes Over time, a pricing change program will likely touch almost all existing pricing processes; new processes may also be established to manage pricing performance long term (e.g., lifecycle pricing and strategic planning for all new products). Early on, however, companies should focus on processes that link closely to the largest opportunities or risks (e.g., instituting tighter compliance management mechanisms to eliminate price leakages). The company should also ensure that the new or refined processes are used as desired by the organization and with the intended outcomes.

Organization Pricing change programs often require organizational changes. Most companies strive to achieve the organizational elements outlined in Chapter 6, "Pricing Infrastructure," as an end-state aspiration. Two elements are worth highlighting here for organizations going through a pricing journey.

First, a company going through a pricing change effort often needs to upgrade the capabilities of its future pricing function substantially. The pricing change program can be an opportunity to recruit fresh internal and/or external talent for the future pricing organization. The senior leader and core team members dedicated to the pricing change effort are prime candidates for these future roles; however, because they are among the best and brightest the company has to offer, they may be needed elsewhere in the business. The important thing to remember is not to aim low when finding new talent for the future pricing function—that talent is what will help secure the benefits of the company's investment in the pricing change effort.

Second, the core pricing team driving the pricing transformation needs to act objectively and with the best interests of the company as a whole in mind. Pricing change invariably requires the reexamination of what may be long-held beliefs (or even entitlement) regarding discounting authority, frontline pricing practices, sales incentives, and so forth. The structure outlined earlier in this chapter, where the senior pricing leader and core team report to an executive-level steering committee, can help ensure that inappropriate biases are weeded out.

Performance Management   A company needs to establish performance metrics, or key performance indicators (KPIs), to track each major pricing initiative during the pricing change program. These KPIs, which are designed so they are consistently used across the organization, should reflect the company's overall pricing aspiration. Chapter 6, "Pricing Infrastructure," provides more information on KPIs, their design, and use. By agreeing on them at the beginning of the pricing change effort, a company can use the KPIs to create a baseline and provide direct feedback on the effectiveness of the pricing change effort. Successful executives insist on such visibility given the substantial resources, management attention, and other investments that are needed to launch and drive the pricing journey.

The company can also use performance metrics to track the progress of individuals or groups responsible for driving specific pricing initiatives. Under-performance by even a few individuals can cripple the best-designed effort. Moreover, individual and group incentives need to align with the overall pricing change program aspiration and goals as well with the individual's responsibilities (be it sales or deal desk).

A carefully designed compensation and incentive structure is one of the principal mechanisms a company can use to motivate individuals to adopt the desired pricing behaviors that may emerge from a pricing change effort. While a comprehensive review of this topic is outside the scope of this chapter and book, companies that drive successful pricing change programs usually establish incentives that promote good pricing behavior for *all* roles that are critical to the pricing change process—not just frontline sales. In addition, they recognize the natural tension between price and volume and aim to strike a balance between these two in the compensation and incentive scheme. Often, the underlying goal is to move the organization from a mostly volume-based mindset to one that weighs pricing and its impact on profit more heavily.

Finally, incentives should not be only about cash compensation—pricing change programs should leverage nonfinancial motivators to alter mindsets and behaviors. Chapter 6, "Pricing Infrastructure," covers all of these topics in more detail.

Systems and Tools   A pricing change program can be swept away in a flood of data or stalled by the lack thereof. Initially, the effort might require extensive, manual work even to get the relevant transaction data (which may be spread across multiple systems, may need significant cleanup, and may require financial analysis—for example, proper cost allocation). Over time, IT-enabled systems and tools can help make this an easy, replicable exercise.

For the purposes of driving a pricing transformation, there are four things to consider with regard to systems and tools. First, visibility into underlying pricing issues and opportunities for the business must be present in an unambiguous, fact-based way. Without some degree of visibility, it will be hard to know what to change and whether change efforts are actually having the desired effect. Second, pricing data (especially early on) should be *just* accurate enough to enable confident decision making. Greater accuracy is always welcome but should not become a bottleneck (e.g., companies do not need 0.1 percent accuracy in pocket prices when their current pocket price bandwidth is 60 percent or more). Third, over time it will be increasingly essential to get the appropriate, up-to-date pricing data in the hands of the relevant decision makers. From real-time negotiation support to setting a new product's release price, getting the right data in the right hands at the right time is crucial. Fourth, automation can minimize the effort required to gather, prepare, analyze, and present data effectively. The specific systems and tools that are most likely to help change organizational behavior and drive pricing performance should be top priority.

CREATING ENABLERS: DEVELOPING TALENT AND SKILLS

Just giving someone a hammer, nails, wood, and a blueprint does not make them a master carpenter. Similarly, providing an individual with pricing tools and guidelines does not create an excellent pricer. Building pricing skills takes time and must be coordinated across all levels of a company, from senior management through to the frontline sales force. Four steps are fundamental to building these new capabilities: defining pivotal jobs; managing and acquiring key talent; developing targeted training and learning programs; and disseminating knowledge and information.

Defining Pivotal Jobs A small handful of jobs are absolutely critical for each pricing process (e.g., new product or transaction pricing). Often occurring at multiple organizational levels, those positions can, if well executed, ensure that pricing is a true performance driver.

In defining the pivotal pricing jobs, managers must be specific and clear about which skills and other attributes are necessary for outstanding performance in each one. For example, a pricing manager who supports negotiations must be well acquainted with the benefits of the company's products and how they rate against the competition; they must also know negotiating processes and strategies inside and out. More importantly, field reps must respect them enough to accept the negotiating advice they offer, especially in tough situations.

Developing Targeted Training and Learning Programs   After the needed skills are defined (e.g., large account pocket price management, competitive pricing intelligence, value-based new product pricing), training and learning become vital components of a capability-building program. Best practice companies often start by identifying sources of relevant knowledge. Although external benchmarking or outside experts offer useful insights, the best sources are often the organization's own people—whether top pricers or internal experts. After identifying these people, a company can conduct workshops with them to codify the skills that make them distinctive. When recognized in this way, these pricers can also inspire a company's entire team to better performance.

Disseminating Knowledge and Information   Spreading pricing knowledge through training is a critical part of institutionalizing *the price advantage* and can be accomplished through a number of formal and informal mechanisms, including external training, formal sharing of internal best practices, online knowledge modules, and real-time learning. Management workshops and role-playing exercises, led by the most skilled employees as part of larger training sessions, can make these tasks easier. Knowledge is retained best when it is shared, practiced, and then used in real customer situations.

ROLE MODELING

Role modeling demonstrates in both words and deeds that leaders across the organization are behaving in new ways. It must come from everyone—from the most senior executives to the frontline sales force. The four elements of effective role modeling highlight the ways it reinforces the messages around *the price advantage*: taking on personal risk; promoting a two-way performance dialogue; reinforcing desired behavior; and penalizing poor behavior.

Taking on Personal Risk   Few change programs carry as much personal risk as pricing. A decision not to discount or to enforce a policy can lose a customer. A salesperson who takes that risk needs to know that senior management stands behind them and shares that risk. If the customer goes straight to a senior executive and gets an additional 5 percent off the price of the deal, word will spread quickly that senior management is not truly committed to pricing excellence, and commitment throughout the organization may suffer accordingly. Even if a logical reason is offered (e.g., a "strategic" account, attractive new market segment), the damage is done.

A visible act of strength—for example, senior management holding the line on pricing with a large account—has the opposite effect. Word will spread like wildfire that senior management has the courage to risk losing an account in the name of pricing excellence.

Promoting a Two-Way Performance Dialogue　An ongoing, two-way performance dialogue should occur between the executive team and pricing staff. This dialogue serves multiple purposes. It helps with goal attainment by establishing a baseline, setting specific pricing targets, and bringing visibility to actual pricing performance. Pricers can then move forward to define corrective measures and apply the pressure needed to find the next wave of pricing opportunity.

It is crucial, however, that top managers treat this as a two-way dialogue. They need to listen to and learn from pricers. The entire organization must stay in touch with changes in the marketplace. Top executives should be as eager to solicit feedback on real pricing challenges in the market as they are to pressure the organization for results.

Reinforcing Desired Behavior　Role models of pricing excellence populate every level of a company. As good pricers surface, whether from the executive ranks or the frontline, their efforts should be recognized and reinforced.

A few questions can help determine whether a company is doing enough to recognize and advance its best pricers:

- How are the best pricers identified and publicly acknowledged? For example, are salespeople praised because they stood firm in the face of intense competitive pressure, holding the line on pocket price (even if a deal fell through in the process), or only because they brought in the most revenue?
- What criteria go into deciding promotions? When announcing promotions, is pricing excellence cited as a factor or is volume growth? Do the reputation and actions of the promoted manager align with the company's pricing objectives?

Along with public recognition of jobs well done, desired behavior can be reinforced subtly, but with wide-ranging impact. At one large services company, the CEO personally called the top three salespeople based on margin percentages at the end of each quarter and congratulated them for excellent work. The praise was specific and private. Still, the first time the calls were made, the entire sales force knew about them by the next morning.

Penalizing Poor Behavior   Of course, with responsibility comes consequences, and one of the more unpleasant tasks during a change program
is to enforce the new direction when parts of the organization resist.
However, without clear enforcement of the new direction, employees will
begin second-guessing the company's priorities if they sense that career advancement is not linked to the new pricing program. As surely as penalties
are noticed, the absence of penalties will also be noted.

COMMON PITFALLS

The four cornerstones seem straightforward and logical. However, our
experience shows that a handful of common pitfalls can throw otherwise well-designed price change programs off-track and reduce companies'
returns from their investments. Some of the most common pitfalls include:

- *Believing it is enough for the CEO to assert that pricing is a priority.* Senior management needs to reinforce this assertion with repeated actions
  and words that assure employees that pricing is not perceived a "flavor
  of the month" improvement priority. Conviction and commitment to
  achieving *the price advantage* are built by clear and repeated messages,
  over a number of years, on the importance of pricing distinctiveness. It
  must be stressed that pricing excellence is not just a one-time project but
  rather part of the lifeblood of a company and the way that a company
  routinely does business from now on.
- *Overemphasizing the building of pricing systems and processes, while
  underemphasizing the building of requisite pricing skills and conviction.* The emotional nature of pricing decisions and the fundamental
  behavior and mindset shifts required to build *the price advantage* require that a fair amount of the change focus on nurturing capability and
  conviction.
- *Thinking a couple of training sessions are enough to build adequate
  pricing capability.* Structured training sessions can only lay the foundation. Real pricing skill is best learned over time and reinforced through
  regular coaching and mentoring. Furthermore, the mentors and coaches
  should continually refresh their pricing excellence knowledge base with
  information about pricing successes across the company.
- *Inadequately rewarding pricing excellence in the incentive system.* As
  we have asserted, pricing done well is hard work that entails real risks.
  Inadequate incentives make pricing superiority worth neither the work
  required nor the risk incurred.
- *Openly rewarding individuals whose pricing performance is substan-
  dard.* If the "Salesperson of the Year" award is given to a sales rep

who excels at selling high volumes of products but whose pricing performance is mediocre, then management assertions on the importance of pricing excellence lose all credibility.

■ *Senior management caving in on pricing under pressure.* As mentioned earlier, few things undercut a pricing improvement initiative more quickly than senior managers capitulating to price discount demands from large customers and failing to act as role models of the new approach to pricing.

* * *

Any company pursuing *the price advantage* is embarking on a journey of operational and cultural change—a journey where it must win and sometimes change the hearts and minds of many. Designing a program for the pricing journey (which shows what must be done) and accelerating and embedding the change throughout the organization are both required before the company can achieve enduring success. But doing the latter is the result of building broad understanding and conviction, reinforcing this with appropriate tools and processes, finding and developing the required skills, and creating role models of the new behavior throughout the organization. Only when all of these work seamlessly together will your company capture and sustain its full price potential and achieve *the price advantage*.

CHAPTER 16

The Monnarch Battery Case

Throughout this book, you have read in-depth discussions of a number of specific pricing topics. We covered the three levels of price management plus pricing infrastructure in considerable detail, showing the approaches and tools at each level and demonstrating their application with targeted cases. We devoted chapters to the unique events of price wars and post-merger pricing as well as to the boundary-expanding topics of legal degrees of pricing freedom, lifecycle pricing, and pricing architecture. We also addressed a wide range of advanced topics that are particularly challenging when they apply—including pricing software, dealing with issues that add complexity to pricing, and tailoring the value that you deliver. And in the previous chapter, we explored the challenge of making sustainable pricing change happen in an organization.

In this chapter, we share a more comprehensive pricing case study that cuts across many of the topics covered, bringing many of our pricing fundamentals together and illustrating how these fundamentals worked in concert in a real-life pricing situation.

THE MONNARCH BATTERY COMPANY

The Monnarch Battery Company makes replacement lead-acid batteries used in automobiles. As Exhibit 16-1 shows, Monnarch's direct customers are auto parts distributors (who resell to smaller auto parts retailers), regional and national auto parts retail chains, and several national general mass merchandisers who have automotive departments within their stores. These various retailers and mass merchandisers then sell Monnarch batteries directly to car owners.

Exhibit 16-2 shows Monnarch's economics and profit structure. With a return on sales (ROS) of 5.2 percent, Monnarch's profitability is extremely sensitive to even small swings in price. A 1 percent increase in price with no

Exhibit 16-1 Monnarch Battery Company

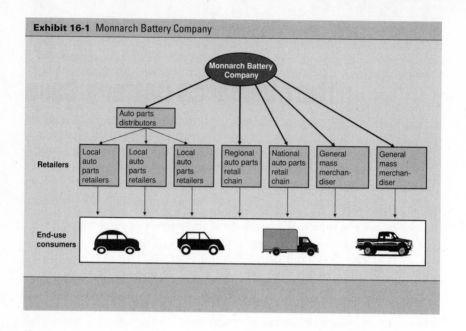

volume loss would increase operating profit by 19 percent. As this figure also shows, that is almost three times the impact of a one percent increase in volume, assuming no decrease in average price levels. As is usually the case, the payoff for Monnarch for improved price performance would be enormous.

Despite successful cost-cutting programs across the entire Monnarch organization, including efforts in manufacturing, distribution, sales, and administration, Monnarch's operating profits declined 50 percent over a period of five years. With a cost structure that was already lean and better than the competition, Monnarch had limited room to cut costs further. Unfortunately, its cost improvements were more than offset by a steady drop in the average prices that Monnarch received from its customers. Monnarch managers finally realized that they would be unable to return Monnarch to acceptable levels of bottom-line profitability without improving their performance in pricing. Monnarch senior managers decided to tackle pricing head-on and to look vigorously across all three levels of price management for opportunities, and to invest in the pricing infrastructure required to sustain these opportunities over time.

We go through each of the three levels, starting with the Transactions level, to show how Monnarch identified potential sources of price improvement. We follow this with a description of the integrated set of actions and

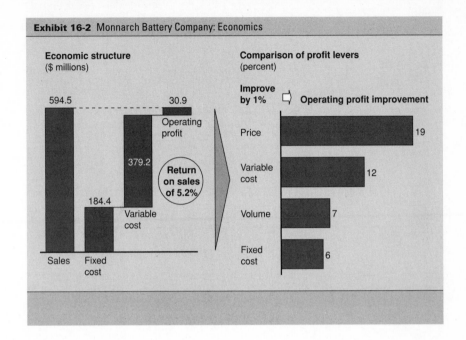

Exhibit 16-2 Monnarch Battery Company: Economics

pricing infrastructure upgrades Monnarch took to capture the identified pricing opportunities.

TRANSACTIONS

Transaction complexity at Monnarch was relatively high given the diversity of Monnarch's customer base and a price structure whose components had grown in number and size over the years. Exhibit 16-3 shows the typical pocket price waterfall for one of Monnarch's common battery models, the Mega-Lyte. From a dealer list price of $68.15, Monnarch deducted several discounts to get to invoice price. There was a standard retailer/distributor discount that differed by account type and averaged $10.22 per battery. Monnarch also provided an order size discount that could reach a maximum of 5 percent, depending on the total dollar value of an order. On average, it was $1.70 per battery, 2.5 percent of list price. Additionally, many transactions included an on-invoice exception discount, negotiated on a customer-by-customer basis to meet the competition. With these discounts, the average invoice price for the Mega-Lyte model was $50.78. What little attention Monnarch paid to transaction pricing was targeted almost exclusively on the invoice price.

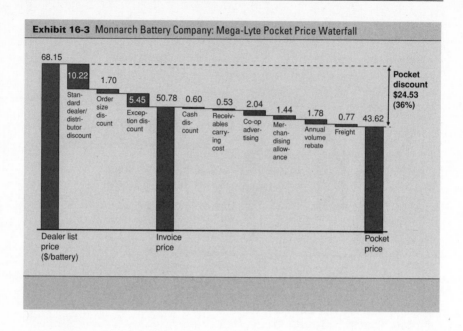

Exhibit 16-3 Monnarch Battery Company: Mega-Lyte Pocket Price Waterfall

That focus by Monnarch management ignored all of the discounting and revenue leaks occurring off-invoice, which averaged $7.16. Monnarch allowed a cash discount of 1.2 percent for prompt payment of invoices. Additionally, it granted extended payment terms of 60 or even 90 days from delivery as part of promotional programs and on an exception basis for select accounts. The extra cost of carrying these extended receivables averaged 53 cents per battery. Cooperative advertising, where Monnarch helped fund accounts' local and regional advertising of Monnarch products, cost an average of $2.04. Another special merchandising program that supported in-store promotions featuring Monnarch products resulted in an average merchandising allowance discount of $1.44. An annual volume rebate, based on the total volume an account purchased across all product lines, represented an additional $1.78 discount per battery. Finally, freight paid by Monnarch for shipping batteries to the retailer cost an average of 77 cents. The invoice price minus this host of off-invoice discounts, allowances, and costs resulted in an average pocket price of $43.62, a full 14 percent less than the invoice price. The pocket discount, which is the total revenue drop from dealer list price down to pocket price, averaged $24.53, a 36 percent drop.

As is typical, not all transactions for the Mega-Lyte had the identical pocket price. Accounts from different channels qualified for different standard dealer discount levels. They ordered in different quantities, which resulted in variations in order-size discounts. And the on-invoice exception

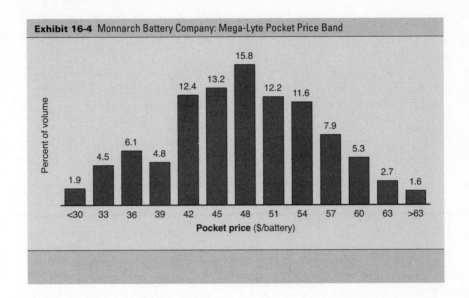

Exhibit 16-4 Monnarch Battery Company: Mega-Lyte Pocket Price Band

discounts were just that—exceptions negotiated on a one-off basis. Further variability extended into the off-invoice items. Accounts paid invoices with varying levels of promptness, resulting in major differences in cash discounts and receivables carrying costs. Not all accounts used all of the cooperative advertising allowance available to them. The merchandising allowance was only paid to retailers who featured Monnarch's products with special displays in their stores, and not all did. Account size, which varied greatly, drove the level of annual volume rebate, and freight paid by Monnarch varied extensively based on retailer location and order pattern.

The result of all of these differences across on- and off-invoice discount elements was the wide pocket price band shown in Exhibit 16-4. While the average pocket price was more than $43.62, units sold for as high as $63 and as low as $30 on a pocket price basis. This wide pocket price band triggered the usual questions: Why are pocket prices so variable, and can that variability be managed? What are the underlying drivers of the price band's shape and width? Does this pocket price variability make good management sense and align with Monnarch's market strategy?

To begin to answer a few of these questions, Monnarch performed the analysis shown in Exhibit 16-5 to see if the wide price band was somehow explained by the volume of batteries that customers purchased. Each point on this chart represents an individual Monnarch distributor or retail account. The horizontal axis shows annual dollar volume of sales through each account. The vertical axis shows pocket price as a percentage of dealer

Exhibit 16-5 Monnarch Battery Company: Pocket Price versus Account Size

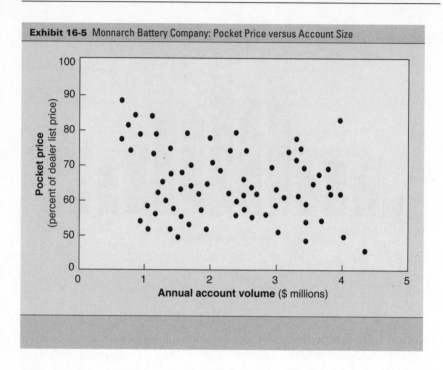

list price for Mega-Lyte batteries sold to each account. It is clear from Exhibit 16-5 that no overall correlation exists between account size and pocket discount. A number of relatively small accounts were receiving very low pocket prices (lower left on chart), while a number of larger accounts were buying at rather high pocket price levels (upper right on chart).

Further analyses were conducted to determine if other characteristics of accounts might better explain the wide pocket price band. Variables tested included customer channel, geographical location, local competitive intensity, and other battery brands carried by each account. However, none of these variables helped much to explain the extreme width of the pocket price band. The apparent randomness of pocket price levels baffled Monnarch managers, who had thought that they were quite careful about setting prices.

Further study showed this randomness had its roots in a transaction pricing process that actively managed only a portion of the pocket price waterfall and paid little attention to the ultimate pocket price level for each account. The standard dealer/distributor discount level was clearly defined and enforced. Order size was also well defined, but a number of "preferred accounts" were allowed to take the maximum order size discount on all orders, regardless of magnitude. Some general rules of thumb existed for the on-invoice exception discount (for instance, retail accounts with annual purchases less than $2 million should never receive an on-invoice exception discount of more than 5 percent), but these guidelines were neither clearly articulated nor carefully enforced.

The situation was even worse for off-invoice elements of the pocket price waterfall. Rules of thumb for these discounts were even less specific, and Monnarch's information systems provided individuals in sales and marketing with no report on these items by individual transaction or even by account. This systems shortfall made it impossible for Monnarch to pay any incentive to sales and marketing people for pocket price realization.

This assessment led Monnarch senior management to realize that its transaction pricing process was out of control, that decision making up and down the waterfall was based on ambiguous rules and discipline, and that no one was focusing on the end results of those decisions as represented by pocket price.

CUSTOMER VALUE

Monnarch managers had for years been laboring under the assumption that the battery industry was becoming increasingly commoditized, making it ever more difficult for Monnarch to distinguish its products from competitors. They assumed that price was the most critical factor driving consumer selection of battery brand, saw low-priced competitive offerings as real threats to their market share, and believed that any attempt to raise prices would result in a significant loss of volume and profit. Against this backdrop, they thought investing in market research to understand the Monnarch value position in key markets was futile and as a result had gone nearly a decade without conducting research on consumer value perception and price sensitivity. However, fundamental shifts in where consumers were choosing to purchase their replacement batteries, along with the merger of two of Monnarch's smaller competitors, convinced managers that it was time to update their understanding of their current value position.

To gain richer insights at the Customer Value level, Monnarch conducted new consumer price research that provided some eye-opening information. The objective of this research was to gain an up-to-date perspective on Monnarch's current price/benefit positioning for major products and the likely impact of price changes at the retail level. Monnarch used discrete choice analysis to simulate the customer battery buying experience and test the effect of changing price and other attributes on consumer choice—that is, retailer at which they shopped and battery brand they chose.

The research was conducted as follows. Researchers identified a sample group of 1,200 people who had recently purchased Monnarch or other battery brands and were willing to participate. They answered a series of background questions about their demographics, vehicles, circumstances around their last battery purchase, and retailers they had considered. Based on these answers, each respondent was put in front of a computer screen, given a set of three discrete choices for buying a battery, and asked a series of questions (see box).

DISCRETE CHOICE AT MONNARCH

Discrete choice analysis is one of several market research tools that can help a company determine the potential impact of changes in price levels and benefit offerings on customer choice of suppliers. Monnarch used this analysis to get a clearer picture of its value position in key market segments and the profit implications of potential price moves, for example, raising or lowering price or adjusting the price gap between different models.

Exhibit 16-6 shows the nature of the choices that were presented to respondents (i.e., battery consumers). Choice attributes included where the respondent might shop, the brand of the battery available at that retailer, and features of the various batteries being offered. The price that the retailer charges for that battery was also included with each choice. This initial set of choices was designed to mirror the brands, features, and prices that the respondents would likely see if they were to shop at their chosen retailers in the local market. Presented with these choices, the respondents were asked to select which battery they would purchase.

Exhibit 16-6 Monnarch Battery Company: Discrete Choice Research

	Choice 1	Choice 2	Choice 3
Retailer	CBA Auto Mart	Jetsen AutoMart	Mass-Mart
Battery brand	Monnarch	Eberist	Qalco
Battery features			
• Cold cranking AMPs	700	700	650
• Warranty	60 months	60 months	48 months
• Nationwide replacements	Yes	Yes	No
Retail price	$89.95	$96.95	$82.95

Suppose in this case that the respondent had selected Choice 1 in Exhibit 16-6, which was the Monnarch battery bought at CBA Auto Mart for $89.95. At this point, the discrete choice software would generate a slightly different set of choices for the respondent—for instance, the same choices as in Exhibit 16-6, but with the retail price for Choice 1 raised to $92.95. The respondent would then be asked to choose again. If Choice 1 were selected again, the next set of choices might have the Choice 1 price raised to $95.95. If the respondent then made a different choice, such as the Eberist brand battery at Jetsen AutoMart for $96.95, then the program might change the pattern for the next set of choices put before the respondent. For example, the warranty period under Choice 3 might be increased to 60 months or the nationwide replacement availability might be changed from "no" to "yes." Each research respondent might be taken through a sequence of up to 15 of these modified discrete choice scenarios, with individual choices at each stage generating a slightly different set of choices for the next stage.

The underlying discrete choice program tracks the choices each respondent makes over the course of the research and analyzes the changes in choice attributes that cause respondents to make different selections.

The research gave Monnarch managers a fresh outlook on their markets and allowed them to create up-to-date value maps for their key products and market segments, like the Mega-Lyte map shown in Exhibit 16-7.

Among key insights gained were these:

- In most product categories, Monnarch batteries were priced at or near value equivalence with competitors.
- Suggested reductions in Monnarch prices of up to 10 percent failed to attract many customers from the economy end of the market being served by Qalco. The research made it clear that there was a small, price-sensitive set of customers who would not consider switching from Qalco until a competitor's price nearly matched Qalco's price.
- There was a small but notable zone of indifference around Monnarch's prices for most of its models. In almost every product category, Monnarch's retail prices could be raised as much as 2 percent with virtually no loss of consumer choice for the Monnarch brand. This was valuable to know, considering the impact of a 1 percent price increase shown earlier in Exhibit 16-2.

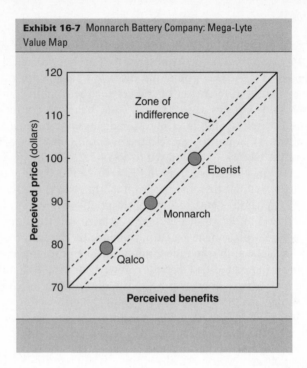

Exhibit 16-7 Monnarch Battery Company: Mega-Lyte Value Map

- Monnarch had underpriced its new stress-resistant, high-performance battery, the Ultra-Lyfe, by as much as 20 percent. In the demanding application niche targeted by Ultra-Lyfe, the innovative battery provided performance attributes that were far superior to Monnarch's own in-house estimates.

These findings unveiled an exciting and unexpected opportunity at the Customer Value level for Monnarch's managers and triggered a number of high-payoff market actions.

MARKET STRATEGY

A number of trends in the replacement automotive battery industry had conspired over the years to place destructive downward pressure on overall industry prices. Improvements in battery design had caused the average life of an automotive battery to increase by more than 15 percent over a decade, resulting in flat unit demand from consumers. Over that same period of time, the three major battery manufacturers had streamlined their manufacturing processes and increased industry production capacity by 11 percent without building a single new manufacturing facility. These trends in demand and supply had resulted in current industry capacity exceeding demand by more than 22 percent.

Furthermore, distribution channels that sold replacement batteries were consolidating drastically. Growing regional and national auto parts retail chains were buying out many of the smaller auto parts retailers. At the same time, an increasing number of consumers were purchasing replacement batteries from the national mass merchandisers and discounters. Battery manufacturers—Monnarch and its competitors—found themselves selling to a smaller number of increasingly powerful retail and wholesale customers who were only too willing to exercise their purchasing power to extract lower and lower prices.

The mass merchandisers and national auto parts retailers frequently advertised their low prices for Monnarch batteries, which fostered intra-brand competition between retailers and further depressed Monnarch's retail prices. Competitors were facing the same channel dynamics. Even the remaining smaller auto parts retailers would pressure Monnarch to give them a price that would allow them to compete with the low prices advertised by the national retailers.

The combination of chronic excess industry capacity, ongoing consolidation in distribution channels, and aggressive intra-brand competition had driven average retail prices paid by consumers for batteries down a real 9.6 percent over five years. As is usually the case, these retail price reductions were basically matched by the lower prices that battery makers could charge their retail and wholesale customers. In the wake of these price declines, profit margins for Monnarch and its competitors were squeezed to unacceptable levels.

Attempts by both Monnarch and its largest competitor, Eberist, to relieve this profit squeeze had been totally ineffective. When Eberist tried to take prices up at some of its largest direct customers, Monnarch received inquires from those customers indicating that they were threatening to leave Eberist and move their business to Monnarch and Qalco. When Monnarch tried to raise prices across the board to small retailers, the most costly channel for Monnarch to serve, the small retailers rebelled, saying they could not compete with low-priced national retailers if Monnarch increased its prices. In both cases, Eberist and Monnarch relented. Meanwhile, Qalco marketed itself in its promotional communications to the market as the lower-priced alternative to Monnarch, contributing to the belief that replacement batteries were undifferentiated commodities.

Mindful that they could do little on the pricing front that would have lasting positive impact unless the decline in industry prices could be slowed, Monnarch managers conducted a thorough assessment of their industry.

Their objective was to understand better the real sources of the price freefall and to devise a plan to stop it. Among their revelations were these:

- Few consumers shopped across different retail channels. In other words, a consumer who goes to a small auto parts retailer to purchase a battery seldom even considers a national mass merchandiser as a viable retail alternative. That consumer values the expert advice of a knowledgeable local retailer. In much the same way, the consumers who purchase their batteries from a mass merchandiser seldom consider the small auto parts retailer.
- While Eberist and Qalco's cost structures were different from Monnarch's, the price/volume/profit tradeoffs (as shown earlier in Exhibit 16-2 for Monnarch) worked essentially the same. In other words, easing downward price pressure was just as attractive for Eberist and Qalco. Furthermore, Monnarch's discrete-choice research showed that if Eberist or Qalco were to cut prices further, they would not gain nearly enough consumer volume to offset the price cut and gain profit margin.
- Although Monnarch liked to see itself as a responsible industry player, Qalco apparently perceived it as an aggressive price competitor—based on comments by Qalco's CEO during their quarterly earnings conference call. The impression came from "introductory prices" Monnarch had offered some of Qalco's high-profile retail accounts during competitive bids for supply contracts. While Qalco retained the customers, it was forced to lower its prices significantly to match Monnarch's bid. As a result, Qalco leaders were likely dubious whenever Monnarch tried to move prices higher.
- Excess production capacity would probably remain a fact of life for the foreseeable future. There were no anticipated developments on either the demand or supply side that would affect that imbalance significantly.

These findings at the Market Strategy level of price management provided fresh perspective and indicated greater freedom for Monnarch to try to relieve some of the downward pressure on pricing that had damaged the industry so much over the past several years.

CAPTURING THE MONNARCH PRICING OPPORTUNITY

So far, we have highlighted the findings of what might be called a pricing diagnostic across the three levels of price management. Crucial pricing issues and opportunities emerged at each of the three levels. Armed with this new knowledge, Monnarch took specific steps to change basic pricing mindsets and behaviors and to build an effective pricing infrastructure to capture and sustain the pricing opportunities it had identified. As discussed in Chapter 6, "Pricing Infrastructure," Monnarch enhanced all of four elements of its pricing infrastructure, including its pricing processes, organization, performance management, and systems and tools. Although many of the price infrastructure improvements taken by Monnarch touch on more than one of the three price management levels (Market Strategy, Customer Value, and Transactions), we summarize these actions within the level that is most appropriate, starting with the Transactions level.

ACTION STEPS: TRANSACTIONS

Monnarch took several steps to bring control and discipline to its transaction pricing. First, it oriented its entire transaction pricing *process and performance management* around pocket price realization. With input from sales, marketing, and pricing managers, Monnarch set overall pocket price targets by account channel and size. These targets were aspirational but not in any way unrealistic, with the dual intentions of actively shaping Monnarch's pocket price band and setting a higher bar, account by account, for pocket price realization. Smaller accounts generally received higher pocket price targets—that is, less total discounting—than large ones. Full-service dealers and distributors who were developing and growing markets for Monnarch and investing in Monnarch merchandising and promotional campaigns had lower pocket price targets than those who were not.

Next, Monnarch compared target pocket price to actual pocket price, account by account. It identified underperforming accounts with large gaps between target and actual pocket price and devised specific account plans to bring their pocket price levels into line. To help account managers identify the individual elements of price that were out of line, Monnarch created an average pocket price waterfall for similar higher-performing accounts and compared it to the waterfall for these over-discounted ones. The account managers quickly saw which elements were excessive and understood what they needed to improve. This targeted approach helped Monnarch bring the majority of its outlier accounts in line within a year.

Simultaneously, Monnarch mounted a program to grow sales volume in select accounts where actual pocket price was already greater than its target. Higher pocket prices made growth in these accounts extremely profitable, so much so that Monnarch earmarked these accounts for special treatment. A marketing and sales team investigated them to determine the nonprice benefits that were most important to them. Monnarch significantly increased their unit sales to these accounts, not by cutting price, but by providing the benefits that were most critical to each: for example, more targeted promotions, higher levels of service, or preferential order fill rates.

Finally, Monnarch instituted an aggressive program to bring greater overall discipline to the transaction *pricing process*. Beyond the pocket price targets discussed above, this program set clear guidelines and decision rules for each element in the pocket price waterfall. Monnarch's IT department created new *information systems* to support and monitor transaction pricing decisions, and Monnarch instituted pocket price as the *companywide metric of price performance* in all of these systems. Each of them measured and assigned, transaction by transaction, all the significant off-invoice waterfall elements that were previously collected and reported only on an aggregate basis. Addressing the crucial *performance management issue of incentives*, compensation for salespeople, sales managers, and even product managers was tied to pocket-price realization against account-specific targets.

ACTION STEPS: CUSTOMER VALUE

Actions at the second level of price management were driven directly from the rich set of consumer and market insights yielded by the discrete choice market research. Knowing the width of the price indifference zone for each product line, the company launched its first broad increase in dealer list prices in years. Although the list price increase was a modest 1.5 to 2 percent for most lines, Monnarch could commit itself to these increases because it was confident that consumers would not switch from the Monnarch brand. Monnarch even shared the detailed market research results with skeptical retailers to help encourage them to charge justifiably higher retail prices in their stores.

Again using the market research, Monnarch relaunched the innovative new Ultra-Lyfe product line with a 16 percent increase in dealer list price. They placed additional advertising emphasis on the benefit attributes that market research had shown to be most important to customers purchasing the Ultra-Lyfe model. And, to help reinforce the high-price, high-benefit positioning of the Ultra-Lyfe line, they refined the central *pricing process* to deny virtually all requests for special or discretionary discounting of the product line (both on- and off-invoice). Furthermore, Monnarch put together a compelling presentation to retailers to convince them that consumers would pay higher prices for the Ultra-Lyfe and to show specific estimates of how this would increase retailer profitability.

In a further adjustment to the core *pricing processes*, Monnarch management no longer even considered requests from the field to discount any Monnarch product lines to approach the price levels of Qalco, the low-end economy competitor, as the discrete-choice research had shown that Qalco's customers were unlikely to switch unless Monnarch prices matched or beat Qalco's.

Finally, the abundant insights drawn from the market research enlightened Monnarch about the value of up-to-date consumer behavior information. Managers realized they had been flying blind for years, and decided to commission similar market research every year or two, or whenever a major discontinuity occurred in their markets (e.g., the launch of a new product)—yet another fundamental *pricing process* shift. These recurring research efforts not only prescribed specific price positioning actions for Monnarch, but also established it as the most informed and credible adviser to retailers on consumer buying behavior for automotive batteries.

ACTION STEPS: MARKET STRATEGY

The action steps and pricing infrastructure upgrades at the Transactions and Customer Value levels were, in most cases, quite direct and explicit, and the impact often seen immediately. Actions taken at the Market Strategy level had less direct and immediate effect but were among the most important taken by Monnarch. If industry prices continued their fall uninterrupted, the hard-fought gains at the Transactions and Customer Value levels might be wiped out by industry-wide price declines.

The first steps taken at this level were designed to decrease the destructive Monnarch intrabrand competition across the different types of retailers. Monnarch took its research on consumer buying behavior to its retailers to demonstrate that the various retail battery channels—mass merchandisers, national auto parts retailers, and small auto parts retailers—were seldom competing for the same customers. The small auto parts retailer did not share customers with the national auto parts chains and did not have to be overly concerned with their advertised prices for Monnarch batteries. Likewise, the national auto parts chains did not have to worry much about mass merchandisers' advertised prices; consumers in their customer base seldom shopped the mass merchandisers for auto parts.

In another significant *pricing process* enhancement, Monnarch next designed and executed a thoughtful communications program to its channel partners and end-consumers around its across-the-board list price increase. Monnarch was upfront that the increase was indeed market-based. Monnarch issued press releases explaining the logic and intent of its price increase and the benefit that it expected Monnarch and its retailers to gain. Monnarch trained its salespeople on how to sell the price increase to retailers and how to respond constructively to their questions and unavoidable objections. Monnarch's president and CEO took every opportunity to explain and reinforce the rationale behind the price increase and even accompanied salespeople on calls to select key accounts where the price increase had encountered some resistance. Again, Monnarch's organizational resolve to making the price increase stick was clear and unwavering.

Finally, Monnarch marketing and sales management went on high alert to make sure that Monnarch was not taking any actions in the marketplace that might be construed as counter to the constructive pricing behavior that they were trying to exhibit. Extra care was taken to avoid aggressive transactional discounting in accounts shared by or visible to Eberist and Qalco. All promotional programs were carefully assessed to assure that the market would not perceive them as price cuts counter to the spirit of constructive pricing behavior. It was clear to Monnarch managers that any market action taken that might be misread by the market could completely undermine the constructive pricing initiative.

HARD-WIRING THE CHANGE

Monnarch's efforts to create and sustain improved performance in pricing went well beyond specific action steps across the three levels of pricing and improvements in pricing infrastructure. As discussed in Chapter 15, "Pricing Transformation," reaching for *the price advantage* requires a dedicated transformational effort. The four primary tasks needed to shift pricing behaviors and mindsets were each explicitly addressed in Monnarch's pricing change program:

1. *Fostering understanding and conviction.* The CEO and president augmented his external market communications on pricing with an ongoing internal dialogue. Pricing became a routine agenda item at all monthly and quarterly management meetings. It was clear to everyone that senior leadership was unambiguously committed to the creation of a sustained price advantage for Monnarch.
2. *Reinforcing with formal mechanisms.* In addition to all the pricing process and systems changes described earlier and the incentive compensation changes, Monnarch senior management took many symbolic steps to further reinforce a positive pricing mindset. For instance, each month the CEO and president made personal commendation calls to the salespeople who had achieved the most significant improvements in individual account pricing performance. These calls made the priority of pricing excellence across Monnarch unmistakable.
3. *Developing talent and skill.* One of Monnarch's most talented marketing managers was assigned the position of pricing director. She not

only helped orchestrate the upgraded Monnarch pricing processes but also took the lead in building pricing capability across marketing and sales. She pushed the development and execution of training sessions on all of the new transactional pricing tools. She led regular field workshops with sellers to brainstorm and share a growing arsenal of pricing improvement ideas that was being created across Monnarch. She also acquired and developed individuals with the additional talents required to support the reconstructed pricing processes, for example, experts in consumer price research.

4. *Role modeling.* The CEO and president provided a positive pricing role model to the Monnarch organization by personally taking tough stands with even large customers who were asking for excessive discounting. Furthermore, care was taken that the "salesperson of the year" award be given only to an individual who displayed exemplary pricing performance in addition to high-revenue volume performance.

* * *

The Monnarch Battery Company case illustrates the intertwining set of initiatives, pricing infrastructure enhancements, and change programs that cut across all levels of price management when a business gets serious about creating *the price advantage* for itself. The journey to create *the price advantage* was a rewarding one for Monnarch. In the first year of full implementation, an ROS increase of 2.1 percentage points was attributed to price performance improvement—that is, ROS increased from 5.2 to 7.3 percent. Incremental improvements continued in the second and third years, resulting in a cumulative ROS increase of 5.4 percentage points from the pricing program. Monnarch more than doubled its operating profits—and has sustained and continues to build on that improvement—through thoughtful pricing infrastructure advancements across all three of the price management levels along with a deliberate ongoing effort to build enhanced mindsets, behaviors, and core pricing capabilities. Monnarch management remains convinced to this day that no other initiative could have yielded the lasting profit impact of their enthusiastic creation of *the price advantage*.

Epilogue

So is now the time to begin to make *the price advantage* one of your advantages—to make excellence in managing the prices you charge for the goods and services you provide a cornerstone of your ongoing success and profitability? Should you strive to execute the pricing function routinely at a level of skill and professionalism that exceeds your industry peers and serves as a source of sustainable competitive advantage?

The reasons to excel at pricing are diverse and compelling. No single management lever available to you can boost profitability more quickly than even a slight improvement in average price levels. As we have discussed earlier, a one percentage-point improvement in price can drive huge increases in operating profits. Just as importantly, however, excellence in pricing requires and pulls along in its wake excellence in other essential management disciplines.

It requires you to understand your customers more richly than ever, to know the benefits that are most important to them, and to deliver those benefits in a manner that is so superior that your customers can easily justify any price premium that you seek. It requires you to understand how customers compare your prices to those of competitors, and determine the pricing architecture that causes your prices to be perceived most positively by customers.

Excellence in pricing also demands that you understand your competitors better, that you comprehend the price/benefit tradeoffs they are offering in your markets, so that you can consistently maintain a position of value equivalence and even value advantage in the eyes of the customers you most want to serve. It requires you to understand with greater clarity the price initiatives and price levels of your competitors, so that the misreads that invariably lead to price wars can be avoided.

And finally, it requires that you understand yourself better, understand your economics of serving individual customers with greater precision, and understand your benefit delivery capability—both what it is and what it could be—so that you can target the market segments and customers that are truly best for you. Excellence in pricing requires you to take a hard look at your own competitive behavior to assess and potentially improve your conduct that places unnecessary downward pressure on price levels in your markets.

Achieving the *price advantage* and all the benefits that come with it does not happen by accident. To excel at pricing is hard work. It compels you not just to react to market and competitive prices but *to manage pricing actively*—with organizational commitment and discipline and structure. It requires you to build a robust pricing infrastructure—the processes, organization, supporting tools, and performance management that will enable and sustain pricing excellence.

But the investment to create *the price advantage* is worth it. Adopting the "profit center" mentality about pricing that we described earlier would justify a company's investing in pricing excellence at the same level as a growth initiative or an acquisition that would increase sales volume by 15 to 40 percent. The investment to create pricing excellence is invariably much less; so the return on investment for creating *the price advantage* is among the most attractive that any business can generate.

We hope that with this book, we have convinced you that *the price advantage* is indeed an advantage worth pursuing aggressively and worth the effort required to achieve it ultimately. We hope also that we have provided you with a practical approach and the tools that will help you begin to routinely capture the full complement of pricing opportunities that remain by and large untapped by most businesses today, and begin to make *the price advantage* your advantage. We wish you the best of luck as you embark on this journey.

Pocket Price and Pocket Margin Waterfalls

In Chapter 3, "Transactions," we presented the pocket price and pocket margin waterfalls. Here, we offer a collection of waterfalls from disguised client situations to illustrate how revenue can leak through a wide variety of mechanisms. This collection not only shows how waterfall elements can proliferate (often unintentionally) and how they can trigger large differences between base and pocket prices, but also how the waterfalls differ across a broad sweep of businesses.

To clarify the nature of the transaction, we have noted the customer on both the waterfall and the contents page. Please note that these waterfalls reflect the situation for a specific product at a specific company during a particular time period. They are not meant to be broadly applicable examples. Also, all list and base prices have been indexed to 100.

Exhibit A1-1 Contents

Pocket Price Waterfalls

Product	Customer
Athletic Shoe	Retailer/distributor
Breakfast Cereal	Retailer/distributor
Candy	Retailer/distributor
Consumer Audio Equipment	Retailer/distributor
Dishwasher	Retailer/distributor
Electrical Controls	Distributor/OEM
Elevators	Contractor/Developers
Executive Recruiting	Business
Fabricated Aluminum Products	Business
Furniture	Retailer/distributor
Laboratory Services	Doctor/hospital systems
Nonferrous Metals	Business
Passenger Car	Dealer
Personal Computer	Dealer/retailer
Polymer	Business
Specialty Chemicals	Business
Surgical Supplies	Distributor/hospital systems
Television	Retailer/distributor
Vinyl Flooring	Retailer/distributor
Voice and Data Communication Service	Business

Pocket Margin Waterfalls

Product	Customer
Automotive Aftermarket Parts	Retailer/distributor
Automotive Glass	OEM
Business Line of Credit	Business
Commodity Chemical	Business
Construction Equipment	Business/distributor
Custom Manufacturing System	Business
Enterprise Computer	Business
Enterprise Software and Service	Business
Maintenance Service	Business
Medical Device	Distributor/hospital systems
Office Products	Business
Plastic	Business
Rolled Steel	Business
Technical Services	Business

Exhibit A1-2 Athletic Shoe—Pocket Price Waterfall

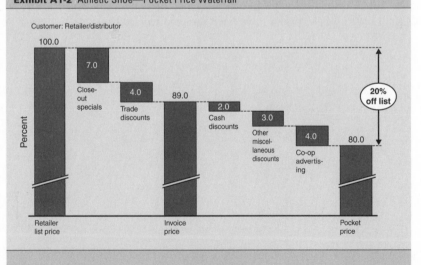

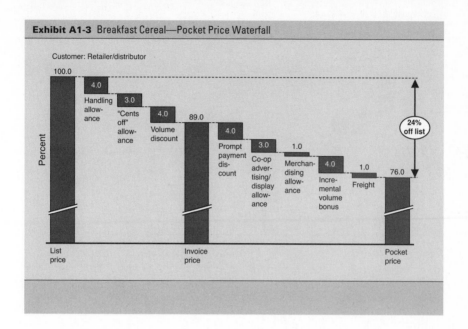

Exhibit A1-3 Breakfast Cereal—Pocket Price Waterfall

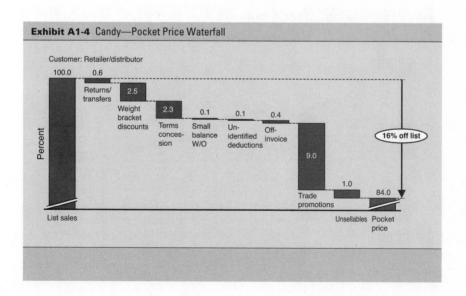

Exhibit A1-4 Candy—Pocket Price Waterfall

Exhibit A1-5 Consumer Audio Equipment—Pocket Price Waterfall

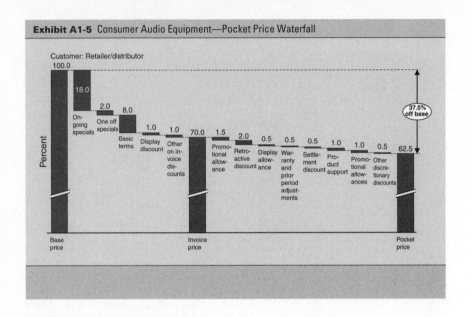

Exhibit A1-6 Dishwasher—Pocket Price Waterfall

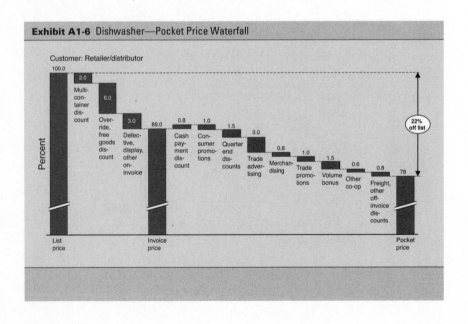

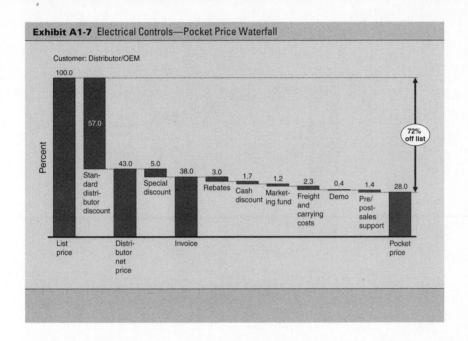

Exhibit A1-7 Electrical Controls—Pocket Price Waterfall

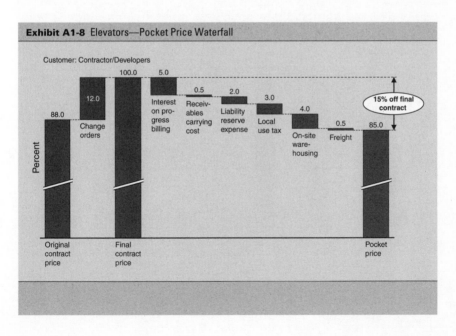

Exhibit A1-8 Elevators—Pocket Price Waterfall

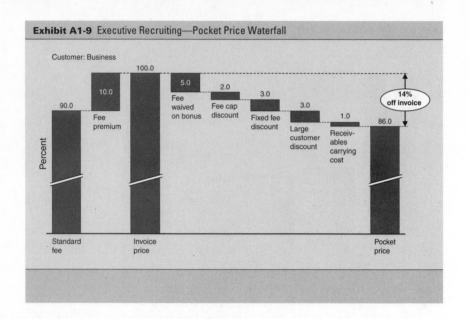

Exhibit A1-9 Executive Recruiting—Pocket Price Waterfall

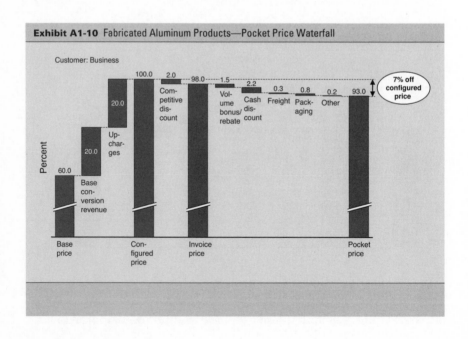

Exhibit A1-10 Fabricated Aluminum Products—Pocket Price Waterfall

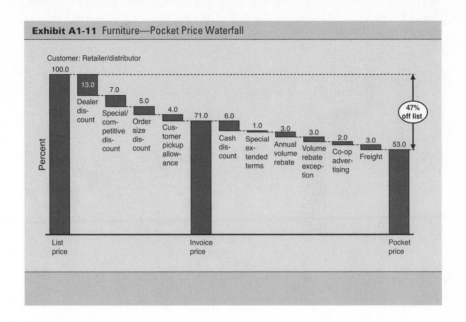

Exhibit A1-11 Furniture—Pocket Price Waterfall

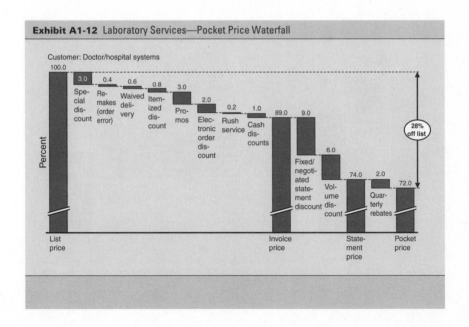

Exhibit A1-12 Laboratory Services—Pocket Price Waterfall

Exhibit A1-13 Nonferrous Metals—Pocket Price Waterfall

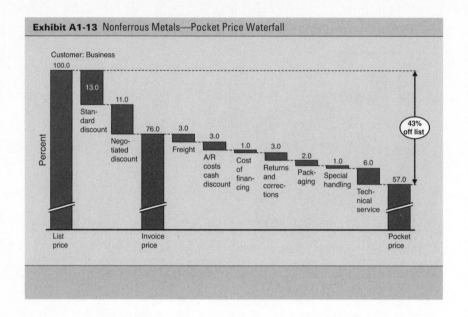

Exhibit A1-14 Passenger Car—Pocket Price Waterfall

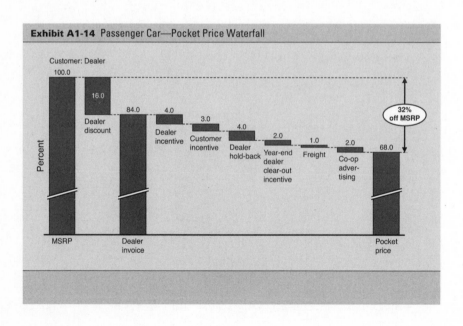

Exhibit A1-15 Personal Computer—Pocket Price Waterfall

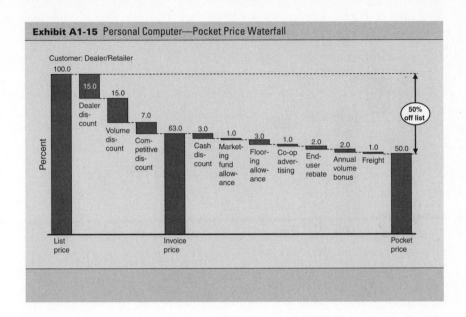

Exhibit A1-16 Polymer—Pocket Price Waterfall

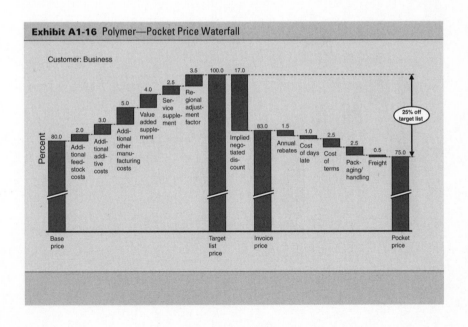

Exhibit A1-17 Specialty Chemicals—Pocket Price Waterfall

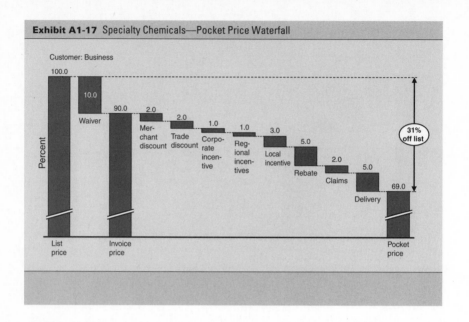

Exhibit A1-18 Surgical Supplies—Pocket Price Waterfall

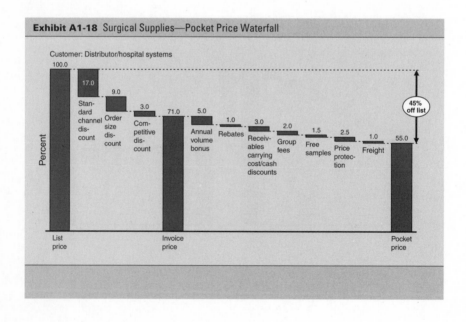

Exhibit A1-19 Television—Pocket Price Waterfall

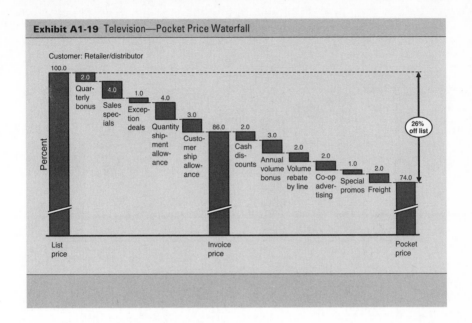

Exhibit A1-20 Vinyl Flooring—Pocket Price Waterfall

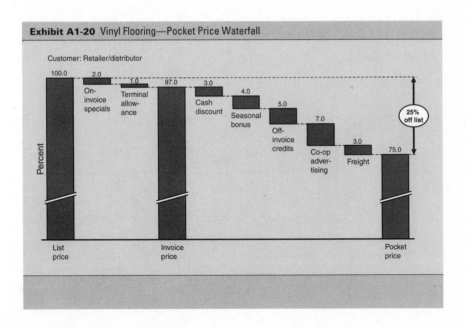

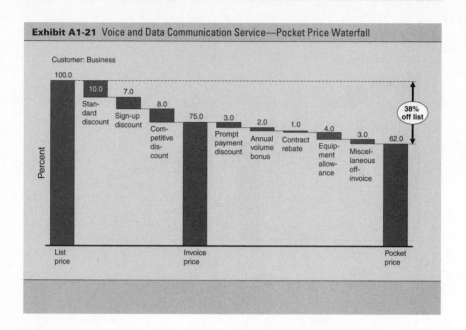

Exhibit A1-21 Voice and Data Communication Service—Pocket Price Waterfall

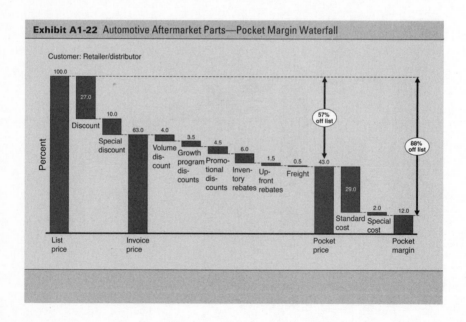

Exhibit A1-22 Automotive Aftermarket Parts—Pocket Margin Waterfall

Exhibit A1-23 Automotive Glass—Pocket Margin Waterfall

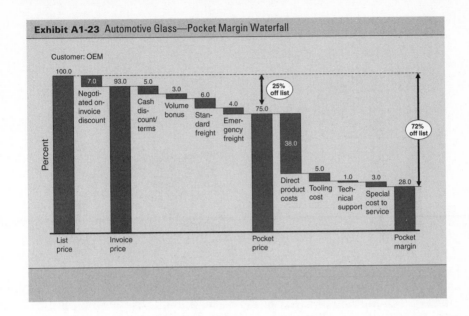

Exhibit A1-24 Business Line of Credit—Pocket Margin Waterfall

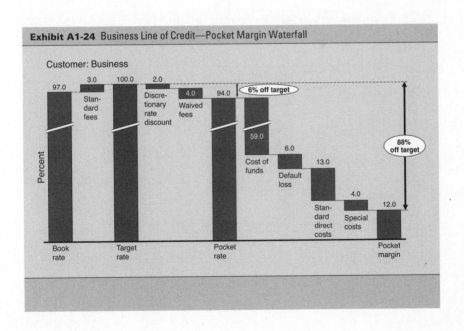

Exhibit A1-25 Commodity Chemical—Pocket Margin Waterfall

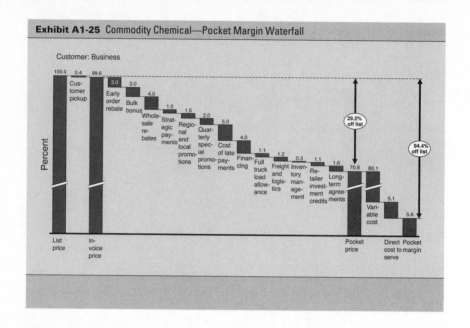

Exhibit A1-26 Construction Equipment—Pocket Margin Waterfall

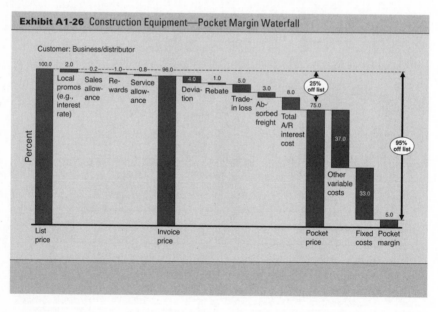

Exhibit A1-27 Custom Manufacturing System—Pocket Margin Waterfall

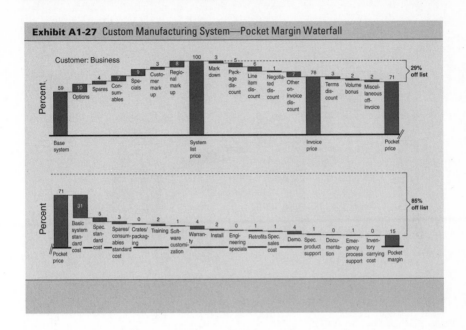

Exhibit A1-28 Enterprise Computer—Pocket Margin Waterfall

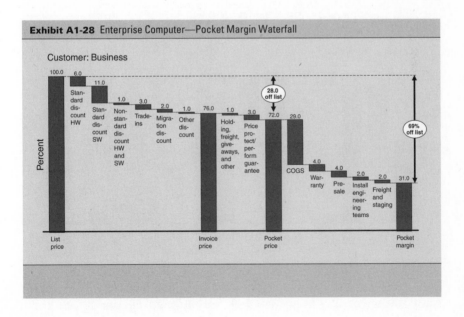

Exhibit A1-29 Enterprise Software and Service—Pocket Margin Waterfall

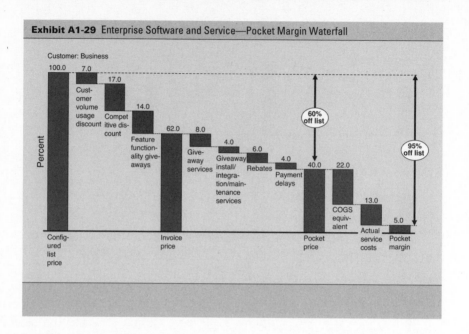

Exhibit A1-30 Maintenance Service—Pocket Margin Waterfall

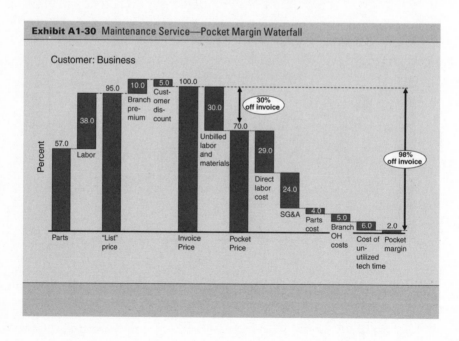

Exhibit A1-31 Medical Device—Pocket Margin Waterfall

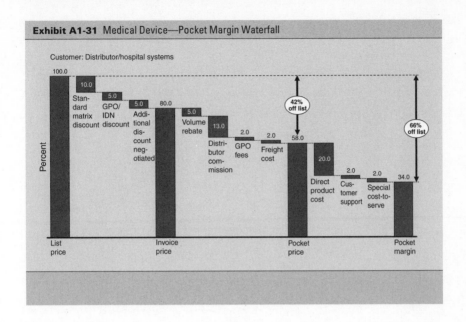

Exhibit A1-32 Office Products—Pocket Margin Waterfall

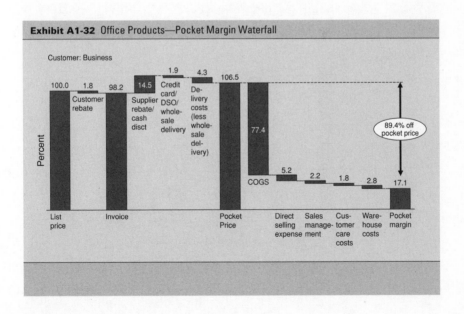

Exhibit A1-33 Plastic—Pocket Margin Waterfall

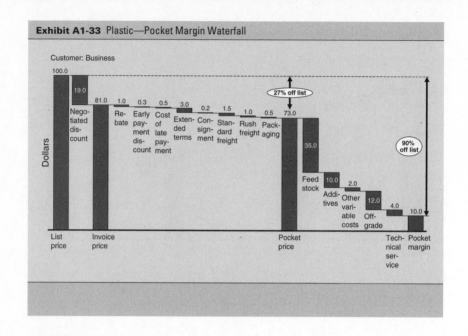

Exhibit A1-34 Rolled Steel—Pocket Margin Waterfall

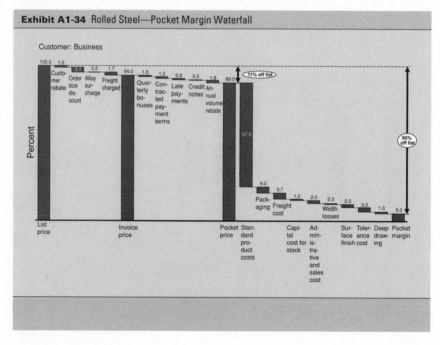

Exhibit A1-35 Technical Services—Pocket Margin Waterfall

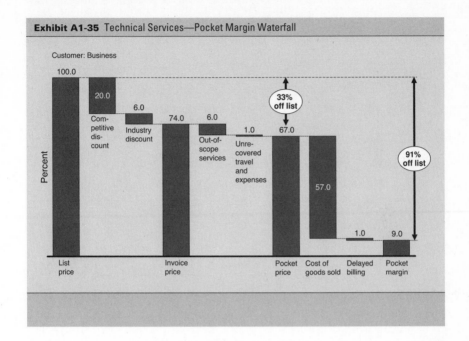

Antitrust Issues

This appendix highlights some of the major U.S. and EU antitrust statutes and regulations relevant to pricing strategy. The descriptions are not exhaustive. Because these laws are continuously in flux, companies should always obtain advice from legal counsel on the current state of the law, how it is applied, and whether the actions being discussed comply with relevant laws. As previously mentioned, this book is descriptive and does not constitute legal advice.

U.S. PRICING LAW

The U.S. experience with federal antitrust statutes has developed over more than a century and has influenced the law in other jurisdictions, such as the European Union and Japan.[1] A common thread that runs through much of U.S. antitrust law is that some practices are always anti-competitive and are therefore considered to be *per se* illegal; by contrast, others are considered good or bad depending on the circumstances, so they are judged under the *rule of reason.*[2]

---

[1]This section examines U.S. laws that apply generally at the federal level. Individual states also have antitrust statutes that tend to be consistent with the federal statutes, but there are exceptions. This appendix does not examine industry-specific laws and those at the state level.

[2]Antitrust laws in the United States are enforced by the government. At the federal level, the Justice Department may file civil and criminal actions, while the Federal Trade Commission (FTC) and private parties (e.g., resellers, customers) may bring civil cases. While criminal violations are felonies, such penalties are usually used only in *per se* cases of price fixing and hardcore cartel activity. Civil plaintiffs often pursue injunctions to stop objectionable behavior, and private parties, if successful, are entitled to three times their actual economic damages (called *treble damages*), plus their legal fees and court costs.

Under the *per se* test, courts require only that the plaintiff prove the presence of the objectionable activity, along with antitrust injury and damages. In contrast, the *rule of reason* adds a third element—that the conduct is unreasonably anticompetitive. This additional point generally makes it more difficult to prove a violation of *rule of reason* because it requires evidence of adverse competitive effect and the defendant has the opportunity to justify its behavior. As a result, more pricing flexibility tends to be available under the *rule of reason* standard.

Significantly, U.S. antitrust law for the last 25 years or so has been moving away from *per se* treatment and toward *rule of reason*. Consequently, the law has become increasingly more forgiving, as many of the old assumptions have been jettisoned in favor of a more fact-based approach.[3]

Despite the changes in the law, we would be remiss if we did not emphasize the fact that the most serious or "hardcore" pricing violations remain strictly prohibited, and that companies and individuals that engage in such violations suffer significant consequences, ranging from large fines to prison sentences for individual directors and managers. For example, a fine of more than $1.2 billion was imposed by U.S. and EU authorities in the vitamins cartel price-fixing case in 2001.

PRICE FIXING OR PRICE ENCOURAGEMENT

There are two types of price fixing: horizontal and vertical. In horizontal price fixing, competitors agree on the prices they will charge or on the key terms of sale affecting price. In vertical price fixing, also known as *resale price fixing*, a supplier and a reseller agree on the prices the reseller will charge or the price-related terms of resale for the supplier's products.[4]

Horizontal Price Fixing   Horizontal price fixing remains *per se* illegal, except when the pricing reflects the collaborative nature of the effort (e.g.,

---

[3]Even the European Union softened its historically more structuralist approach in 2000, creating a safe harbor that permits a supplier to control how its products are resold in certain situations by allowing the seller to impose territorial and certain other vertical nonprice restrictions as long as the supplier's market share is 30 percent or less. (Case reference: OJ (L 336) 21.)

[4]In the United States, the supplier cannot be charged with vertical price fixing when the intermediary does not take title to the goods or services from the supplier. So a supplier may tell an independent sales representative or sales agent (in an agreement or otherwise) what price to charge for the supplier's goods or services. The same is true for a party that holds the supplier's products on consignment until they are sold to the end user.

competitors bring a joint product to market and must agree on a price that does not create a negative effect). However, such circumstances are closely watched and narrowly defined. Under such circumstances, the *rule of reason* applies.[5]

Vertical Price Fixing   The principal points of U.S. law in this area are Section 1 of the Sherman Act, an 1890 statute that prohibits "every contract, combination . . . or conspiracy in restraint of trade," and the subsequent cases that have shaped its application. Two important points bear mention. First, the "contract, combination, or conspiracy" requirement means that there must be an express or tacit agreement between two or more individuals or entities. If a company is acting alone, there can be no illegal price fixing.

Second, written contracts and other direct evidence of price-fixing conspiracies are rare, so evidence of agreement usually must be inferred from the actions of the parties involved.[6] For example, based on case law, courts are more likely to find illegal price fixing when there is parallel pricing behavior and one of two situations:

1. Such conduct would be against the self-interest of each party if the party acted alone, but consistent with their self-interest when they all behave the same way. An example would be near-simultaneous price increases when the companies involved all have excess production capacity and input costs have not increased.
2. Such conduct is preceded by an opportunity to collude, such as direct communications between the parties, and the actions taken cannot be supported by legitimate business explanations.

The rule of reason was used to liberalize the federal law of resale price setting in 2007 in the Supreme Court in *Leegin Creative Leather Products, Inc. v. PSKS, Inc.* It permitted a supplier to set a minimum or exact resale-selling price by agreement with its wholesalers, distributors, dealers, or retailers. This is the identical rule that has governed such common practices as defining reseller territories, confining reseller sales to particular locations,

---

[5]In *National Collegiate Athletic Association v. Board of Regents*, 468 U.S. 85 (1984), while competitors getting together in an athletic conference served many useful purposes, broadcast restrictions, which affected output and price were struck down under *rule of reason*. See Federal Trade Commission and U.S. Department of Justice, *Antitrust Guidelines for Collaborations Among Competitors* (April 2000).

[6]The practice of imitating a competitor's pricing or other moves in the market—something called *conscious parallelism*—is not illegal. There must be proof of an agreement to meet the Sherman Act standard.

or allocating reseller customers for the last 30 years. It is also the same test that the Court determined 11 years ago applies to maximum resale price setting by agreement.

The *Leegin* decision has not been popular at the state level or with certain members of Congress, and may be challenged in the future. Many state antitrust laws follow it, but there are exceptions.

It is important to note that when a supplier sets resale price unilaterally, it is outside the scope of the antitrust laws and therefore lawful. The *Leegin* decision did not disturb *U.S. v. Colgate,* a 1919 case that held that a supplier could lawfully announce the terms or policies under which it will do business with its customers—including a minimum resale price—and cease to do business with those that choose not to follow its terms. Moreover, compliance by the supplier's customers does not create an agreement. Many high-end brands of consumer durables have successfully adopted minimum price policies in the United States to protect their brand price positions from erosion.

If a company decides to go the more conservative route in adopting a resale price policy (e.g., to further protect itself if states challenge the *Leegin* decision), it needs to be more cautious. The way it implements its policy makes all the difference between legality and illegality under the *Colgate* precedent. The supplier typically announces the desired resale price as a policy and then refuses to do business with any reseller that does not comply.[7] No contracts can establish or enforce the policy. Similarly, discussions with resellers regarding this matter must be limited to explaining the policy, as no assurances of compliance can be sought or accepted. In addition, a violator of the policy cannot be placed on probation. In its least risky form, this approach is zero-tolerance, one-strike-and-you're-out, although it is entirely up to the supplier when, if ever, to reinstate the violator.

Because of the narrowness of the exception for unilateral acts, it is imperative that the supplier's headquarters and field people be instructed carefully on what they can and cannot say and do. Moreover, the policy should be applied uniformly; otherwise, an appearance of an illegal agreement can occur.

---

[7]Compliance with the policy is not considered to be an agreement to maintain a price. In addition, the policy can apply to some or all products, channels, or geographic areas. Moreover, failure to comply may result in the loss of only the covered product or products upon which the violation occurred, a product line, or all of the supplier's products.

PRICE SIGNALING

Sometimes companies communicate pricing or other intentions to the market, which facilitates parallel behavior by competitors. While this phenomenon is not illegal, care must be taken to avoid the inference of an illegal contract, combination, or conspiracy. The communications must be public and have a clear business purpose apart from giving early warning to the competition (e.g., providing customers advance notice of a price increase, furnishing investors with insight into the company's pricing strategy). Two examples illustrate these points. In the first, the court found nothing unlawful when manufacturers of gasoline additives provided advance public notice of price increases beyond that required by their customer contracts. The stated purpose was to aid buyers in their financial and purchase planning.[8]

In the second example, eight major airlines and their jointly owned data company had to settle price-fixing charges centering on a nonpublic computerized system that communicated intended fare changes and promotions and permitted later modification or withdrawal of them.[9] The system apparently served as a virtual smoke-filled room in which the parties privately discussed and effectively coordinated pricing.

PREDATORY PRICING

A supplier engages in predatory pricing when it tries to drive competition out of business by setting its prices below its marginal cost or average variable cost, which is easier to measure over time. Such practice is unlawful only if the resulting market structure allows the supplier to recoup its losses by raising prices. This factor makes it difficult to bring predatory pricing suits successfully.

PRICE DISCRIMINATION

Price discrimination is simply charging different prices to different customers, but it is unlawful in the United States only under certain

---

[8]*E. I. Du Pont de Nemours & Co. v. FTC*, 729 F.2d 128 (2d Cir. 1984), decided under Section 5 of the Federal Trade Commission Act, 15 U.S.C. § 45, a statute that is more regulator-friendly than the Sherman Act. The court upheld the legality of price signaling where there was no evidence that it was collusive, predatory, coercive, or exclusionary.

[9]*United States v. Airline Tariff Publishing Co.*, 1994-2 Trade Cas. (CCH) ¶ 70,686 (D.D.C. 1994); 836 F. Supp. 12 (D.D.C. 1993).

conditions.[10] The law in this area—usually referred to as the Robinson-Patman Act[11]—balances the economic efficiency justification for price discrimination with the goal of preserving competition by maintaining the viability of numerous sellers, erring on the side of the latter.

In order to prove illegal price discrimination under the Robinson-Patman Act, *each* of five elements must be present:

1. *Discrimination.* Different prices are charged to different customers. But there is no discrimination if the price difference is based on a discount or allowance available to all or almost all customers—for example, a prompt payment discount. This is called the *availability* defense.
2. *Sales to two or more customers.* Different prices must be charged on reasonably contemporaneous sales to two or more purchasers.
3. *Goods.* The sale must be of goods, not services or bundles where services predominate in value.
4. *Like grade and quality.* The goods must be physically the same or essentially the same. For this element, the willingness to pay more for branded products is irrelevant.
5. *Reasonable probability of competitive injury.* There must be substantial competitive injury or the reasonable probability of it, usually at one of two levels. In *a primary line case,* a company may file suit against a competitive supplier for the latter's discriminatory pricing, but the law requires proof that the competitor's prices are below its costs and that the market structure is such that the competitor may recoup its losses.[12] In a secondary line case, a supplier's disfavored customer may sue the supplier for price discrimination, as long as the customers in question compete with each other.[13]

---

[10] Price discrimination can also be charging the same price to different customers in different circumstances, although this situation arises much less often in practice.

[11] *15 U.S.C. § 13.* The U.S. Justice Department and the FTC may enforce this law, but neither is particularly active in this regard. By far, most cases are brought by one business against another (consumers have no standing to sue).

[12] *Brooke Group Ltd. v. Brown & Williamson Corp.,* 509 U.S. 209, 221-24 (1993). This standard is so onerous that the threat of a primary line case tends to be rather remote.

[13] If they don't compete, the Robinson-Patman Act does not prohibit price discrimination. The lack of customer overlap may occur naturally or it may be engineered with the use of vertical nonprice restrictions discussed later in this appendix. The customers in question can be either resellers or end users that compete.

Even in cases where all five of the elements of price discrimination are present, there are three defenses that may be used to avoid a finding of unlawful discrimination:

1. *Cost justification.* A price disparity is permitted if it is based on legitimate cost differences.
2. *Meeting competition.* Discrimination is permissible if it is based on a good faith belief that a discriminatory price is necessary to meet (but not beat) the price of a competitive supplier to the favored customer or to maintain a traditional price difference.
3. *Changing conditions.* Special prices may be provided to sell perishable, seasonal, obsolete, or distressed merchandise.

VERTICAL NONPRICE RESTRICTIONS

There are several ways a supplier can control how much its resellers compete with each other on price or otherwise using the suppliers' products, a situation known as *intra-brand competition*. Fortunately, U.S. law affords suppliers a good deal of flexibility in the name of promoting competition between rival brands, or *inter-brand competition*. Each of the three approaches described below is judged under the *rule of reason* (or something substantially similar) and may be implemented using the carrot approach, the stick approach, or a combination:[14]

1. *Customer restrictions.* The supplier specifies that the reseller may sell only to certain customers or may not sell to certain customers.
2. *Territorial or market restrictions.* The supplier defines a certain geographical area or market in which the reseller may sell and prohibits or discourages the reseller from selling outside of it.[15]
3. *Product restrictions.* The supplier determines which of its products a reseller may buy, prohibits reseller or end user purchases of certain products from another supplier, or ties the sale of a desirable product or service with the purchase of a less desirable product or service.

---

[14] Under the carrot approach, financial incentives are provided by the supplier to reward compliance. Under the stick approach, a failure to comply results in a termination of the relationship due to breach of the distribution agreement or otherwise.

[15] This tactic can be combined with the grant of an exclusive distributorship, where the supplier agrees not to supply anyone but the reseller in that market. When an exclusive distributorship is combined with absolute confinement to a geographic territory, the result is referred to as an *airtight territory*.

PROMOTIONAL DISCRIMINATION

Promotional discrimination is providing different benefits, such as advertising allowances, to different customers, effectively achieving discriminatory pricing through other means. While the Robinson-Patman Act also governs promotional discrimination, the standards here are more flexible in some respects than those for price discrimination.

Promotional discrimination is unlawful if *each* of three elements is present:

1. *"The provision of allowances, services, or facilities . . ."* The supplier grants advertising or promotional allowances or provides services or facilities, such as free display racks or demonstrators.
2. *". . . in connection with the resale of the supplier's goods . . ."* The law applies only to resellers and only to the sale of goods, not services.[16]
3. *". . . which are not available to all competing customers on proportionally equal terms."*[17] As with price discrimination, only competing customers must be treated alike. The greater flexibility here is based on the fact that competing customers do not have to receive the same level of benefits—only benefits that are proportionally equal based on unit or dollar purchases, the cost to the reseller of the promotional activity, or the value of the promotional activity to the supplier.

Notably, there are also three ways in which the standards for promotional discrimination are more restrictive than those for price discrimination. First, the same sort of evidence of competitive injury is not required, so in certain respects, promotional discrimination is treated as a *per se* offense.

Second, the only defense when all three elements are proven is meeting competition, as cost justification and changing conditions are irrelevant. Finally, if the supplier provides promotional benefits to direct buying resellers, it must also furnish them to competitive resellers that buy the same products through intermediaries.

---

[16] Due to differing standards, deciding whether a pricing action under consideration is to be judged as price discrimination is important As a rule, price discrimination applies to the sale of goods by the supplier to the end user or reseller, while promotional discrimination applies only to the resellers of such goods.

[17] While availability is a defense to price discrimination, functional availability is required to avoid illegal promotional discrimination. The benefits or the performance necessary to earn them must be usable or attainable in a practical sense by all competing customers. If not, alternatives must be offered.

PRICE SQUEEZES

When a producer has monopoly power in an intermediary product and both *sells* the product to others for further processing and *does* such processing itself, it engages in a something known as a *price squeeze* when it prices the intermediary and finished products so that competitors cannot compete in the finished product market. The same effect can occur when a company sells at both the *wholesale* and *retail* levels, has monopoly power at wholesale, and prices so that wholesale customers cannot compete against it in the retail market.

EU PRICING LAW

This section highlights the relevant European Union (EU) regulations and the primary ways in which EU law differs from U.S. law. The descriptions are not exhaustive, and companies should always consult with legal counsel for specifics on whether a certain program complies with the laws described. There are two key differences between the EU law governing pricing and U.S. law. First, there is a crucial distinction in the European Union between a company deemed to be *dominant* and one that is not. Most EU pricing law applies only if a company is dominant.[18] Second, the EU supports the use of rules to promote the creation of a single European market—including pricing rules. Analyses of the relevant products and geographic markets and the market share of a company can be key determinants of whether its pricing practices are legal or illegal.

As shown in Exhibit A2-1, while a market share of 50 percent or higher raises a presumption of dominance, the European Court of Justice (ECJ) has found dominance in a company with a share as low as 39.7 percent.[19] In addition, the European Commission (EC) has stated that a dominant position cannot be ruled out when market share is between 25 and 40 percent. There are other factors the EC and the ECJ consider to determine dominance, including relative market share compared with competitors, barriers to entry, and the period of time the company has held its market position.

---

[18] The European Court of Justice (ECJ) has defined dominance as "a position of economic strength . . . [enabling a company] to prevent effective competition being maintained on the relevant market by affording it the power to behave to an appreciable extent independently of its competitors, customers and ultimately of its consumers." Case 27/76 *United Brands* [1978], ECR 207, ¶ 65.

[19] Fifty percent presumption: C-62/86 AZKO [1991] ECR-2585; 39.7 percent finding: *Virgin/British Airways*, OJ [2000] L 30/1, [2000] 4 CMLR 999.

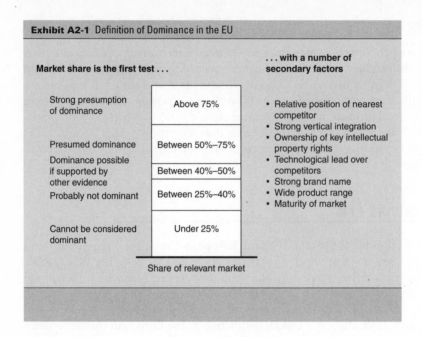

Exhibit A2-1 Definition of Dominance in the EU

Market share is the first test . . .

		... with a number of secondary factors
Strong presumption of dominance	Above 75%	• Relative position of nearest competitor • Strong vertical integration • Ownership of key intellectual property rights • Technological lead over competitors • Strong brand name • Wide product range • Maturity of market
Presumed dominance	Between 50%–75%	
Dominance possible if supported by other evidence	Between 40%–50%	
Probably not dominant	Between 25%–40%	
Cannot be considered dominant	Under 25%	

Share of relevant market

Further, duopolistic or oligopolistic markets can lead to a finding of *collective dominance* and cause companies that otherwise would not be dominant to be deemed dominant for the application of pricing laws. An explicit agreement or other legal link is not necessary for companies to be considered collectively dominant. EU law is not clear on this subject, so in situations where there is a potential oligopoly, companies should be careful even when engaging in practices that are prohibited only for dominant companies.

The second key distinction between U.S. and EU pricing laws regards the unique structure of the European market. The European Union has a strong focus on market integration of its member states, and the EC and ECJ support the use of the EU competition rules to promote market integration and the building of a single European market. Thus certain actions, such as restricting export from one EU country to another, are especially prohibited as contrary to this single-market goal.

The relevant EU statutes in this area are Articles 81 and 82 of the European Community Treaty (formerly Articles 85 and 86). Article 81 deals in general with collusive pricing, whether the companies involved are in dominant positions or not; Article 82 addresses abuse of a dominant position and only applies to companies deemed to be dominant. For a nondominant company, price fixing and resale price fixing are restricted, but most other pricing practices are legal so long as they do not represent collusion with competitors.

Specific national laws are not within the scope of this book. Companies operating within the European Union must comply both with EU law and also with any local laws, which may be stricter. Most of these laws are similar to EU law in the areas of pricing, but in some cases national laws carry a stricter punishment for violation or provide a broader standing for others to bring a case against potential violators. The major exceptions to the similarity in legal rules are France and Germany, where the national nondiscrimination laws are more restrictive on pricing policy. In most cases companies will need to remain cognizant of both EU law and national laws when setting pricing policy.

PRICE FIXING OR PRICE ENCOURAGEMENT

As mentioned previously, there are two types of price fixing: horizontal and vertical. In horizontal price fixing, competitors agree on the prices they will charge or on the key terms of sale affecting price. In vertical price fixing, also known as resale price fixing, a supplier and a reseller agree on the prices the reseller will charge or the price-related terms of resale for the supplier's products.

Horizontal Price Fixing   As in the United States, horizontal price-fixing agreements are essentially *per se* illegal. This prohibition applies to both dominant and nondominant firms. Even in cases where participants failed to comply with agreed-upon prices, such agreements are a violation of the law.

Price uniformity among competitors does not as such violate Article 81, but it may lead to an inference that unlawful concerted action has taken place when additional factors—such as escalating prices when there is large unused capacity and several competitors present—exist.[20] For example, *parallel pricing* when the competitors have met or made contact has been held illegal when deemed to limit competition. While neither the ECJ nor any European court has found companies guilty of an unlawful concerted practice where

---

[20] The leading case on this subject is the *Dyestuffs* case, Decision 69/243 OJ 1969 L195/11, in which several uniform price increases in the aniline dye market throughout Europe in the mid-1960s led to a EC investigation of 17 producers. The investigations resulted in a ruling of "concerted practice" and fines for all but one company. The court ruled that "concerted practice" can be a form of coordination, without amounting to formal agreement, which purposely substitutes practical cooperation for the risks of competition.

they have not met, European rules take a strict approach to the notion of concerted practice, which covers communication of a company's actual or intended policies on pricing with the intent that competitors will react. If the industry is oligopolistic, competitive companies' prices moving in tandem can give rise to suspicion of collusion or even abuse of collective dominance.

Vertical Price Fixing   EU law governing vertical price fixing (particularly resale price fixing) also applies to both dominant and nondominant companies and is more restrictive than U.S. law. Minimum resale prices, even if part of a stated policy and enforced unilaterally, are generally illegal in the European Union, based on the idea that any policy decision by a company toward its dealers can become a part of the dealership arrangement and not merely a unilateral policy.[21] Although a recent appellate decision indicates a potential movement toward seeing some of these policies as unilateral acts rather then agreements, the outcome of the case is still uncertain and the case itself covers a relatively limited set of circumstances.[22]

A minimum resale price restriction is also considered a policy that can make an otherwise legal vertical agreement illegal. Fixed resale price restrictions are equally illegal. Recommended resale prices, and in some cases maximum resale price policies, have been permitted as long as the recommendation is not reinforced by any pressure or incentives that could make the prices operate essentially as minimum or fixed resale prices. These restrictions on resale price fixing apply equally to actions by an individual supplier and actions by a trade association on behalf of all suppliers in the trade. National law technically governs resale price maintenance systems operating at a purely local level. However, if experts think they will deflect likely trade between EU countries from its natural patterns, the systems may come under the scope of EU law.

---

[21] *Ford-Werke AG v. EC Commission* (Joined Cases 25 and 26/84) [1985], ECR 2725.

[22] In *Bayer AG v. EC Commission* (Case T-41/96) [2000] ECR II-3383, the EC found that Bayer's pricing policies regarding its Adalat product supplied to pharmaceutical wholesalers in Spain—Bayer attempted to provide it at lower prices than in the UK but only provided a limited quantity to cover local market demand and prevent export—were part of a set of unlawful agreements and concerted practices. On appeal, the Court of First Instance agreed with Bayer that the action was unilateral. The case is currently on appeal to the ECJ.

PRICE SIGNALING

Intentionally disclosing pricing or production information to send private signals to competitors or to elicit an anticipated reaction from them is strictly prohibited in the European Union for both dominant and nondominant firms. If companies choose to disclose future pricing information publicly, they need a legitimate business purpose for doing so.

While exchanges of price information between competitors, such as *open price systems*, may in some circumstances be prohibited under Article 81, published price lists that competitors can see do not alone constitute an unlawful exchange of information. In fact, it is likely that such systems would be found legal so long as they serve a clear bona fide commercial purpose. It is only when communication of prices or anticipated prices to competitors occurs with the intent that they will modify their behavior that the specter of illegality appears. For example, the EC has stated that trade associations may compute and disseminate aggregate output and sales statistics so long as they do not identify individual companies and transactions.

PREDATORY PRICING

The ECJ adopted a two-part test to gauge whether predatory pricing is illegal as an "abuse of a dominant position." First, if prices are below average variable costs there is a *per se* violation, because the only justification for such prices is deemed to be the elimination of a competitor. Matching a competitor's prices is not considered to be a valid defense. Second, if prices are higher than average variable cost but below total costs, then there must be a demonstration of intent to eliminate a competitor.[23] However, such practices as introductory offers, end-of-season sales, or other temporary price reductions with generally legitimate business purposes are likely to be legal in the European Union as long as there is no specific intent to eliminate a competitor.

---

[23] *Tetra Pak International SA v. EC Commission* (Case C-333/94P) [1996], ECR I-5951. In this case, sales below average variable costs were deemed to be part of an eviction strategy designed to eliminate competition. However, the Commission noted that not covering total costs may be economically justified in the short term if the activity still covers fixed costs in part, but that any activity for which the profits would remain permanently inadequate to cover variable costs would be illegal and must be terminated.

PRICE DISCRIMINATION

Generally, as long as a company is nondominant, it may legally discount quoted prices however it chooses to each customer, even competing customers, as long as it does not collude with its competitors or agree with some customers as to what other customers will be charged. However, a nondominant company may not discriminate for an unlawful purpose, such as to exert pressure, provide an incentive around resale price maintenance, or create territorial limitations or indirect restrictions on exporting or importing within the European Union. For example, a discount linked directly to products resold for local consumption was found to be an unlawful restriction. Furthermore, French and German laws regarding price discrimination are broader in scope than equivalent EU rules for both dominant and nondominant companies.

When a company is dominant in the European Union, the rules are similar to U.S. law and prohibit discriminatory pricing to customers in the same or similar circumstances. Two main defenses exist for such action. First, the discount can be based on genuine cost savings. Second, different prices can reflect differing values of services provided by the buyer, such as in IT where value-added resellers provide demonstrable value to the seller or in groceries where a supermarket provides a favorable display location. As a result, quantity discounts (where larger orders reduce unit costs) and prompt payment discounts (where fast payments reduce financing costs) are justifiable, while a loyalty rebate is not. For example, in *Hoffman LaRoche*, the classic case on loyalty rebates, the ECJ ruled that a rebate tied to a purchaser obtaining all or most of its requirements from a dominant seller, even when that rebate was willingly accepted by the buyer, was a violation of Article 82.[24]

Certain specific actions are likely to trigger a finding of discriminatory pricing, such as defending against a new entrant by offering loyalty discounts to those customers targeted by the new entrant. Other acts that could prompt discriminatory pricing concerns include securing a long-term, exclusive contract with a reseller, withdrawing discounts if the customer satisfied some or all of its requirements from other suppliers, and including contractual provisions that require the customer to allow the supplier to match the best prices offered by other suppliers.

It is important to note that a meet-the-competition argument is not necessarily an acceptable justification for price discrimination in the European Union. It is no defense that the company offering the discriminatory prices had low profits or losses or that customers requested the discounts. It is also

[24] Case 85/76 [1979], ECR 461.

important to note that the ECJ is more likely to find price discrimination in cases where prices are not transparent, or where, if they are transparent, they are clearly unequal.

GEOGRAPHIC DISCRIMINATION

The European Union's single-market objective is a central driver of EU competition policy enforcement. As such, it supports strict treatment of both dominant and nondominant companies that engage in practices that effectively segregate countries from one another. For example, if goods are marketed in the European Union, there must be no agreement or understanding that directly or indirectly prohibits or restricts their subsequent export and trade within the Union. Such policies as pricing differently to customers from different countries, even if the prices were claimed to be "what the markets would bear," are illegal for a dominant supplier. Similarly, offering discriminatory discounts to certain customers to discourage them from importing from or exporting to certain other countries has been held illegal regardless of dominance.

A qualified territorial agreement, in which a supplier gets dealers to agree not to actively market and sell outside their territory, is sometimes allowed, so long as the agreement does not restrict passive sales (responding to unsolicited orders) that come from outside the agreed territory of the dealer.

PROMOTIONAL DISCRIMINATION

Under EU law, promotional discrimination does not have a special set of rules. Actions that in the United States might be covered by promotional discrimination laws are judged in the European Union under price discrimination law.

PRICE SQUEEZES

Similar to U.S. law, it may be illegal for a dominant European company to engage in price squeezing, in which a dominant supplier of intermediary products that also produces finished products prices the intermediary products to other players in such a way that they cannot compete effectively.

EXCESSIVE PRICING

Excessive pricing can be construed to be an abuse of a dominant position, but it is very difficult for the EC to prove its case in such situations because there is no clear definition of what constitutes *excessive*. Generally the only companies found guilty of this conduct have been absolute monopolies. The ECJ has defined a price as excessive if it has no reasonable relation to the economic value of the product or service provided. It has also suggested several ways of measuring what is excessive, including: comparison of prices charged for the same product in different geographies; comparison of the dominant company's price charged in its geographic market to the price charged in competitive markets in other geographies for the same product; and, where possible to measure, comparison of price to production cost.

ANTITRUST INFORMATION SOURCES

The following is a representative list only; it is not comprehensive, but includes enough sources of information about local antitrust laws to give you a flavor of the scope of data available. It is absolutely crucial that companies consult legal counsel in this area and ensure that they access the correct sources for their area.

Argentina

Comisión Nacional de Defensa de la Competencia
Ministerio de Economía y Obras y Servicios Públicos
Julio A. Roca 651 4to Piso
CP: 1322
Ciudad de Buenos Aires
Argentina
Tel: (54) 11 4349-3480/4097 4349-4104/4107
Fax: (54) 11 4349-4125
www.mecon.gov.ar/cndc/
(Spanish only)

Asia-Pacific

Asia-Pacific Economic Cooperation
35 Heng Mui Keng Terrace
Singapore 11961
Tel: (65) 68 919 600
Fax: (65) 68 919 690
www.apec.org/

Australia

Australian Competition and Consumer Commission
Adelaide office

Street Address:
Level 2
19 Grenfell Street
Adelaide SA 5001
Postal Address:
GPO Box 922
Adelaide SA 5001
Australia
Tel: (61) 8 8213 3444
Fax: (61) 8410 4155
www.accc.gov.au

Austria

Federal Ministry of Economy, Family and Youth
Stubenring 1
A-1011 Vienna
Austria
Tel: (43) 43/1/711 00-0
Fax: NA
E-mail: service@bmwfj.gv.at
www.bmwfj.gv.at/

Belgium

Service des prix
Ministère des Affaires Economiques
Régulation et Organisation du Marché
North Gate III
Boulevard du Roi Albert II, 16
1000 Bruxelles
Belgium
Tel: (32) 2 277 51 11
Fax: (32) 2 277 52 52
E-mail: eco.regul@economie.fgov.be
www.economie.fgov.be

Brazil

Conselho Administrativo de Defesa Economica
Ministério da Justiça
SCN Quadra 2 ProjeçÃo C
70712-902 - Brasilia - DF
Tel: (55) 61 3221 8599

Fax: NA
www.cade.gov.br
(Portuguese only)

Canada

The Competition Bureau
50 Victoria Street
Gatineau, Quebec
K1A 0C9
Canada
Tel: (1) 819-997-4282
Fax: (1) 819-997-0324
www.competitionbureau.gc.ca/eic/site/cb-bc.nsf/eng/home

China

Ministry of Commerce the People's Republic of China
2 Dong Changan Jie
Beijing 100731
China
Tel: (86) 10 65284671
Fax: (86) 65599340
www.english.mofcom.gov.cn

Czech Republic

Office for Protection of Economic Competition
tr. Kpt. Jarose 7
604 55 Brno
Czech Republic
Tel: (420) 542 167 111
Fax: (420) 542 167 112
E-mail: posta@compet.cz
www.compet.cz/en/

Denmark

Competition Council
(Konkurrenceraadet)
Norregade 49
DK-1165 Copenhagen K
Denmark
Tel: (45) 33 17 70 00
Fax: (45) 33 32 61 44
www.ks.dk/english

Egypt

Ministry of Trade and industry
2 Latin America, Garden City,
Cairo, Egypt
Tel: (20) 2 792-1202
Fax: (20) 2 795-5025 (Minster Cabinet)
www.mfti.gov.eg

European Commission

Direction Générale Concurrence
Commission Européenne
DG Competition
rue Joseph II / Jozef II straat 70
1000 Bruxelles/Brussel
Belgium
Tel: 00 800 6 7 8 9 10 11 (From the 27 member countries)
(32) 2 299 41 07 (Members of the press)
Fax: NA
E-mail: comp-mergers@ec.europa.eu
www.ec.europa.eu/competition/

Finland

Finnish Competition Authority
Pitkänsillanranta 3, P.O.B. 332,
FIN-00531 Helsinki
Finland
Tel: (358) 9 731 41
Fax: (358) 9 7314 3328
E-mail: kirjaamo@kilpailuvirasto.fi
www.kilpailuvirasto.fi/cgi-bin/english.cgi

France

Autorite de la Concurrence
11, rue de l'Echelle
75 001 Paris, France
Tel: (33) 1 55 04 00 00
Fax: (33) 1 55 04 00 22
E-mail: communication@autoritedelaconcurrence.fr
www.autoritedelaconcurrence.fr/user/index.php

Germany

German Cartel Authority
Bundeskartellamt
Public Relations Section
Kaiser-Friedrich-Strasse 16
D - 53113 Bonn
Germany
Tel: (49) 228-949-9-0
Fax: (49) 228-94-99-400
www.bundeskartellamt.de/wEnglisch

India

Monopolies and Restrictive Trade Practices Commission
Ministry of Corporate Affairs
'A' Wing, Shastri Bhawan
Rajendra Prasad Road,
New Delhi - 110 001
India
Tel: (91) 11 23384158, 23384660, 23384659
Fax: NA
E-mail: dr.navrang@mca.gov.in
www.mca.gov.in/MinistryWebsite/dca/mcaoffices/mrtpc.html

Indonesia

Ministry of Industry
Jl Gatot Subroto No. 52-53
Jakarta 12950
Indonesia
Tel (62-21) 5252194, 5271380, 5271387-88
Fax: (62) 21 526-1086
www.dprin.go.id/default_e.htm

Ireland

Competition Authority
14 Parnell Square
Dublin 1, Ireland
Tel: (353) 1 804-5400
Fax: (353) 1 804-5401
www.tca.ie

Italy

The Italian Competition Authority
Autorità Garante della Concorrenza e del Mercato
Piazza G. Verdi, 6/A,
00198 Roma - Italia
Tel: (39) 06 85 82 11
Fax: (39) 06 85 82 12 56
www.agcm.it/eng

Israel

Israel Antitrust Authority
22 Kanfei Nesharim Street
P.O. Box 34281
Jerusalem 91341 Israel
Tel: (972) 2-655-6103
Fax: (972) 2-651-5329
www.antitrust.gov.il/pratim.htm?Lang=HEB

Japan

International Affairs Division
Fair Trade Commission
1-1-1 Kasumigaseki Chiyoda-ku
Tokyo 100-8987
Japan
Tel:(81) 3 3581-1998
Fax: (81) 3 3581-1944
www.jftc.go.jp/e-page/aboutjftc/

Korea, Republic of

Korea Fair Trade Commission
648 Banpo-ro, Secho-gu
Seoul
Republic of Korea
Tel: (82) 2-2023-4238/4248
Fax: (82) 2-2023-4241
E-mail: webmaster@ftc.go.kr
http://eng.ftc.go.kr/

Mexico

Federal Competition Commission
Av. Santa Fe 505 (piso 24),
Col. Cruz Manca Santa Fe,
Del. Cuajimalpa,
C.P 05349
México, D.F.
Tel: (52) 2789 - 6500/6501
Fax: (52) 2789 - 6672
www.cfc.gob.mx/english/

The Netherlands

Netherlands Competition Authority
P.O. Box 16326
2500 BH The Hague
The Netherlands
Tel: (31) 70 330 33 30
Fax: (31) 70 330 33 70
www.nmanet.nl/engels/home/Index.asp

New Zealand

Ministry of Commerce: Regulatory
and Competition Policy Branch
33 Bowen Street
P.O. Box 1473
Wellington, New Zealand
Tel: (64) 4 472 0030
Fax: (64) 4 473 4638
www.med.govt.nz/templates/Page__3408.aspx

Norway

Norwegian Competition Authority
Konkurransetilsynet
P.O. Box 439 Sentrum
NO–5805 Bergen
Norway
Tel: (47) 55 59 75 00
Fax: (47) 55 59 75 99
E-mail: post@konkurransetilsynet.no
www.konkurransetilsynet.no/en/

Pakistan

Competition Commission of Pakistan
4-C Diplomatic Enclave, G-5, Islamabad, Pakistan
Tel: +92-51-9247530-32
Fax: +92-51-9247547
E-mail: info@cc.gov.pk

Poland

The Office of Competition and Consumer Protection
Powstancow Warszawy 1
00-950 Warsaw
Poland
Department of Competition Protection
Tel: (+48 22) 826 91 06, (+48 22) 556 02 99
Fax: (+48 22) 826 30 51
www.uokik.gov.pl/en/

Russia

Federal Antimonopoly Service
Sadovaya Kudrinskaya, 11,
Moscow, D-242, GSP-5, 123995
Russia
Tel: + 7 495 252 70 48, + 7 495 254 56 43
Fax: NA
E-mail: international@fas.gov.ru
www.fas.gov.ru

Saudi Arabia

Ministry of Commerce and Industry
P.O. Box 1774
Riyadh 11162
Saudi Arabia
Tel: (966) 1 401-2220
Fax: NA
E-mail: info@commerce.gov.sa
www.commerce.gov.sa/english/default.aspx

Slovakia
Antimonopoly Office
Drienǎová 24

826 03 Bratislava
Slovakia
Tel: +421 2 43 33 38 80
Tel: +421 2 48 29 71 11
Fax: +421 2 43 33 35 72
E-mail: pusr@antimon.gov.sk
www.antimon.gov.sk/

South Africa

South African Competition Commission
Private Bag x23, Lynwood Ridge 0040
South Africa
Tel: (27) (012) 394-3200
Fax: (27) 394 0226
www.compcom.co.za

Spain

Comisión Nacional de la Competencia
C/ Barquillo, 5
28004 Madrid (España)
Spain
Tel: (34) 91 568 0510
Fax: (34) 91 568 0590
E-mail: informacion@cncompetencia.es
www.cncompetencia.es

Sweden

Swedish Competition Authority
Malmskillnadsgatan 32
SE-103 85 Stockholm
Sweden
Tel: (46) 8 700 16 00
Fax: (46) 8 24 55 43
E-mail: konkurrensverket@kkv.se
www.kkv.se/t/SectionStartPage__257.aspx

Switzerland

Federal Competition Commission
Effingerstrasse 27
CH-3003 Bern
Switzerland

Tel: (41) 31 322-2040
Fax: (41) 31 322-2053
www.weko.admin.ch/kontakt/index.html?lang=en

Taiwan

Fair Trade Commission
12-14F, No2-2, Sec.1, Chi Nan Road
Taipei
Taiwan, R.O.C.
Tel: (886) 2 2351-7588
E-mail: ftcpub@ftc.gov.tw
www.ftc.gov.tw/english.asp

Turkey

Competition Council
Bilkent Plaza Blok B3
Bilkent, 06530, Ankara
Turkey
Tel: (90) 312 266 6966
Fax: (90) 312 266 7920
www.rekabet.gov.tr/english.asp

United Kingdom

Office of Fair Trading
Fleetbank House, 2-6 Salisbury Square
London EC4Y 8JX
United Kingdom
Tel: 08454 04 05 06 (Consumer Direct)
www.oft.gov.uk

United States

Federal Trade Commission Antitrust Division
Office of Policy and Evaluation, Room 394
Bureau of Competition
600 Pennsylvania Ave NW
Washington, D.C. 20580
USA
Tel: (1) 202-326-3300
E-mail: antitrust@ftc.gov
www.ftc.gov/ftc/antitrust.htm

Venezuela

Pro-Competencia
Superintendencia para la Promocion
Y Proteccion de la Competencia
Torre Oeste, Piso 11, Parque Central,
Caracas, Venezuela
Tel: (58) 212 577 9919, 576 5101, 576 8421
Fax: NA
E-mail: info@procompetencia.gov.ve
www.procompetencia.gov.ve

Vietnam

Ministry of Trade
21 Ngo Quyen Str., Ha Noi
Vietnam
Tel: (84-4) 9360733, (84-4) 08046947, (84-4) 8262538
Fax: NA
www1.mot.gov.vn/en/NewsDetail.asp?id=20&kind=0

World Trade Organization

Centre William Rappard
Rue de Lausanne 154
CH-1211 Geneva 21
Switzerland
Tel: (41) 22-739-51-11
Fax:(41) 22-731-42-06
www.wto.org/english/tratop_e/comp_e/comp_e.htm

List of Acronyms and Abbreviations

ABC	Activity-Based Costing
AP	Asia-Pacific
ASP	Average Selling Pricing
ATM	Automated Teller Machine
B2B	Business-To-Business
COGS	Cost of Goods Sold
CPG	Consumer Packaged Good
CRM	Customer Relationship Management
EBIT	Earnings Before Interest and Taxes
EBITA	Earnings Before Interest, Taxes, and Amortization
EC	European Commission
ECJ	European Court of Justice
EDI	Electronic Data Interchange
ELA	Enterprise License Agreement
EMEA	Europe, Middle East, Africa
ERP	Enterprise Resource Planning
EU	European Union
FDA	U.S. Food and Drug Administration
FTC	U.S. Federal Trade Commission
FTE	Full-Time Equivalent
HR	Human Resources
IT	Information Technology
KPI	Key Performance Indicator
M&A	Mergers and Acquisitions
MACs	Moves, Adds, and Changes
MAP	Minimum Advertised Price
MRO	Maintenance, Repair, and Operations
MSRP	Manufacturer's Suggested Retail Price

OEM	Original Equipment Manufacturer
PDA	Personal Digital Assistant
PPR	Pocket Price Ratio
PTMC	Price-To-Meet-Competition
R&D	Research and Development
RACINS	Responsibility, Approval, Concurrence, Input, Notification, Support
Rep	Representative
ROI	Return on Investment
ROS	Return on Sales
SaaS	Software as a Service
SKU	Stock Keeping Unit
SUV	Sports Utility Vehicle
T&C	Terms and Conditions
VAR	Value-Added Reseller
VEL	Value Equivalence Line

About the Web-Based Tool:
Periscope

Your purchase of *The Price Advantage, Second Edition*, gives you access to a demo of *Periscope*, a web-based tool that has been preloaded with realistic transaction data for a hypothetical company. Please refer to the insert card that accompanies this book; it contains instructions and the *unique registration code* and *temporary passcode* you need to access the web site.

Periscope is a proprietary analytic and technology toolkit from McKinsey Solutions that helps companies improve their commercial performance management (with a particular focus on pricing and sales in B2B environments). It was developed based on McKinsey's deep pricing expertise and experience driving commercial excellence and change management across multiple industries.

By logging onto the *Periscope* web site, you can explore some of the transaction pricing concepts from this book. A fictitious but realistic transaction data set helps you experience firsthand a few typical analyses you might use and then allows you to interpret the results. You will see that *Periscope* is structured around three basic objectives: (1) *getting insights* through a set of core analytics including pocket margin waterfalls, price/margin scatter plots, variance analyses, and Pareto analyses; (2) *capturing value* through what-if simulations and planning tools; and (3) *driving performance* by leveraging heat maps, dashboards, and other KPI reports.

For additional information regarding *Periscope*, its capabilities, and applications to real-world pricing issues, please visit:

http://solutions.mckinsey.com/periscope

About the Authors

The authors are partners at the international management consulting firm of McKinsey & Company, Inc. With more than 60 years of collective experience, they lead the Pricing Practice at the firm. McKinsey has done more pricing work than any other pricing consultancy in the world, having conducted more than 1,700 pricing engagements during the past five years.

WALTER L. BAKER

Walter Baker joined McKinsey in 1998 and is based in Atlanta, Georgia. Walter has worked with numerous clients across a broad range of industries in the areas of pricing, sales, marketing, and strategy. He regularly leads clients and consulting teams worldwide as an expert on pricing strategy, tactics, and capability building.

Walter is a graduate of Harvard University and M.I.T. At Harvard, he earned a doctorate in engineering sciences in 1997 and a master's in applied mathematics in 1995. At M.I.T., he earned both a master's and bachelor's in mechanical engineering in 1987 and 1985, respectively. Walter has published articles on pricing in *CMO Magazine*, the *McKinsey Quarterly*, and the *Harvard Business Review*, and regularly presents at industry conferences.

MICHAEL V. MARN

Mike Marn joined McKinsey in 1977 and is based in Cleveland, Ohio. Mike has developed many of the most universally used analytic approaches for identifying and capturing opportunities in pricing.

Mike is a 1974 graduate of Hiram College with a degree in mathematics, and he holds a master's degree in operations research from Case Western Reserve University, which he received in 1976. He has written a variety of articles on pricing, appearing in such publications as the *Wall Street Journal*, the *New York Times*, *Boardroom Reports*, *Sales and Marketing Management*, the *Harvard Business Review*, and the *McKinsey Quarterly*.

Mike was named to *Consulting Magazine*'s 2005 list of the world's top 25 most influential consultants.

CRAIG C. ZAWADA

Craig Zawada joined McKinsey in 1997, is based in Calgary, Alberta, and lives in Kimberley, British Columbia. His experience spans a wide range of B2B and consumer products. Craig has developed innovative new pricing concepts and ideas in the areas of market strategy, postmerger pricing, Internet pricing, pricing in distribution, price implementation, and pricing infrastructure.

Craig earned his bachelor's degree in business administration in 1992 and his MBA in 1993, both from the Schulich School of Business, York University, in Ontario, Canada. Craig is widely published on pricing strategy, with articles appearing in the *Harvard Business Review*, *Mergers and Acquisitions*, and the *McKinsey Quarterly*. He has also been interviewed and quoted in *Fortune Magazine*, *Canadian Business*, and *Business 2.0*. He has spoken on pricing strategy at industry conferences in North America, Europe, and South America.

Index

Important Registration Information for
The Price Advantage Readers

Your purchase of *The Price Advantage, Second Edition*, gives you access to a demo of *Periscope*, a proprietary commercial management tool developed by McKinsey Solutions that will let you explore some of the concepts in this book. For more information, please see Appendix 4 of this book.

Accessing McKinsey Solutions *Periscope* Demo

- Using a web browser, enter the following URL:

  http://solutions.mckinsey.com/periscope/demo

- Register as a new user by entering your **unique** registration code:

  JuysWd

  and **temporary passcode:**

  Bix*E7tLiU

- Follow directions online to gain access to a working version of *Periscope* loaded with dummy transaction data for a hypothetical company.

For additional information regarding *Periscope*, its capabilities, and applications to real-world pricing issues, please visit:

http://solutions.mckinsey.com/periscope